OKANAGAN UNIVERSITY COLLEGE LIBRARY

D1459796

P

"Paul Shepard is the most brilliant a[...] our time."

DAVE FOREMAN, CO-FOUNDER, EarthFirst!

"In this superb collection, Paul Shepard once again discovers the poetry that lies at the heart of biology. There is no question but that Shepard is our premier environmental philosopher."

THEODORE ROSZAK, AUTHOR OF *The Voice of the Earth*

"Shepard's work beats at the palpable heart of the reanimation of the human psyche. All who care about the ongoing course of life and the animal others should heed these provocative words."

MAX OELSCHLAEGER, AUTHOR OF *The Idea of Wilderness*

"Paul Shepard shows us how the roots of our environmental destructiveness lie in a failed development of the self. Before the modern era, for thousands of years, small children played freely in wild nature. Adolescents became adults through nature myths and rituals that took place in a community that included both humans and the more-than-human world surrounding them. We can free this 'original' human deep inside each of us by a change in the way we rear our children. Shepard's work explains how we can begin."

DOLORES LA CHAPELLE, AUTHOR OF *Sacred Land, Sacred Sex*

"Paul Shepard's work represents one of the most important syntheses available today on the subject of the human condition. He remains in that category of thinkers who are imaginative, intellectually rigorous, and disturbingly on target, all at the same time."

MORRIS BERMAN, AUTHOR OF *The Reenchantment of the World*

OTHER BOOKS BY PAUL SHEPARD

THE PICTORIAL HISTORY OF THE 493'D ARMORED
FIELD ARTILLERY BATTALION

MAN IN THE LANDSCAPE: A HISTORIC VIEW OF
THE ESTHETICS OF NATURE

ENGLISH ATTITUDES TOWARDS THE NEW ZEALAND
LANDSCAPE BEFORE 1850

THE SUBVERSIVE SCIENCE: ESSAYS TOWARD THE ECOLOGY OF MAN,
ED. WITH DANIEL MCKINLEY

ENVIRON/MENTAL: ESSAYS ON THE PLANET AS A HOME,
ED. WITH DANIEL MCKINLEY

THE TENDER CARNIVORE AND THE SACRED GAME

THINKING ANIMALS: ANIMALS AND THE DEVELOPMENT
OF HUMAN INTELLIGENCE

NATURE AND MADNESS

THE SACRED PAW: THE BEAR IN NATURE, MYTH AND LITERATURE,
WITH BARRY SANDERS

THE OTHERS: HOW ANIMALS MADE US HUMAN

OKANAGAN UNIVERSITY COLLEGE
LIBRARY
BRITISH COLUMBIA

A *Paul Shepard Reader*

THE ONLY WORLD WE'VE GOT

edited by Paul Shepard

SIERRA CLUB BOOKS
San Francisco

The Sierra Club, founded in 1892 by John Muir, has devoted itself to the study and protection of the earth's scenic and ecological resources—mountains, wetlands, woodlands, wild shores and rivers, deserts and plains. The publishing program of the Sierra Club offers books to the public as a nonprofit educational service in the hope that they may enlarge the public's understanding of the Club's basic concerns. The point of view expressed in each book, however, does not necessarily represent that of the Club. The Sierra Club has some sixty chapters coast to coast, in Canada, Hawaii, and Alaska. For information about how you may participate in its programs to preserve wilderness and the quality of life, please address inquiries to Sierra Club, 730 Polk St., San Francisco, 94109.

COPYRIGHT © 1996 BY PAUL SHEPARD

"The Metaphysical Bear" from *The Sacred Paw* by Paul Shepard and Barry Sanders. Copyright © 1985 by Paul Shepard and Barry Sanders. Used by permission of Viking Penguin, a division of Penguin Books USA Inc.

All rights reserved under International and Pan-American Copyright Conventions. No part of this book may be reproduced in any form or by any electronic or mechanical means, including information storage and retrieval systems, without permission in writing from the publisher.

LIBRARY OF CONGRESS CATALOGING-IN-PUBLICATION DATA
Shepard, Paul, 1925–
    The only world we've got : a Paul Shepard reader / by Paul Shepard.
    p. cm.
    ISBN 0-87156-396-7 (pbk. : alk. paper)
    1. Environmentalism.   2. Environmental sciences—Philosophy.
3. Human ecology.   I. Title.
GE195.S48   1996
363.7—dc20   95-39899

Production by Janet Vail

Book design by James Robertson, The Yolla Bolly Press

Composition by Wilsted & Taylor

Printed in the United States of America on acid-free paper containing
a minimum of 50% recovered waste paper of which at least 10%
of the fiber content is post-consumer waste

10 9 8 7 6 5 4 3 2 1

In the most sophisticated way we can summon,
we must return to the awe, and even fear,
in which primitive man held the mysterious world about him,
and like him we must strive to live in harmony
with the only biosphere that we can be certain
will be occupied by our descendants.

J. V. NEEL

CONTENTS

PREFACE

FOR REASONS that are not entirely clear, much of my adult life has been marked by allusion to the past, consciously in more recent years, by inference always. I suspect that this was in part a habit shaped by three years of military service in World War II when I was first out of high school, and by the remembrances and the enduring idealism fostered by this experience. I arrived at my twenty-first year suffering from two kinds of inquietude. One was a lament for the land and its fate, a painful sense of the vanishing wild and, what had seemed to me as a boy, its perfection, a yearning that made me a typical target for the antienvironmentalist accusation that "nature lovers" are incurably fixated on nostalgia for an illusory past. My academic interest in the study of the romantic poets, painters, and travelers, who represent a special attitude toward nature, was a sort of professional extension of this predilection and its yeasty intuition. The second, more provocation than uneasiness, was generated by the study of biological evolution and a growing sense of my own distant ancestry, no less emotionally felt than the lost landscapes of my childhood, and yet intellectually satisfying in a way that no other religious ideas are.

I spent a lot of time with frogs and fish and reptiles, more still with birds and mammals. These boyhood companions are also relicts of a past out of whose primal darkness I too have come, and with whom I still share the world. I don't doubt that I created a concept of human evolution from my own ontogeny and have seen my personal sensibilities as arising in analogous ways to the origins of consciousness in the human species. I am aware that such atavistic thinking is widely disapproved, that science scorns the notion that "ontogeny repeats phylogeny." Yet that despised idea drives my fascination with human prehistory. To have lived through a large part of the twentieth century, with its catastrophes of violence and greed, is to have realized ruefully that during the three million years of the Pleistocene—the era of our becoming—humankind was few in number, sensitive to the seasons and other life, humble in attitude toward the earth, and comfortable as one species among many. Group size was ideal for human relationships and human freedom, health was good despite (or perhaps because of!) high infant mortality rates, diet was in accord with our omnivorous physiology and sapient flexibility, and our ecology was stable and nonpolluting. These generic sensibilities are with us still, unmediated, at levels prior to what the social sciences celebrate as "culture." Humans all share a prototypic or archetypal relationship to nature. It was shaped by a lifeway of hunting and gathering, in which the season of personal existence from birth to death was celebrated as a small cycle within that of the larger universe.

Yet we have been led to think that the true self is largely free from biology—from "determinism"—as though our biology were a kind of tyranny that we can deny. Our industrial culture tells us daily that we can do anything we want, create our world according to taste, make any sexual and social relationships, and become whatever self pleases us: all this on the grounds that we are fundamentally different from other life. Periods of such swagger come and go, but none has resulted in such devastation as the ecological insolence of the last century. At last the new genetics and molecular biology reconfirm our bonds to the past. We are whatever our DNA—in response to our environment—makes us. The impact of being 99 percent identical in DNA to the chimpanzee and 80 percent identical even to horses falls on us with staggering impact. Even the lizard is represented in our presence, although we are "only" its cousin. Of course, DNA does not operate in a vacuum: the genetical heritage is constantly interfacing with our experience and environment. The old question of nature or nurture was always pointless, as the constraints are biological and the opportunities are circumstantial.

The hunter-gatherer context of our emergence was based on primate omnivory. Our teeth, alimentary system, metabolism bear it out; neither carnivore, nor herbivore, nor frugivore, nor granivore, we are all these at once. To get by on a diet of any one of these is to be either painfully stressed and malnourished or preoccupied with substitutions and additives. To willfully "be" an herbivore—i.e., a vegetarian—is a special arrogance masquerading as ethics. Even within omnivory it is possible to get the proportions wrong or to be misled in the quality of foods, for instance, to overdo on meat or to omit fruit. Or worse, to eat plants and animals of varieties bred for appearance, size, keeping, or the convenience of machines, which tend to be deficient in nutritional value *because* our bodies are keyed to the wild varieties of our evolutionary past, of which they are the depleted representatives.

To harvest any food is to kill living beings. This realization has become painful to us because of our lack of a philosophy of death as part of life and because in industrial societies we pay someone else to do the killing. Such a philosophy would include not only the moral necessity of killing, as the source of life, but recognition that we too are food. This continuity is basic to the whole of organic existence; the kinship of life requires it. Embalming, that civilized nicety pioneered by the ancient Egyptians and made law by us, is a desperate hope of escaping the cycle of bodily existence. Cremation is a half effort in the same direction.

In societies in which people individually kill their own food (be it the embryos in seeds or whole animals) there is no escape from the physical network; the perception, acknowledgment, and finally embrace of the hard truth as part of an affirmation of life. Thus the killing and eating of other beings is understood by most tribal peoples as part of a larger gift of life rather than a victory over nature or submission to a "bestial" nature. The individual hunter is not solely responsible, nor is she who tears the root from the ground or pulverizes the seeds more to blame than those who share the feast. Rites of celebration, purification, homage and veneration are group-wide. Virtually all religious concerns for these matters, among such peoples, bond death to both physical and spiritual renewal in some way or other.

The celebration of Pleistocene life (human life before twelve thousand years ago) seems to always hit two snags. One is that there are "no universals." I was made painfully aware of this objection at a large public meeting in Washington, D.C., in 1978 when, having given what I thought was a good paper on child development in primitive societies, I was assailed before the audience by Margaret Mead. The famous anthropologist, garbed in huge-brimmed hat, a flowered mumu reaching to the floor, and carrying a six-foot staff, was utterly regnant. "We all know there are *no universals*," she sniffed, and down I went. For years I dreamed of the reply I should have made, then I began to realize that she was mouthing the conventional wisdom not only of anthropology and the social sciences in general, but of modern society. Of course there are no universals: not everyone is born with two legs. Species characteristics were of no interest to most anthropologists, who were hell-bent on the study of cultural differences.

Hunter-gatherers may not always live in perfect harmony with nature or with each other, nor are they always happy, content, well-fed, free from disease, or profoundly philosophical. Like people everywhere, they are in some sense incompetent. Some tribes live in fringe environments that place special stress on their humanity. Deep tropical forests and the extreme arctic are such places, if one is to judge from the examples of homicide, suicide, sexual and child abuse. But these hardly compare to the destitution and demoralization of the human personality, the total amount of human suffering in modern cities, or the catastrophes of industrial greed that have so impaired natural and human life in the name of progress everywhere in the arctic and the tropics. We should not be mistaken about our terms. It is not technology or materialism that is the problem. The love of materials and the physical world and the extraordinary craftsmanship in its use have made us human. By catastrophes of industrial greed I refer to the corporate organization of the economy, with its destruction of the human community, its blindness to place, its obscene disregard for scale, its garbage, its rapacity, and its excessive desire for "products." Worst of all, these chronic disasters create a bizarre double bind in which people believe that the solution to their problems lies in more of the same, so that the collapse of human dignity and the ravaging of its environment are perceived as evidence of insufficient industrial growth.

The second snag in the acceptance of the Pleistocene as a model is that "you can't go back." As a student I knew about time's arrow and evolution. Extending that to social process seems only natural. It worried me for years. Then it finally came to me why it was wrong. It is not necessary to "go back" in time to be the kind of creature you are. The genes from the past have come forward to us. I am asking that people change not their genes but their society, in order to harmonize with the inheritance they already have.

Finding practical ways to translate our DNA into environments is difficult. Five minutes into this subject and my students immediately start asking, "All right, what do we do?" After forty years I feel that I am only beginning to understand the problem. As Ivan Illich says of his social critiques, I have spent my whole life trying to understand these matters, working on the nature of the question. How we got where we are and where we came from is part of the problem.

There were a few people some years ago who began to doubt that the rise of agriculture was the "greatest human revolution." Indeed, historians have generally credited the emergence of agriculture with the very possibility of civilization, that is, supporting the necessary density of people to have cities. For two centuries they have blandly repeated and foisted on the public this ideology of progress, the same old assumptions about literacy, inventiveness, security from want and natural dangers, leisure, great art, political organization, health, and so on through the litany of good things. Reality is the opposite. At the level of the individual, the quality of human life began to deteriorate with the domestication of plants and animals. In the shift from primal human groups to states we graduated from homicide to war, from murder to genocide, from family hunger to the starvation of populations, from diversity in every aspect of life to homogeneity, from sickness as individual organic failure or parasites to mass epidemic death, from council and group-centered power to the hierarchy of empires, from occasional craziness to group insanity.

But of course we cannot believe that. The ideology of progress and the double bind of the industrial catastrophes commit us not only to what we strive for but to what we reject. The issue is one not only of public mood and emotion but of philosophy and religion; it implicates historical changes in paradigms of organicism and mechanism, of the nature of deity and of the spirit, of the meaning and purpose of life, of what it means to be human. If philosophy guides action then events make philosophy. We cannot blame our concepts for our actions, but we cannot overlook them either.

My own take on this is that a basic economy is a generator of values. Before agriculture there was only one economy. Despite the majority of twentieth-century social opinion to the contrary, generalizations can be made about that primal way of life and its beliefs and cultures. When people began cultivating plants, moving from a world of perennials to annuals, they created a new mode of perceiving reality, an altered sense of time. For example, an economy based on annual plants has an amputated perspective on the future.

Botanically it centered on hardy, quick-growing, short-lived plants, takers from the soil, not givers, dependent on man-created fields, on disturbance and uniformity rather than diversity. Likewise, domesticated animals were a deformed fauna with exaggerated features (milk-giving and plow-pulling), reduced social and physical requirements, diminished intelligence, vulnerability to epidemic disease and psychopathology. Inevitably this led to their infantilizing. Humans replaced their surround of wild diversity, maturity, and a rich, mysterious Other in elaborate webs of life, with a simplified biota of a few species, dependent on humans for their existence.

Is it any wonder that we came to think of the natural world as inferior, as created by a human-like deity, as an enemy to our civilized interests? What could religion do in such circumstances but invent God the maker, place evil in the wilderness, reserve the soul as a human possession, and locate heaven somewhere else? What could philosophy do but abandon the natural world altogether and become obsessed with the ethics among humans or their obligations to their gods? Instead of "nature," a random play of forces, how much better a mathematicized, abstracted, and alphabetized world?

The main certainty in the agricultural, civilized world was overwhelming uncertainty. Would the one-crop seeds come up? Would the weather be right or disease wipe out the plants? Would flood wash it all away? Would there be adequate labor for tilling, seeding, weeding, cultivating, fertilizing, harvesting, hauling, storing, and distributing—or would the labor force be drafted for war or die from communicable disease? Would enemies burn the fields again? In the boom-or-bust economy of all agriculture (except perhaps its "garden" form), nature in the bad years seemed to withhold (like a cruel mother) that to which the farmer felt he had a right. Or on the contrary, the earth (like a good mother) nourished the people as they hoped. Does this analogy not imply the infantilization of human thought?

The worldview of early farmers centered on the earth's fecundity. The seed was analogous to semen, the rain or sun to paternity, the earth to the womb, sowing to impregnation, cultivation to gestation. These ideas marked a shift away from a previous epiphany of wild plants and animals toward the deification of the human figure. The transition reflected the idea that sacred power was exercised by a being with human characteristics who relished power and obeisance in ways and to an extent that sacred animals did not. And because of the association of the female with the reproductive earth, the first sculpted humanized deities were probably female.

Yet there is a benign quality in subsistence farming that attracts us still, a nourishing, protecting sense that seems somehow associated with nonviolence, appealing to the feminine and the caregiver in us all. How can we explain the fear and hatred of the natural world in the light of this feeling we have about the soil and its cultivation? The answer is in part that we are the victims of the fiction of the "happy yeoman." More importantly, the animal-keeping side of agriculture is the source of masculinization, which historically produced the patriarchal tone in Western culture. Herding is not so much concerned with the fecundity and nurturance of the soil as with the possession of livestock, the control of resources amid endless conflict and chafing. The dominant male god arose in pastoral cosmology and defeated the goddess as nomadic pastoralists sundered sedentary peoples again and again during the six thousand years after the domestication of the horse and the llama. Mounted, herders became the first cavalry, as professionals completing the one element that the kings of the ancient agricultural states lacked. As these conquerors transformed sedentary society there was for them not a good and a bad side to the feminine but a schizoid split of her into the mother and the prostitute, an ambivalence fired with an overheated sense of female virginity, male honor, and vengeance. The modern forms of "pastorality" are the corporation and the politics of power, traditionally male provinces in which the earth and woman are reduced to objects of ownership.

Some anthropologists have been quick to observe that "gender wars" occur in all societies, but in truth most hunter-gatherer groups show little actual subordination of women, and the matter is frequently treated with humor. Councils of the whole are not unusual. "Vernacular gender" is the rule, which is to say, different gender tasks but not suppression.[1] Modern gender wars are different because pastorality was on a different track in defeating the goddess and raising men to gods, and by inference subordinating women to men.

This turn of mind "invented" ritual sacrifice, the attempt to placate or obtain favors from a sacred power by offerings, by bargaining with an arbitrary—a "royal"—power. What had been participation among foragers became manipulation. The cosmic game changed from chance to strategy, from measuring one's state of grace in nature's bounty to bartering, from a sacramental gift to a negotiated blessing.

Clearly, the "new" relationship to nature (one three-hundredth of human time since the beginning of the Pleistocene) leads to the necessity of control. The idea of regulating one's body, pests, predators, plants, animals, and microclimates is familiar to us but is relatively new to the human mind, and it may lead to an intoxication with power. If the farmer can destroy his competitors, be they beetles, fungi, birds, or deer, and the pastoralist-rancher can kill lions and wolves, they will be inclined to do so. Wild things become adversaries; they take up space, sunlight, or water that the farmer can use for his crops, or they invade the crops, eating, trampling, or infecting them with disease. As soon as people began to kill wolves to protect sheep and to squash grasshoppers ("locusts") to protect crops, nature became an opponent and wild forms became enemies of the tame in ways analogous to a war between human armies. The domain of power is a continuum, extending from control of people to control of all the Others, in which the only outcome is surrender or domination.

It is very difficult for us, removed by so many generations from our hunter-gatherer forebears, not to project the fear of nature upon them. If wild nature is threatening, how much worse we think for those primitive people who had no buildings, guns, or chemicals, who "must" have spent much of their lives cowering in caves. But the evidence is to the contrary. Protection by black magic, voodoo against evil, even the late forms of shamanistic defense against demons, and ritual sacrifice are characteristic of planters and herders, not hunters.

Another side to this mentality is the premise of the "limited good." This is a way of understanding the given world as insufficient for the wants or needs of people. The constant shadow of scarcity, fundamental to modern economics, arose in the era of agriculture. It was not a fundamental human condition. Lean times may have occurred among primitive peoples, as they do occasionally among all species, but in general small numbers, ecological flexibility, and the richness of the earth worked toward stability among the primal groups. Culturally we have inherited an inability to see that our human numbers are at the root of our problems, directly in the form of insufficiency of all kinds, but also through the fallout in the form of social chaos: tyranny, the little wars everywhere, deprivation, human abuse, terrorism, and poverty.

Despite some feminist insistence, bringing back the Neolithic goddess is not the solution to our present troubles. True, we need new stories and enactments, new myths and rituals. But insofar as these are fundamental communications to ourselves of what we most deeply believe, their veracity and power will depend on convictions of the heart, growing out of instinct or inherent psychogenic sources which come from ways of life. This is why "New Age" efforts to start with rites and resurrect old tribal myths will not work in changing our attitudes toward the earth. We may dance the Maypole till the cows come home but it will not recover for us the sense of the cycle of the seasons, which can only be regenerated in our own context.

The myth that epitomizes our present beliefs is the myth of history. Historical events are not the myth of history, but are merely its data. The story—the myth—of history is that change and time are inextricably linear. Created and set in motion by an outsider, the world goes on toward its end, as Buckminster Fuller said, "utopia or oblivion." This "maker" or "potter" story denies the self-creating character of planetary systems, of life in its most creative sense. It is a declaration of independence from the deep past (prehistory) and its peoples, from primal tribes today or ancestors long dead. History denies the earth as our true home and regards nonhuman life as incidental to human destiny.

For history the alternative to itself is in a *"heart of darkness."* Joseph Conrad's novel is a terrifying adventure into history's idea of the primitive soul given a geographical setting in the tropical jungle, where the male, rational, corporate mind confronted wild savages who personified their own inmost emotions and impulses—their instincts. This fear of the wild self was supported by Sigmund Freud's misguided notion of aggressive and destructive beasts living in the wilderness of the unconscious: no place for a civilized person. Yet we are not happy in our present situation. Could it be that those beasts are terrible not because of their nature but because they are contained? Our spontaneous sense of connectedness to nonhuman life— itself positive and not fearful—should make us feel at home on earth. The problem may be more difficult to understand than to solve. A journey beneath the veneer of civilization would not reveal the barbarian but our ("romantic") recollection of a good birth, a rich plant and animal environment, the reception of food as a gift rather than as a product. The generic human in us knows how to dance the animal, knows the strength of clan membership and the profound claims and liberation of daily rites of thanksgiving. Hidden from history, this secret person is undamaged in each of us and may be called forth by the most ordinary acts of life.

THE ONLY WORLD
WE'VE GOT

ONE

The Eye

THE HUMAN—THE VERTEBRATE—eye originated in the sea. Its basic structure is the same for all vertebrates, the most primitive of which are aquatic. When it is compared to eyes invented in the air, such as those of the insects, the differences are enormous; compared to eyes independently invented by invertebrates in the sea, such as those of the squids, the similarities are astonishing. An important difference between the sea eye and the land eye is the number of chambers, being multiple in the latter and single in the former. The single-chambered eye is apparently more effective in the murky, homogeneous, three-dimensional world of the sea. The flicker effect, which seems to be the advantage of the multiple ommatidia of the insect eye, is unnecessary in the sea, where, even on the bottom, light and dark are blurred in a universal penumbra, a gentle uniformity where total light gathering rather than flickering contrast is important.

With some slight additions and modifications, especially in the external protective structures and the size and shape of the lens, the vertebrates carried this eye onto the land. It was further perfected by terrestrial quadrupeds, probably both the amphibian labyrinthodonts and reptilian therapsids, before it came to the first of the mammals. But it was debased by the early mammals as excess baggage in their nocturnal lives and underground ways. In time certain of these insectivore-like creatures shifted back to daylight activity. Modern tree shrews may be very similar to the ancestors of the Primate order, to which lemurs, monkeys, apes, and man belong. One species, the Philippine tree shrew, is diurnal, nervous, fussy, intelligent, inquisitive, omnivorous, clean, and nimble. It has binocular vision, a round pupil, color vision, expressive eyes, and even humanlike ears. Some authorities think it is actually a primate, and it is indeed disconcerting to see these humanlike traits in a creature so much more primitive than a monkey.

The primates undertook a seventy-million-year struggle to reestablish the primacy of vision. They returned it to the daylight and built their lives around it, reinvented color vision, and made other improvements. Our thoughts are teased by the consequences of a rebuilt sea eye on the delicate ego of a grounded primate or, more exactly, the role of a salvaged reptilian-amphibian-ichthyoform eye in making the man.

What the earliest mammals, scrounging a living at night through the mid-Mesozoic, bequeathed to the primate ancestors was probably not much better than the wasted remains of the elegant structures of the reptilian forerunners. Night eyes need not be degenerate if the animal remains eye-minded, as did the cat, owl, and tarsier, but near the ground or under it, where food is fat grubs and crunchy roaches, there is no visual imperative. The smallness of the eye is itself a weakness. It contains fewer sensory cells, and in the night eye these are entirely rods, the type of receptor functioning in dim light, their communication to the brain pooled by neural connections so that the message is "summated" and the ultimate picture coarse and colorless.

The first arboreal preprimate forms may have clambered up trees at night as though following vertical trails. These were "nosy" animals who rediscovered the use of vision only after electing to remain in trees. An animal heavily dependent on the sense of smell is a good candidate for the progenitor of a brainy one relying on sight, as "braininess" specifically means elaboration of the cerebrum of the forebrain, whose enlargement was begun for the receiving, mixing, analyzing, and storing of information from the nose.

The combination of ground and tree life, or even of traveling on the vertical and horizontal trails of tree trunks and branches, is a kind of reentry of the sea eye into a three-dimensional world. In both, gravity is the principal orienting force, so that the proprioceptive sense of weight, the inner ear, and the eye work together to separate experience into vertical and horizontal planes. Perhaps our esthetic feeling for symmetry and balance, our inclination to abstract the vertical and horizontal lines and to follow them with our eyes, belongs to the following of trunks and limbs, first with bodies and then by sitting and looking. When art critics talk about the "tension" or "motion" created in sculpture or painting by oblique lines, I am inclined to remember the primate preoccupation with the horizontal planes of the ground and forest canopy, the vertical trunks that connect them, and the occasional leaning tree that is neither one nor the other.

As for following these trails, much depended on how it was done. Creatures who crawl, such as the raccoon and some of the lemurs, keep their long snouts—a liability for jumpers. Not only does the nose get in the way of landing, but it also obscures the view ahead. Smell is not very important anyway in the trees, at least not for diurnal forms who depend upon seeing their enemies as well as their food. Within the broad scope of omnivorousness, emphasis shifts from insects to fruit and plant material; in primate arboreal life, walking feet are modified into squirrel-like claws, tarsierlike pads, or fingerlike digits. Judging jumping distance is accomplished mainly by having both eyes in front, as in tarsiers, cats, and monkeys. Though by no means the only approach to seeing depth, binocular stereoscopic vision is the most efficacious, depending on central fusion of unlike images from the two eyes. In man the total visual field is about 180 degrees, the zone of overlap or stereoscopy about half the total. When the slightly convergent eyes look at an object, every part of it falls on corresponding parts of the two retinas, and the two eyes normally move in conjunction.

Animals are binocular for two reasons: predation and jumping, either or both. That much of the human eye is a product of life in the crown of a tropical forest is indicated by its similarity to the monkey eye. Our binocularity developed in jungle treetops where primate ancestors jumped and later swung from limb to limb. An extraordinary effect of this convergence of the lines of vision of two eyes is that all objects at greater or lesser distances than the point of fixation are out of focus. Focusing is accomplished in each eye by adjustment of the tension of the fibers holding the lens and allowing the lens to change shape so as to focus the image at exactly the right distance away from the retina. The amount an object is blurred depends on the distance it is short of or beyond the point of fixation. Of course, the "point" of fixation is not a point at all, but part of a continuous curved "surface," each part of which is equidistant from the eye. All of this surface or horopter is not only in focus in each eye, but all parts of the image fall upon "corresponding points" in each eye—at least in animals whose eyes are conjugate, or moved together. All other objects and points, short of and beyond the shell-like horopter, are blurred and are seen double. Our visual life is spent in the center of a nearly hemispheric transparent shell whose distance from us we fixate. The rest of the world is a jumble of subliminal double images. These double images serve depth perception, however, because they are wider apart the farther they are from the two-dimensional screen of the horopter. Objects deliberately blurred by a landscape painter to suggest distance and nonfocus can give only weak approximations of actual distance. Our conscious awareness of this duplication is not normally great, but its possible implications for our more basic mental events may include our widespread philosophical tendency to see the world dichotomously, as infinite antinomies. Horizontal lines are one component of the environment that are not seen double when the head is in a normal position. The practical effect of this is that jumpers in trees do not have to focus before leaping to another limb.

Experimental work on visual habits shows that the eye, in a random examination of the surroundings, tends to follow flat lines and vertical lines. This contributes to our rectilinear sense of the world, a sense certified by the gyroscopic activity of the canals of the inner ear in their control over posture, motion, and equilibrium. We experience a kinesthetic relation between the sense of motion and the visual field, oblique lines giving a sense of motion as the eye moves swiftly along them in a search for the symmetry of verticals or horizontals on which to rest.

The sense of continuous distance is due to the continuous array of surfaces whose reflected light is projected upon the two-dimensional surface of the retina as gradations into the distance. These are perspectives of texture, or changes in the density of patterns such as leaves, perspectives of size, convergent lines, amount of blur, the disparity gradient of double imagery, and motion perspective (the amount of displacement of a distant object relative to a nearer one as the observer moves). Together with such clues to distance as overlapping and upward location in the visual field, all contribute to the estimation of distance by the two-dimensional retinal surface. The result of these gradients is what we perceive as relief or terrain. The diminishment of texture creates not only the impression of continuous distance by a regular gradient, but represents contours by breaks in the gradation. The same is true of grades of illumination, gradual transitions indicating curved surfaces, and abrupt changes showing protuberances and indentations in the terrain. These variations in shading and textural density, functions of the orientation of surfaces to light, give relief to a surface and are more important to sight than separate points of light.

As white light passes through the lens, its colors refract at slightly different angles. The two ends of the color spectrum, at the limits of the frequencies that we see, cannot both be focused on the retina at once. For example, when we fixate adjacent red and blue patches the red seems close and the blue far away. This is because we are unconsciously aware of the ciliary muscle in the eye, whose contraction focuses the lens at points within about twenty feet. We are also clued to distance by the degree of convergence of the two eyes as the external eye muscles contract to keep them each directed at an approaching object.

That there are so many sources of distance information confirms the crucial necessity of accuracy by a rapidly moving creature. The well-camouflaged sloth adopted one way of avoiding eagles and predatory cats, the squirrels another, and the ape ancestors still another. I doubt that the sloth cares much about judging distance or could very easily produce descendants who would make good test pilots or polo players.

Both monkeys and squirrels are concerned with spotting food that holds still and enemies that move. But it is not only the movement of an object that causes its image to shift on the retina. When the object is fixated, or looked at, its image is focused on the area of sharpest vision, the central area, and on a pitlike depression, the fovea, whose visual cells and geometry combine to produce extreme resolution and visual acuity. The eye roves or scans just sufficiently for the image of the object to wander somewhat on the fovea. So, even when the object sits still, the set of gradients composing the image do not simply sit on the retina but shift constantly, producing an adjacent order of excitation of the visual cells. The image flows across the retina in a patterned arrangement of focused light, somewhat like the shifting of light flashes on an animated electric sign.

The curved surface of the retina does not deal uniformly with the image. Light entering the eye from a fixated object travels close to its geometric axis on its way to the central area. Here the retina is rich in cone cells, which maintain a high proportion of separate neural connections to the brain, so that the fovea conveys more separate bits of information to it than do other parts of the retina. The cone cells function in daylight and mediate color. The diameter of the fovea is about one degree of arc and represents an emphatic refinement of keen vision. Most sharp-eyed forms have one or two foveae, especially if they are also intelligent. To "look at" is to bring the image of the object of attention into the fovea. The philosopher's capacity to "look at" an idea is related to the primate's recovery of the object of attention onto the fovea, and they—the philosophers—should give thanks for it. Without it they could do no better than be generally alert, their ultimate limits of philosophical speculation to isolate this or that in their world and their thinking. In view of the primate invention of the human fovea, the comic statue of the monkey meditating on Darwin's skull assumes a new, tender sense of mutuality.

Eye movement is also affected by body motion, turning of the head, and rolling of the eyes, all of which tend to displace the image. In addition, there is an extremely rapid vibratory scanning of only about half a second of arc, oscillating about one hundred times per second. This produces a flux in the input to any given visual cell, which adds the ultimate touch of keenness, so that lines and points are discriminated more finely than would otherwise be possible. The system cannot deal with a steady input; blindness to an object occurs if the object is vibrated so that its image holds a set position on the retina.

In addition to being a pattern-locating system, the eye is attracted by movement or motion of an object in the field of vision. Good-eyed animals are "interested in" moving objects. A headlong dash through the treetops, the pursuit on foot of a woolly mammoth, and the broken-field running of a football player are part of the heritage of the vertebrate eye, as it was carried from flight to pursuit, from tree to ground. Travel produces apparent displacement and skewing of the whole visual picture. If the traveler looks ahead, the point of fixation on the horizon becomes a germinating bud of landscape, from which the world dilates as he approaches. It flows on either side and above him in gradients of velocity and direction, finally diminishing and contracting toward a vanishing point behind which whole visual fields are swallowed up as new ones are born in front. To the side, nearby points pass rapidly, distant objects slowly, in a graceful, parallactic shearing. Every object in this fantastic deformation grows exponentially as we approach and shrinks as we depart. Only the clear sky is free of this deformation, its great vault serenely substantial because it has no surface. The impression of space varies according to illumination, weather, clouds, and its figure-ground relationship to terrestrial objects. Objects seen against the sky or against the terrain seem to contract as the field of view expands; that is, objects seem smaller when seen by an observer in the open than by one looking through a window. Life in the treetops is almost entirely one of looking through the windows, and so is the terrestrial visual effect of stalking.

As we pass through a forest, the graded motion of vegetation overhead does not seem a jumble of branches and leaves; on the contrary, the elaborate mesh and interlacing seem to untangle and each twig to take its proper place in space. Here too the visual world is different from a painting. A stationary observer tends to presume that all objects extend at right angles from his line of sight, as they do in a painting. But as he moves through an actual terrain the sense of being at the center of a three-dimensional world falls upon him, a continuous unfolding revelation. Perhaps this suggests to him that he is the center and therefore the master of all the world. We might expect the eagle, lion, stag, and man to have more egocentric personalities than such creatures as mice, grouse, opossums, or even whales.

The foveate retina does not eliminate the role of the periphery. Fovea and periphery partake of the gestalt of figure and ground. Yet the peripheral portion is more even than a context, the mind is not wholly seduced by concentration. The whole is continually perceived. The object centered in the fovea is not separate from its environment. The surroundings give and take on meaning relative to the object. The complete abstracting of the object from its environment is one of those higher intellectual activities that can deliver new insights at new and unimagined risk.

The peripheral retinal image is not uniform. The relative proportion of rod to cone cells increases away from the center, so that the rim of the retina at its outer edges near the pupil is almost entirely rods. Here, acuity and color are minimal. Light strikes this peripheral area at acute angles. An image in motion produces an exaggerated displacement as it sweeps across this part of the retinal surface that is oblique to the entering light. The combined effect of the diminished acuity and accentuated motion is that information from the limits of the visual field is almost entirely about motion rather than appearances.

A squirrel's eyes are set in the head in a compromising position to gain the widest possible visual field for safety against attack without losing an area of binocularity in front. Their eyes are about intermediately placed in the head between two extremes—those of the rabbit, which are set laterally for a 360-degree view, mostly monocular, and the complete frontal vision of the gorilla, who apparently doesn't have to worry about who might be coming up behind him, or who has other ways of finding out.

Man could not have been produced by any other than a diurnal arboreal ancestor. Of all the possible candidates for the honor of being the human ancestor, it is noteworthy that tree squirrels did not become monkeys and produce bipedal forms and human descendants. Certainly the order of rodents is a potent and vigorous group; rats are capable of enough braininess to tax the ingenuity of psychologists. The reason partly lies in the temperate center of origin for the squirrels as opposed to tropical origins for the monkeys, apes, and man. The frugality of the winter fare limited the squirrel to nuts and seeds; the season exposed him by either blowing away his leafy cover and driving him into the hollows of trees, thus keeping him small to fit holes, or, if we mean squirrels in coniferous forests, keeping him small enough to climb to the tips of the branches for cones. In either case the vicissitudes of living in a cold climate depleted his numbers so rapidly that a half-dozen young were necessary for replacement each year, in contrast to the higher primates.

In spite of the squirrel's genuine horticultural contribution of planting whole forests, there has not been as much mutual evolution between nuts and squirrels as between fruits and monkeys. Locating colored fruits may have been the making of the primate fovea, which lends itself so well to finding fleas and the arts of mutual grooming such as we see at a cocktail party. It is possible that the lack of brightly colored nuts as much as anything else keeps squirrels from becoming human. If he knew this the squirrel might be very grateful and have an annual holiday, shouting "Hooray for the monochrome nuts!"

It is true that some monkeys eat pods and seeds and leaves and small animals as well as fruits, but not all monkeys are like the ancestors of man or ape. Colored vision is a great help in finding brightly colored durian fruits in the tropical sea of green—and possibly in spotting some kinds of dangerous snakes. It helps in differentiating all sorts of things in a world much fuller of things than the relatively sparse environments where squirrels coldly eke out their existence. Color vision, binocularity, and retinal acuity are a powerful combination in a diurnal eye. Sorting things out visually, at a distance, helps one to know before coming close to them whether to eat them, run from them, or signal to them (and the brilliant posteriors of some baboons clearly show a mating esthetic based on color). Sorting out has to do with leisure time and intelligence. It has to do with time for working out group communications and a general plucking, picking, poking, and manipulating. If curiosity killed the cat it was because the cat extended it beyond the question of whether yonder moving spot was edible. It occasionally kills the monkey, as when a baboon cannot resist approaching and teasing a leopard feigning sleep. But to his advantage, curiosity put the monkey in touch with the extraordinary richness of the tropical world and excited him intellectually, just as it aroused the imagination of Charles Darwin during the voyage of the *Beagle*.

The monkey was prepared to examine objects that seemed to be nonessential. Perhaps for the first time foveal vision was not merely a searching for a specific signal or sign to which the animal was internally ready to respond in a stereotyped manner, but a searching at once aimless and more fertile. Freedom from a life governed by a limited repertoire of signs means the difference between driving on a well-regulated thruway and flying your own aircraft; there are rules in both cases but the number of choices, the opportunity, and the risk are greater above ground than on it.

In our eagerness to identify what is uniquely human we have not been warm to the primate heritage. Man makes symbols and through this capacity acquires culture. A sign is a resistant, commonplace, and simplified symbol. New work in linguistics compares the language of bees, chimpanzees, dolphins, and men, finding common underlying structure: sign and symbol are part of the same series of communicative forms.

Our spontaneous joy in the colors of crayons and delight at sunlight penetrating a dusky room are examples of uncensored, visual innocence. "There are two sources of pleasure in the visual aspect of scenery," says Vaughn Cornish, "the association of ideas and the physical satisfactions of the eye. The latter are not experienced as a local sensation, and so, being apprehended purely as emotions, their origin is apt to escape recognition. When no association of ideas can be found to account for the ecstatic mood it is often attributed to some spiritual faculty higher than ordinary thought and thus further removed from the mere senses."[1] That is, of course, what many painters have aimed to produce.

Are visual signals inherent or learned? The person born blind lives in a world of sequential tactile impressions and comprehends nothing of his visual experience if he is granted sight by surgery. He sees a painful blur of floating color patches, a chaos of pure sensation without localization or meaning, only uncomfortable brightness, and senses a new insecurity. He has not lived in a spatial world; even the extension of his arm was not a movement into depth but a muscular sensation; walking, not the penetration of space but a psychophysical goal-directed posture and activity. Shapes have not been spatial but felt successive contours. The most familiar objects are strange. He can learn them only by following their contours with his fingers and counting corners with his eyes. The transition is difficult. He becomes discouraged and irritable. Deluged by an overwhelming flood of meaningless impressions, he learns with great labor to differentiate a square from a circle without touching it. He loses the serenity of blindness and may despondently and peevishly refuse to make the effort to distinguish one form from another and then to associate its name with its visual image. He learns signal sets or signs, which are abstractions of essential features, with progressively less conscious effort, until he builds a scheme of elementary form and structure. Eventually all the variations on the theme "chair" are comprehensible; he has freed vision from its tactile crutch and may then even learn to read.

How similar is his experience to the visual awakening of the infant? There are some extremely important differences, although prognosis of the newly sighted blind man suggests that there is almost nothing inherent to perception except the organs of sight. Yet the clinical record indicates that even the newly sighted starts with a sense of spatiality insofar as the objects around him are never assumed to be touching his eye but located at a distance. They are perceived immediately as solids rather than only surfaces. His unlearned visual behavior includes scanning, fixation, accommodation, and convergence. The congenitally blind person is not a native impressionist but is immediately involved in constructing a world of association from a sequence of visual fields. He does not enjoy meaningless forms. His struggle to posit significance or else to disregard the visual world implies that artistic impressionism is not a recapturing of the joy of sight either in childhood or in paradise.

The sea eye was first connected to a fishy brain and body. When taken on land it continued to see only the spectrum of light transmitted by water and to commutate the "coolness" of the blue depths and "warmth" of the reddish, sunlit surface in a hundred ways. Parts of the aquatic temperament may have been lost or adumbrated or transposed in amphibian and then reptilian life. The reptile added much that was new as parts of the brain expanded to receive, store, mix, and control. It had "learned" the joy of periodic return to water from an amphibious ancestor. How the joy is experienced may not be discoverable, but it remains, perhaps as the pleasure of individual cells immersed in an optimum level of body fluids.

In the treetops of our pre-apehood, a now extinct monkey expanded visual learning in a new direction: the social context. To him we trace the perception of and anthropomorphic perversion of the world as a whole. Creatures who learn from each other socially extend their learned perceptions to the world, as though saying, "Who is my teacher now, Mother or Mother Nature?" But the nature of the anthropomorphism can only be understood in terms of the nature of the society. Among higher primates, society is highly organized, its forms mostly learned by the members. Learning, associated with plasticity and growth, is most efficacious in the young. There has been a natural selection among these creatures for the extension of immaturity and a reduction in the number of young born at a time.

Sociality, delayed development, and leisure have given the higher primates time to develop a fine capacity for subtle visual communication. Postures, gestures, and facial expressions are well developed in monkeys and apes. Eyes can give as well as receive information; the palpebral fissure or opening between the lids, the lids with their lashes, the nictitans or third lid, fissures and wrinkles, the brows and other bristles, the colored iris with its changing pupil, moisture and tears on the cornea, the reflection of light by retinal devices causing eyeshine, highlights on cornea and lens, and the visible part of the sclera or white have all assumed a secondary communicative nature. The monkey, dog, and parrot watch man's eye and he theirs. More than any other single factor, eye communication transcends the profound barriers of communication between species.

Few other than the higher primates can roll the eyes and expose much of the white. This ability is supposed to correlate with high intelligence. Perhaps rolling the eyes was at first a way of following the flight of an eagle without the added peril of head movement, but at the same time communicating to companions the direction of danger. Once it had become communicative, new meanings could emerge, such as rolling the eyes in concentration as though "to see" an idea clearly. The colored iris set in a white background is one of the most compelling features of the human physiognomy, part of the evolution of the face. The meaning of a face is related to the invention of esthetics by ancient apes or monkeys. Although the dogs seem to make the best of it in some of their greetings, it is difficult to imagine creatures with long snouts and lateral eyes embracing face to face. The application of esthetics to the whole body may have been a factor in the reduction of hairiness and the retention of certain patches of hair. It seems probable that the ancient pre-man *Australopithecus* was probably not so hairy as cavemen are often pictured, but that hair reduction developed with increased sensuousness of the body surface very early among the human family. Man has strongly emphasized the infantile trait of diffuse eroticism of the erogenous surface of the body.

A great deal had happened to the sea eye in the canopy of hot forests. It had found in the gloomy arboreal depths a home more like the sea than the amphibians or reptiles or primitive mammals had given it. It favored a mentality that a porpoise might understand better than a dog or horse. Movement through the dense crowns of trees is not at all like moving across open spaces. There is a more emphatic streaming, a clearer before and after. Three-dimensional travel requires more decisions and perhaps better planning, in which past experience is critical. Seeing ahead in space was inextricably bound with seeing behind in time; seeing ahead in time was a metaphor of seeing ahead in space. By translating adjacent order to successive order, time and space became interchangeable, with an incipient cross-symbolism.

When this sort of mentality was carried once again to the ground, it may have opened new vistas to thinking, a widened capacity for tradition. In transmitting cultural information, "I see" means "I understand" when applied to events in the past. A "seer" is one whose vision extends forward through the unity of time and space in which the tradition-oriented society lives.

Tradition also incorporates a new self-consciousness, increased awareness of being part of a larger context. Flexibility of head and eye and the assurance through peripheral vision of the eternal presence of brow and nose give a sense of "being here" and of putting us in history. The constant sight of our noses assures us that we are not disembodied observers. One goes ahead thrusting one's nose into all sorts of things and places in a confident way impossible for rabbits because they cannot see much of their noses or for possums who are not visual enough to care much about what they see.

The bush apes ancestral to man gradually worked farther from the forest. They took the sea eye out of the gloaming and into the radiance of the open day, though not without some enduring nostalgia. The awareness of glare in the open air and a sense of vulnerability when in it have not been completely dispelled. An affinity for shade, trees, the nebulous glimmering of the forest interior, the tracery of branches against homogeneous surfaces, climbing, the dizzy child-like joy of looking down from a height, looking through windows and into holes, hiding, the mystery of the obscure, the bright reward of discovered fruits are all part of the woody past. Restfulness to the eyes and temperament, unspoken mythological and psychic attachments, remain part of the forest's contribution to the human personality.

It was not possible to see the forest while in it. Once out, we acknowledge the bond by remaining near its edge, cutting it back the right distance or planting forest-edge growth near us. The temperate or deciduous forest is not at all the same as the tropical, yet our attachment for it seems very great. Perhaps this has to do with its remarkable geometry when leafless and its cool half-openness, or perhaps because it happened to have just those elements in common with the jungle for which compatibility predestined us, or yet again, our affection for it may be a relatively late acquisition. The rain forest scarcely evokes our affection, but instead the impression of a formidable and implacable foe, but perhaps our feelings are shaped and named too quickly. The confrontation is profoundly subjective and disturbing in the same way that an ape agitates us more than a dog. Our relationship with the ape is still close enough to awaken vestigial memories or emotions, perhaps once associated with survival or competition.

The brain seems to demand flux in the sensory input from the eyes, and the mind needs variety. Without diversity the mind creates autonomous, hallucinatory experience. The mobile animal that flits through space meets this demand for multiformity. Perhaps the changing habitats in the evolution of an animal from water to air, from day to night and back to day, from ground to trees and back to ground, created that demand.

Art also contributes sensory novelty. Art is not a thing in itself with a life of its own. It is not an improvement on or an escape from life. It is never free from the past. To suppose that because it is abstract it has detached itself from the environment is to ignore the biological role of abstractions, which is the representation of essentials. We sometimes hear that an art object has a "meaning" of its own and refers to nothing in "the world," but we and the painter chimpanzees of England share a delight in abstract color schemes, curves and vertical and horizontal lines, a mutual sentiment for the forest—a heritage from mutual ancestors. Man does not have a priority on creativity, which is a pervasive activity of life, and perhaps of the universe.

Rebecca West says that an artist works like a nervous system, selecting highly significant details of the environment and synthesizing from them an "excitatory complex." He manipulates some bits of his environment in such a way as to confirm his experience of some part of the world, washed through his nervous system as sense data. He incidentally loans this extension of his nervous system to others, some of whose circuits and processes are sufficiently similar to lock onto the object. It is a communication, despite the highbrow scorn for art as "communication." Taken as information, the identifications of art with communication may widen the horizons of those who think art and nature are antithetical.

The art object is a message projected by the painter to himself and to others by a route through the external world. When the observer looks now at the forest and then at a painting of the forest a feedback is turned on, a circuit of constant comparison, discovery, and modification. The sensory input from the painting and from the trees interact so that the perception of each is affected. Recurrent cycles are initiated with the production of a succeeding painting, though this does not mean that the next picture will resemble the trees any more naturalistically or abstractly than the first.

The overall event has to do with "vision," a word connoting a sublime, sometimes traumatic, event or an extraordinary sight. The phenomena of ordinary sight begin with the penetration of our eyes by quanta of energy. The modulation of this energy in the retina activates an electrochemical code of impulses to the brain. The energy for these impulses comes from our oxidation of foods ultimately derived from light stored in green leaves. The input to the brain is shunted in a lattice of circuits. Its information value is partly due to what has come before; information of high value probably increases the orderliness of brain activity, perhaps even brain structure.

The round of energy from environment to artist and its return in his manipulation of the canvas is an aspect of a greater energy flow that binds man to his world. Even the rocks he paints are transitory, their temporary presence an expression of the mortality of the crustal drama of the earth, the irreversible arrow of planetary evolution. The motion of rocks is rhythmic; they are fragments of the breakup of land slowly rising. This destruction and creation is marked by flexes in atmospheric and oceanic chemistry. In a still shorter pulse, transient atoms migrate in cycles like seasonal workers, now part of the body of a miner, now of a tomato picker. They slip from the dead husk of a body into the soil, water, air, or rock and back again into a series of living systems, at once part of many overlapping systems. The living cell has its foundations deep in the physical structure of the world, where boundaries between life and death are indefinite. Patterns in this incessant flow, even the most elaborate social organizations, are no more stable than an atom.

Just as the artist's eye captures a shaft of light, plants take from the rain or solar radiation enough to do the work of gathering materials to build themselves. Each has self-informing arrangements for creating order from disarray, sucking from the sea of elements and

showers of rays. The orderliness so created is at once health and perception of the universe. Striving for order is sometimes manifested
by creating external designs such as bird nests or paintings and is
continuous within organisms and between them. Like a cell, a forest
regulates energy dispersal. In each there is a symmetry of transmission between and within levels. Transmission involves communications, sometimes accomplished by the joining of molecules to form
a protein, sometimes by putting brush to canvas.

There are two consequences of this. Many creatures create a large
proportion of the environment in which they live. The most extreme
example is the termite, but each species of termite builds a predictable form of termitarium. In no species is the exact form of the built
environment less predictable and more variable than in man. There
are undoubtedly underlying constants, but there has been great diversity in the humanized landscapes of the past ten thousand years.
The amount of deliberateness in this diversity has also ranged widely,
from the "accidental" but practical forms of the city slum or Bantu
village to the design of Brasília or a Japanese garden. When the Renaissance enlarged the idea that life and the state were works of art,
it simultaneously discovered modern landscape esthetics, thus linking the fortunes of the landscape arts and the exploitation of nature
by man's hand. This has sometimes resulted in the manipulation of
the natural world in such a way as to communicate back to us something we want to believe about nature, fitting it to our scheme of the
world. Art is sometimes regarded as a kind of superfluous luxury
which can be afforded as a fringe benefit by wealthy civilized societies. Where art is misunderstood in this way, this evaluation may
be transferred to the natural environment, by the assumption that
natural forms not created by economic man, such as forests, are
merely pleasant but unnecessary amenities.

Another consequence of modern model building has to do with
the ultimate abstraction of the visual process. The final quality to

which an analysis of vision and landscapes leads is light. As the supreme abstraction, light has a way of bringing abstraction full circle,
as it is also an immediate, natural physical event. It is the means by
which most of our information about the world reaches us and, as I
have mentioned, the principal source of energy in life. If plants have
theologies and herbivores can worship, light must surely be at the
heart of their prayers and philosophies. Man, an omnivore-carnivore,
receives his substance at somewhat further remove, insofar as he eats
meat, but even he has a metaphysics of light. In Europe the Gothic
cathedral, for instance, is a model of the medieval universe, representing both the order of the world and the perfection of the world
to come. Its central feature is a special luminosity, as light was regarded at the time of its construction as the source and essence of all
visual beauty. "To the medieval thinker," says Otto Van Simson in
The Gothic Cathedral, "beauty was not a value independent of others,
but rather the radiance of truth, the splendor of ontological perfection, and that quality of things which reflects their origin to God.
Light and luminous objects, no less than musical consonance, conveyed an insight into the perfection of the cosmos, and a divination
of the Creator."[2] This was an adaptation of a Platonic idea that light
was the closest approximation to pure form, and the Middle Ages
raised light to the status of mediator between bodiless and bodily
substances, both spiritual body and embodied spirit. As the cause of
all organic growth light was conceived as the transcendental reality,
engendering the universe and illuminating our intellect for the perception of truth. As the Virgin is the "temple and sanctuary of the
trinity," the garden enclosed, she is the cathedral itself and her impregnation with the Holy Spirit is represented by light through the
windows, beams coming down into the gentle, dusky gloom—like
rays entering the sea—making the seeing eye possible and inviting
it into unimagined habitats.

TWO

On Animals Thinking

PREPARING THE SOIL FOR THOUGHT

A WORLD WHERE PEOPLE are beginning to crowd one another intolerably is a world too small for animals. Until recent centuries, big clusters of people were widely separated. In the towns some animals, such as pets, sparrows, and cockroaches, thrived, but the realm of the wild birds and mammals was between towns. Now the planet is becoming a city. Animals that once lived on farms or simply away from civilization soon will no longer find space. They use "our" air, land, food, and water. If that nonhuman life is to continue, it will be only because it is purposely included in the human designs on the Earth, because animals are more valuable than the resources they use. In a world of periodic starvation and widespread poverty, where wants are created daily by civilization itself, that will be a hard value to prove. A huge, well-fed human population, sustained by global manipulations of our island planet, cannot afford animals—not unless they are essential to us.

What necessity could this be? Technology is rapidly replacing animals as both workers and material substances. Research in medicine is increasing with tissues and cells rather than whole creatures. Our pleasures and our esthetics can find alternatives. Oil, nuclear power, and solar energy make the man-animal partnerships of the past obsolete. In a Buckminster Fuller world there is no time, room, or need for creatures bigger than yeasts and bacteria. The great passion for human betterment is endless, repeating around the globe the theme of a world garden, green lawns, and plastic domes. After centuries the brutes and monsters that for so long contended with and haunted us have all been put down.

So it seems. Such is the myth of fossilfuelman. But there is a profound, inescapable need for animals that is in all people everywhere, an urgent requirement for which no substitute exists. It is no vague, romantic, or intangible yearning, no simple sop to our loneliness or nostalgia for Paradise. It is as hard and unavoidable as the compounds of our inner chemistry. It is universal but poorly recognized. It is the peculiar way that animals are used in the growth and development of the human person, in those most priceless qualities that we lump together as "mind." It is the role of animal images and forms in the shaping of personality, identity, and social consciousness. Animals are among the first inhabitants of the mind's eye. They are basic to the development of speech and thought. Because of their part in the growth of consciousness, they are inseparable from a series of events in each human life, indispensable to our becoming human in the fullest sense.

This claim will seem extravagant and even offensive to some. At the center of our humanity is pride in our independence from animals and animality. We have bodies as they do, but we also have minds. We tell ourselves that minds can free us not only from the animal in us but also from the animals around us. In our mortal life this mind is the focus and the means of all we most prize, our hope for making something of ourselves, of rising above mere existence.

My thesis is that the mind and its organ, the brain, are in reality that part of us most dependent on the survival of animals. We are connected to animals not merely in the convenience of figures of speech—a zoological equivalent of "flowery speech"—but by sinews that link speech to rationality, insight, intuition, and consciousness. It is not the same as thinking *about* animals. The connection is in the act and nature of thought, the working of mind.

Animals themselves have brains and probably share some aspects of our mental experience. Our animal ancestors were in this way, as in others, intermediate between ourselves and other kinds of animals. Mind is a universal and very ancient dimension of life, widely shared in varying degree. But to claim that living animals are a necessary part of the mental growth of humans goes far beyond our casual, poetic sharing of a generalized quality. What follows is not so much about animals as about people: the ways people must use animals because animals evoked, during the long stretch of the past, our human capacity for minding. We cannot avoid the subject of the evolution of intelligence in order to understand its workings. Every child is committed to the use of animal images in the shaping of his own consciousness because thought arose in the past as an interaction between different animals and between people and animals.

It is customary in describing the evolution of intelligence to arrange the creatures in ascending order, and to find correlates of the details of the human brain in the different levels of animal life. But there is an emptiness to such an approach that cannot be avoided. It dumps us into the present as a unique fulfillment, the survivor of all the sunken hulks of the past. This kind of human thinking of evolving from animals turns the rest of the world of life into a vestigial zoo. Our frustration with this isolation from other life makes us resent its otherness. Our culture is hostile to the physical, material world. By their very presence the other creatures haunt us as beings we have evolved from; their being seems to affirm that our consciousness sets us free in an unprecedented cosmos, surrounded by ghosts, loosed from all guidelines, each of us a bundle of wandering thoughts.

But there is another way of understanding that evolution. What is to be known, even in our self-conscious distance from other life, is predicated by the nature of mind. Man is a unique combination of qualities and organs like those of other animals. They are the framework in which his thought is given and in which it works. This

23

history of nature is the history of what to think, what conclusions the probing mind can arrive at, what questions it can raise. We do not graduate from animality but, in our most prized capacity, into it and through it.

The necessity of animals is psychological. Its roots are in the history of intelligence. That history is like a busy atelier of active, crucial figures and events. Among them are flowers, fruits, seeds, insects, soil, birds, primates, and other large mammals. From our view in the present, that arena of moving forms making up evolutionary time seems almost like a dance whose purpose and objective was ourselves.

But the evolution of mind is not like a great river of species, emptying only into us. It is a tangle that diverges instead of coming together. It is not a single great crescendo of emergence, but a pulsing or surging, separated by still pools of time. Its background is the era of reptiles, played out in vast swamps and low-lying forests of evergreen: conifers, horsetails, algae, mosses, and ferns. The flowering plants and mammals which were to revolutionize that world were at first a minor part of it. Then, amid worldwide volcanic activity related to collisions of the great tectonic plates bearing the drifting continents, whose bent edges were riddled with deep fractures and outpourings of molten materials, new upland habitats appeared, the climate was altered, and the world was dappled with the first blooms.

Gradually the flowers evoked and responded in their own evolution to a growing host of insects. The insects supervised flower pollination, engaging with them in alliances that would gradually spread color and deepen the organic blanket across the Earth for a hundred million years. This collaboration was probably the most fateful event in the history of mind. It created soil, the world of color, fruit, and the seed. Seeds, with their nutrient and energy-storing capacity, would eventually support whole families of primates and dynasties

of large prey and predators, the mammalian herbivores and carnivores.

The plant-insect symbiosis gave birth to a true humus and soil,
the most complex organic system in the world. Until then, the land
was only freckled with life. Afterward, the soil (and ooze at the bottom of lakes) became a skin, mediating the mineral and biological
kingdoms. Intelligence is a fragile thing, and the soil was its nest,
the flower its first encyclopedia, and the seed its source of power.

Because of flowers, a thin, sour, silent world was turned into a
sweet nursery, and out of its microbial ferment came three-quarters
of the world's million species of animals, the insects, still being discovered at more than a thousand new species per year. We acknowledge (as grassland primates) the roots of our existence in their gift to
the prairie community. Their marvelous perceptual systems involve
the distinctions of color, odor, number, symmetry, and even sound.
They are attuned to the pigments, oils, vitamins, and other special
compounds of plants to a degree beyond our experience and understanding. They have exquisitely sensitive organs and behaviors that
are phased and synchronized over life cycles that last as much as sev-
enteen years. These complex cycles, mostly spent underground or
inside plants, are keyed to the seasons and to other organisms. They
are able to locate precisely what they need, care for their young, and
communicate. Yet all this does not require or develop in them reflective thought or imagination. It is almost as though they are the
secret chemical ingredients that make the prairie's thinking possible.

The soil was, and is, their main incubator, a placenta modulating
the world's rawness, otherwise too wet or dry, hot or cold, too acid
or too barren to dependably share out the compounds generated by
decomposition. The diversity of flowering plants and the complexity
of plant structure, especially of the flowers proper, and the vast array
of insects associated with particular species are the foundation upon

which the world's ecological stability rests. That stability is the forerunner of warm bodies, and only warm bodies have keen minds. Complex natural communities make complex bodies, make intelligence.

The most characteristic feature of such communities is their multiplicity. The variation of the flowering plants and of the parts of plant anatomy, especially flower and fruit parts, and the profusion of associated insects are like so many tributaries of the life stream. Such variety and diversity are not only the source of intelligence but the necessary subject of all thought, for the thing mind must do above all else is make distinctions and choices. Beyond that, benefiting from experience and communicating the decisions are marks of superior brains.

Diversity is relative, but there may be some yet undiscovered relationship between the number of kinds of things in a world and the possibilities open to intelligence. Why are there not ten times as many or ten times fewer animals than there are? Ecologist G. Evelyn Hutchinson has suggested that the number of terrestrial forms is the result of the number of food chains, that is, the routes that energy can flow within a natural community.[1] The chains begin with plants. The question becomes one of the diversity, size, and complexity of plant species and their support, in turn, of specialized herbivores. Beyond that, diversity is limited by the number of links in food chains, usually about six. By the time F eats E, which ate D, which ate C, which ate the herbivore B, which ate the plant A, there is not enough energy left to pass on to a level G.

As for the relationship all this has to human intelligence, Anthony Wallace once observed that the number of kinship terms in folk cultures corresponded roughly with semantic spaces; that is, our ability to discriminate between stimuli, such as sound frequencies or colors. The number is indicated both from perceptual testing and lexicons or collections of names. The cognitive limit is said to be characterized by the 2^6 rule. Beyond about 64 the complexity of sets ceases to increase, giving way simply to the number of sets. Whether this rule of six binary dimensions is in any way associated with our taxonomies of animals has not been studied.

There is a physical as well as psychological aspect to natural complexity. Diversity is generally recognized as a stabilizing dimension. Rich communities of plants and animals fluctuate less in all ways than sparse ones. Nervous systems are delicate and complicated. No one yet knows how many kinds of plants and animals are needed to stabilize natural systems enough for any given level of brain complexity.

If mind, in this view of history, begins with insects, one still hopes not to slight the tribes of life that had previously come and gone, or the great families of fish, amphibians, and reptiles, some of whom remain, none of whom should be considered only as links in a chain connecting the beginnings of life to ourselves or seen as totally lacking in intelligence. Their orders, together with the precursors of the insects, the rich, unseen world of the invertebrates, and the ancestors of the first mammals need no apology.

So the era of intelligent life as *we* understand it was initiated at the end of a long geological peace. It went in five directions, all of them ultimately dependent on the concentrated packaging of the embryos and nutrients by the flowering plants.

One was the way of insects, masterpieces of finely tuned sensory systems with precise, preprogrammed muscle responses and elegant social unions. A second was the way of birds, eaters of seeds and insects, each of whose minds are conscious instruments of extraordinary visual and auditory integration for following instructions to move through a space defined by a map in the head. The third and the fourth are interrelated. They are the large mammals: the predators on the one hand and prey on the other. The dynamic of pursuit and escape is the great sculptor of brains. While this includes the dolphins and whales, as well as the elephants, we know less about the genesis of their psyches than we do about such terrestrial carnivores as the big cats and members of the wolf family or their prey, the deer, antelope, and other hoofed forms. Hunter and hunted are engaged in an upward, reciprocal spiral of consciousness with its constituents of stratagem and insight. (The small animals are predators or prey, too, but their skulls are too small for good brains; their size in relation to terrain and plants gives a different cast to their mobility; and their habits in the dark are more mechanical than tactical.) The final group is the primates, especially the monkeys and apes, those graceful, highly social fruit-munchers for whom experience forms a perceptual world. Zoologically, this is "our" group and the evolution of human intelligence is incomprehensible except in the primate framework. Unlike that of the apes, however, our past is ecologically intertwined with that of the large mammals of the open country. So it is to them and the clues from the grassland prepredator system that we look first for intelligence in general and then for the special episodes in our own beginnings.

The grasses are central to this intricate history of the relationship among seeds, nervous systems, and minds, even though they themselves do not have bright blooms and pollinating insects. The story—our story—is one of the cycle of events relating flowers and mammals in grasslands, starting more than fifty million years ago.

THE POSTARCHAIC WORLD; OR HOW THINKERS STARTED THE DAY WITH CEREALS

Progressive intelligence is the evolutionary sharpening of mind due to the interplay between animals. Except among the primates, it is not so spectacular in forests as in open country. It is easy to imagine great trees and giant forests as the acme of plant evolution, but there is actually something about endless woods that is stultifying, and even relatively simple. Far more complex and elegant are the grass-lands: the prairies, tundras, steppes, and savannas of the world. Forest trees are comparatively shallow beings and the earth beneath them a cool veneer. Wood and tree leaves are mostly cellulose and lignin, indigestible for most animals, materials that fungi and bacteria slowly recycle. In contrast, the prairie plants are high in pectin and protein, available in the whole tissue of the plant, substances rich in the compounds of life. The deep roots of grasses, interlaced across whole chunks of continents, penetrate, absorb, store, transport, deliver from bedrock to the bright surface, yet tunnel and build their own organic substances into the mineral substrate. They die and decompose as humus, processed by hordes of microbes into the world's richest soils. These soils support prairie and steppe habitats. We call them grasslands because we recognize that the grass seeds support large mammals. The term is botanically misleading. Although grasses are a conspicuous part, a typical modern prairie has only about 20 percent grasses and at least that many legumes and composites; that is, the nitrogen-fixing and conspicuous flowering forms. The remainder of the flora is a mix of hundreds of species, from algae to mosses to rare orchids. The vast flowering spectacle of the plains is not due to grasses, whose flowers are small and mostly independent of insects. But the whole community supports the perennial grasses, the grain-makers.

The grassland flora are composed of the most advanced kinds of plants from the whole experimental laboratory of evolution, and they are accompanied by the most diverse and complex animals: the insects and vertebrates. Perhaps with the exception of the coastal zone of the sea, it is the ultimate community of life, a chemistry so intricate that it remains, late in the twentieth century, mostly an enigma. The intelligence of its native mammals and insects and birds is the mind of the grassland. The brainy things exist by dint of their prairie home, which they pollinate, ventilate, disperse, fertilize, and crop.

Because of the energy they could store, seeds made big bodies and big brains possible. But at first it was only bigger bodies. The early millions of years of this history do not point toward more than minimal intelligence. The most ancient mammals seem to have been honed for size by evolution in the open, while their brains increased only enough to serve their greater mass. Such size changes in brain and body follow an allometric rule: the brain is enlarged at two-thirds the rate of body enlargement. Brain efficiency makes up for the difference. Hence, big animals tend to have proportionately smaller brains and heads than little animals.

This two-thirds relationship between brain and body was typical of the ancestors of the grassland mammals for several hundred million years. As each new species emerged with more weight than its ancestors, it kept the conservative brain-body map. Meanwhile the prairie itself slowly grew in complexity, its soils deeper and reserves greater. The progenitors of the hoofed mammals appeared in the savannas among their massive, relatively sluggish cousins, the carnivores, crude by modern standards, committed to an uncomplicated search-and-destroy pattern.

Very slowly something quite different began. The fossil record of skull sizes shows emphasis on brains. This change foreshadowed the end of the simple rule of chance and strength for predator and prey. Unlike their archaic ancestors, these new forms began to develop brains beyond the minimum needed to coordinate bodies in fixed patterns and serve the mechanics of physiology. Sheer roulette of the open tablelands, in which eater happened onto his victim or prey happened not to be found, gave way to stalking and escaping.

Over the past one hundred million years four whole groups of such progressive mammals have come and, except for the last, gone. The record of disproportionately bigger brains is indisputable. It signifies an investment in brains as specialized adaptations by hunters and hunted with large bodies. The carnivore ceased searching at random and began to track, stalk, intercept, and coordinate. Instead of seeking the prey itself, the hunter would start by seeking signs of the prey. From largely automatic responses and reflexes the hunt shifted to persistence, combined sensory modalities, memory, experience, and skill. The older predators had simply searched, like the herbivores themselves roving through a world of scattered but abundant food. That strategy of search-and-find was associated with reflexive and mechanical patterns of attack, simple response chains. The techniques of the newer stalkers began to vary with the species hunted, to be aimed at selected individuals, and to take advantage of special features of terrain, wind, and group interaction. Out of this progressive predation came hunting skills so highly timed and carefully coordinated that the old became leaders and the young had to be taught.

The prey, on the other hand, would not last long unless it could respond in its own capacity for stratagem. Indeed, the archaic forms did not last. Only a progressive prey could withstand the emphasis on intelligent assault. Being faster or bigger was not enough. Natural selection from the pressure of increasingly intelligent predators produced clever escape tactics. Recognition of differences in the behaviors of different predator species, insight into the body language of distant hunters, the employment of terrain or water as barriers, deliberately confusing the trail, decoying the pursuers from the more vulnerable individuals, complex group movements and defenses— these are only a few of the sorts of behaviors that emerged from the more flexible capacity for learning and the development of social integration by which the herbivores countered the tactics of the carnivores.

The ratio of brain to body size, or "encephalization quotient," among both predators and prey can be compared for the four series of grassland-inhabiting mammals.[2]

MAMMAL GROUP	HERBIVORE	CARNIVORE
I (archaic)	.18	.44
II (60–30 million years ago)	.38	.61
III (30–13 million years ago)	.63	.76
IV (recent)	.95	1.10

Notice that the hunter always has a relatively bigger brain than its prey. This must be so; the contest cannot be equal or the predator would die as a species. But too much success is also destructive. The predator must have an advantage but not reduce the prey too much. The result is an upward spiral of intelligence occurring over the ages among interacting big-bodied mammals, mostly in grasslands. The combination of circumstances, habitats, and interactions is essential to our understanding of mind. The animal groups to which it refers are the hoofed animals and the wolf and cat families.[3]

It is fair to ask at this point what this has to do with our intelligence, since we belong to none of these groups. The answer will be forthcoming. First, some further observation on this system of brains and plains.

Popular zoology often gives the impression of evolution running all-out in certain directions. The fifty million years of mutual honing and selection between prey and predators was never unqualified. Every mutation has its price, especially where brains and behavior are involved. Brains put heavy demands on nutrients, energy, and oxygen. They affect prenatal and postnatal life for both mother and offspring. The time committed to immaturity and growth, the delicacy and fragility of the brain itself, and the probabilities of going wrong, by interfering with other neural and behavioral systems, and of psychopathology all act conservatively to dampen increased braininess. Calculated choices do not necessarily lead to survival more often than spontaneous responses. The slow working toward better brains among the hunters and hunted was not isolated feedback, independent of the rest of the species' requirements; it had to be subordinated to the function of the whole animal and every aspect of its life. Only four or five orders of mammals among twenty have some species specialized in big brains: the primates, the two orders of hoofed animals, their terrestrial predators, and the marine mammals. For each group, or for each community of life, there seems to be a balance struck, like distribution along a normal curve, requiring or distributing other specializations that inevitably diminish intelligence. When all this is taken into account, and when we reflect on what a mess man is making of the planet, we can see the wisdom of the genes in a highly restrained commitment to flexible behavior.

In the popular image, evolution not only races along in certain directions, but sweeps all before it. For example, the anthropologist Pierre Teilhard de Chardin and his followers perceive the evolutionary emergence of mind as a kind of shell growing around the planet, a "noosphere." This gives the mistaken impression that all brains are growing. But there are not only more large-brained forms today than in the past, there are also more small-brained species. There seems to be some kind of ecological ratio at work, like taxpayers supporting the privileged. Insects, for all their sensitive ways, do not have the intellectual freedom to embarrass the community. Mind among the mammals moved toward the calculating consciousness for which part of the ecological price is a wide base of "traditional" animals with conservative brains.

YOU THINK WHAT YOU EAT

With these cautionary words about popular zoology, let us return to our theme: that mind advanced in the grasslands as sparks from the friction between two ecologically synchronized groups of mammals, the clawed carnivores and hooved herbivores. Predator and prey are the means of a dialogue that the prairie carries on with itself. Intelligence has been used as a catchall to include all the improved brain functions, but certain of its components were improved more than others.

The kind of intelligence favored by the interplay of smarter catchers and keener escapers is defined by attention—that aspect of mind carrying consciousness forward from one moment to the next. It ranges from a passive, free-floating awareness to a theta or slow-wave rhythm, which is investigatory, to a highly focused, active fixation. The range through these states is mediated by a brainstem structure, the limbic or arousal system, a network of tracts converging from sensory systems to integrating centers. From the more relaxed to the more vigorous levels, sensitivity to novelty is increased. The organism is more awake, more vigilant. Vigilance is that aspect of attention especially improved by progressive predator and prey. It is sensitive to signals from the surroundings. Prompted by these signals, ever more subtle with more vigilance, the processes of arousal and concentration give attention its tone and direction. Arousal is at first general, with a flooding of impulses in the brainstem, then gradually the activation is channeled. Thus we begin to concentrate, to hold consistent images.

A more proper meaning of intelligence is the way in which this keenly gleaned and alertly searched information is used in the context of previous experience. Consciousness links past attention to the present. It helps tie signs and possibilities together, past and present, manipulating the world by first attending to images from memory, causal chains, and the integration of details with perceived ends and purposes.

These elements of intelligence and consciousness come together in different styles in predator and prey. Herbivores and carnivores develop different kinds of attention, related to their lives of escaping or chasing. Arousal in herbivores or prey species produces adrenaline from the adrenal glands, which is fear-inducing. In predators, the substance produced is its reciprocal, norepinephrine, resulting in aggression. For both, arousal attunes the animal to what is ahead. Perhaps it is not forethought as we know it, but something like it, using past events as a gestalt for the hunter's anticipating. The predator is searchingly aggressive, inner-directed, toned by the sympathetic nervous system and the adrenal hormones, but aware in a sense closer to consciousness than, say, the reflexive snap of a hungry lizard at a passing beetle. The large mammal predator is working out a relationship between movement and food, sensitive to possibilities in cold trails and distant sounds and to yesterday's unforgotten lessons.

The herbivore prey is of a different mind as well as digestive system. Its mood of wariness rather than searching and its attitude of general expectancy instead of anticipating are silk-thin veils of tranquility over an explosive parasympathetically tuned endocrine system.

The smattering of clinical language and technical terms to describe differences of mind in predator and prey may be helpful to some or seem unnecessarily scientific and detailed to others. I hope it conveys the idea that the differences are real and not impressionistic. The impressionist differences between predator and prey are grievously misleading when seen as a kind of viciousness versus sweetness. The polarity of predators and prey has nothing to do with the widespread sentimentality that projects meanness into carnivores and kindness into herbivores.

Indeed, the polarity is simply a convenience in a scale of characteristics. Like male and female, predator and prey share much more than they separately possess. Even so, rabbits, deer, and sparrows all have qualities in common that we recognize. The ferocity of the lion and the persistence of the wolf are not only part of their hunting

35

behavior. In repose they do not become gazelle-like or rabbity. Their carnivore traits are whole-body, whole-life saturated. The differences between predator and prey are character differences in the deepest sense of the term—organically rooted effects on personality.

We can now move to ourselves and our place in the prairie dialogue. There is a third group of animals standing at various distances between the two polar extremes, sometimes carnivores, sometimes herbivores. They are omnivores, the versatile meat- and plant-eaters. They have their expectant side, a kind of fruit-minding, danger-watchfulness, an outward-turned, keen receptivity. At other times they stalk with a yet more flexible attention, subliminal, investigatory, and focused at different moments. The following table compares some omnivores to carnivores and herbivores.

I. CARNIVORE	II. HERBIVORE	III. OMNIVORE
hawk	sparrow	crow
mink	rabbit	raccoon
cougar	deer	bear
wolf	sheep	man

In terms of behavior and personality, this grouping is more important than genetic relationship. Psychologically, hawks and cats have more in common than hawks and sparrows. Bears, raccoons, crows, and foxes all possess qualities which we not only recognize but for which we feel affinity. They have flexibility, a readiness to try things, to meet the demands of the occasion. They are our omnivorousness speaking to us. Our fellow omnivores hold a special place in our thoughts though we may never have consciously classified them as such. What we count as intelligence, adaptability, and diversity are given generic shape by reality, not by us or our art.

Omnivorousness integrates the two poles of catching and escaping. Sometimes it is one, sometimes the other. The cunning, relentless stalker and the silent, cautious prey are in equilibrium. The characteristics are ecological, not social. Our herbivorousness is not in us that passive, loving, and tender feeling for others, nor is our carnivorousness the basis of savagery in our purely human relations. Lions and tigers have their socially tender side, while some of the interpersonal behavior of rabbits and sheep is exceeded nowhere in nature for its brutality.

The omnivore is not simply balancing two opposite tendencies, but integrating them in novel ways. It is a creative duality. For example, we might expect that the carnivore in us and other omnivores would dominate our relationships with other animals, while our plant affinities, our herbivorousness, would be the master shaper of our perception of all plants. But we are not so simple. Part of the strangeness of human experience and history is the capacity for directing the restless psychic force of the meat-mind upon the nonprey world, to experience forests and fields in some strange sense of pursuit and capture. Or is it our ability to attend to animals with the impressionistic, subliminal attention of the browsing consciousness? We can translate our ecological vision so that the carnivore in us makes new prey of the plant world and the herbivore in our heads creates environment from the animals. This psychology of omnivorousness may also make a new vision of one's own preyship, turning toward aggression by scrutiny rather than the knee jerk of flight.

To feel these possibilities is in a sense to be informed by our own possibilities. To put into words what these feelings are is to name those inner beings. With Adam and Orpheus as the namers of creatures, we celebrate a mastery over our inner zoo which that naming seems to give us. Only when they are named and we can speak of them can the animals speak to us in this way, as the means of our reflection and discussion of the forms of our own transient emotion. By means of named images our own behavior becomes subject to our own consciousness.

In this way we come to the use of our ecology for thinking about our humanness. Other omnivores, however, do not seem to have come to this concern with the inner landscape. To see why, we must consider our primate nature.

WHAT THE ARBOREAL EYE KNOWS

Early in the chapter we said that the evolution of the terrestrial mind followed two streams. One was the grassland or savanna. The second was the tropical forest. Keeping in mind the importance of flowering plants in the evolution of insects and soil, which made complex terrestrial life possible, and the progressive refining of mind by cycles of predator and prey whose dances became less and less random encounters and more and more choreographed, there is yet another aspect to the growth of the psyche as we experience it. We have seen how larger bodies, more energy, more complexity, and more stability in the ecosystem are related to one another, but that relationship omits a peculiar sequence of events in mammalian evolution without which the biological anomaly of human thought is unthinkable.

The daytime or diurnal reptiles and amphibians whose behaviors have been studied have fixed connections between eyes and brains and muscles. Bodies are activated by just the right visual signals. For example, if the right-sized image moves across the retina of a hungry frog's eye, the frog reacts by eating it. If the image is not right, the "food" signal will never reach the frog's brain or trigger its food-catching movements. The filtering device is located in the eye, not the brain.

The same is true of reptiles and probably of that reptile-like ancestor of the earliest mammals, who were small ground-dwelling creatures at the time of the first flowers. The new plant communities opened up wider opportunities for all kinds of animals, among which were nocturnal beings. Some paleontologists think the early mammals were "driven" into the dark. This entailed a shift from vision to hearing and smell in obtaining information. Hearing gives distance, movement, and direction of another creature. This requires successive stimuli. Perceiving these signals as a pattern meant ordering them in time rather than visual space, translating them into the all-at-once of a spatial map.

Like the olfactory part of the brain, the auditory centers are located deep inside. That is, the stimuli go directly from the sensors to the brain for analysis and storing. Sniffing conveyed information about the environment close at hand for these ground-dwelling nocturnal forms.

Sound and smell were analyzed and integrated cortically, not sensorially—in the brain rather than in the sense organ. Though hearing and smell are not basically spatial, their temporal analysis creates a kind of analogue to space. Because we descended from these sniffers and smellers, the first step in human-like intelligence was the encephalizing or deep-brain elaboration of tissues for storing information. The perception of patterns from signals coming at intervals meant holding what had gone before, putting it into a spatial code. And it meant the reverse: calling and marking by scent were actions scattered through time by which the individual conveyed information about its location and movements.

The second step in this evolution was the further opening of new niches in the trees, made possible by elaboration of the flowering, fruiting plants in the tropics. After some fifty million years of mammalian life, opportunities arose for visual or daytime movement and food-finding. Night tree-climbers can scarcely go leaping about, nor can they find fruits as efficiently by random searching as they could by color vision—that is, flowers and fruits already co-evolved with birds and insects to reflect light as color.

When the primates emerged once again into the dawn or twilight from that long night passage of their earliest history, they had already at hand a deep-brain integrating and storing ability, created through the interaction of the senses other than vision. It related time to space, a time-binding capacity through the sense of hearing. The kind of temporary storage that made melodies from tones was now transferred to vision. Holding of images would in time become the imagination. Much earlier in the evolution of terrestrial animals, the old reptilian retinal vision system gave way to the primacy of audition for creating nocturnal space, and this was replaced in turn by a new visual center of the brain based on time-coding like that of sound. A perceptual visual world was created in which distance could mean time or space, and those events distant in time were remembered as mental images in the space of the mind's eye. The visual world became, as it were, constant or continuous rather than sporadic illuminated fields.

The integration of sounds over time into a recognized pattern was discovered independently by the birds, and the neural structures to do this are an important reason for their relatively large brains.

The primates redefined the whole idea of the stimulus. It ceased to be simply a releaser and became entrained in sets, patterned as objects making up a perceptual world, subject to autonomous representation or recall. This recall of images establishes an imaged past and imagined future framing the present. This capacity for the visual presentation of objects from the past to one's self and the way it sensitizes us to a stream of time is not a general capacity. Consciousness is a very highly specialized mode of modeling and learning, dependent on specific brain elements and functions.

In sum, the evolutionary sequence was: (1) hearing replaced vision as a distance sense when mammals became nocturnal; (2) this required a capacity to translate successive signals into spatial maps, to perceive sequences of sounds as wholes and to re-hear or re-cognize them simultaneously in space; and (3) with reemergence into daylight activity and vision, the same kind of temporal encoding of visual imagery created a continuous visual world of objects. The oldest reptilian hearing analyzer was deep in its head, the vision analyzer in the eye itself. Its descendants became night creatures, centering their attention on hearing. When, much later, their evolutionary heirs, the primates, emerged once again to live in daylight, their new visual analyzer was connected to the deep-brain hearing centers. Like the primates, the marine mammals also renewed their visual emphasis, using the deep centers of a powerful, time-integrated, auditory heritage. If this use of the old hearing-smelling apparatus for linking visual images into a continuous visual world—with a re-called (re-viewed) past and an imag-inary future—is the foundation of mammalian consciousness rather than the old "hand and eye" theory, it becomes easier to comprehend how the dolphins may have achieved their high intelligence without hands.

The interim of early mammalian evolution in the dark may have made later brain enlargement possible by the advantage it gave to body-temperature regulation. Keeping warm without sunlight may have been initially a physical or behavioral adaptation, but out of it came the warm, constant internal environment, or "warm-bloodedness," necessary to higher brain activity.

The progressive brain repacking by which terrestrial predators and prey honed their respective intelligences on the whetstone of each other's strategies and the enlargement of brain centers for visual time-binding among the primates were the sources of the increase of certain brain tracts, of reticular clusters of neurons, specific interconnections, and of brain cell and intercellular glial mass in areas governing these behaviors. We can now see that they were essential to our past and made possible the even more unusual steps that followed.

SPEECH AS THE SUMMONS TO IMAGES

Man is a primate, the beneficiary of the shift of the deep midbrain, nose-ear information storage into a time-binding visual coding process. The primates use this special kind of attention for learning and communication, even for consciousness. Man's special form of communication is speech. Like brains, speech did not emerge as a blank check to be drawn against the future. It was the outcome of something, not just practice or need, but a set of selective events in human prehistory.

Since none of the other primates has speech, it apparently arose in the protohuman line after that line had separated from other primates. Our prehuman ancestors lived in semiopen country, and they shifted from primate omnivorousness in which their protein was acquired from such things as insects, nestling birds, eggs, and crayfish toward the hunting/gathering omnivorousness of root digging, grain foraging, scavenging, and large-mammal hunting.

What was the correlation between speech and this shift in ecology? It is unlikely that hunting alone was the selective force in the evolution of speech and its brain centers (at the confluence of three lobes: temporal, parietal, and frontal). There are many animal hunters who are extremely efficient and highly evolved, but none has speech except man. Nor is speech simply an accessory to the neural needs of a warm body, of learning, of hands, upright stance, or even tools. Yet somehow language is related to them all.

The clue to language is in the nature of the *primate* hunter. Consider what happened when the typical predator attention system was joined to the incessant communicative turmoil and total self-absorption in the group. Few other kinds of vertebrate terrestrial animals even approach the monkeys and apes in the intensity and subtlety of personal interaction impelled by a sound-linked visual intelligence. From birth to death the primate is swept by currents of taking and yielding, rank-order anxiety, expression and response, play, learning, all the relentless commitment of the social contract. It often seems manic, the nuances of posture and intention more like chemical reactions than intermittent signals made across space.

Everything in its life—food, enemies, weather, danger, movement in space—is experienced through a social screen. Intelligence is wrapped in a social skin. Self-assessment is a perpetual concern: in relation to parents, siblings, competitors, and mates. A tenuous, vibrant personal status is the nucleus at the heart of all primate experience and action.

The nonprimate predators also interact, reproduce, protect, and nourish. But primate food is at hand, like that of most herbivores. Feeding is almost incidental to social interactions. Many large carnivores are social, and yet the hunt focuses their attention away from themselves. From their persistent search, energized tracking and interception to the rush of pursuit and kill, their attention is on another species. The intelligent predator learns from experience, and the strategy of the hunt itself is a tactical whole needing attention to past and future: what is ahead, some image of a prey perhaps yet unseen, and a sense of continuity with past experience. Here the predator and primate cross trails, both have temporal concerns, a kind of protohistorical sense, a forward and backward looking. They are deeply different: one haunted by social identity, the other engrossed with the mystery of movable feasts; one fixated on relationships with its kindred, the other absorbed in its symbiotic relations with prey species.

What happens when you cross the two types of attention? What hybrid emerges from the mixing of the furiously solipsistic world of the primate with the rage of pursuit of the other—political stratagems and ecological tactics? Obviously, such a combination cannot be simply additive. We might expect a fusion centered on some integrating factor not found either in the primates or among true carnivores, and we might expect novelties of attention.

For example, our hypothetical new breed would extend primate perception of sexual pursuit into the hunt. That is, the hunt would not only take on social implications, but the prey might themselves be seen in their social relationships, as subjects as well as objects. Or the social contract among primate hunters might also be transformed: personal relations seen as having ecological dimensions, so that the role of the individual emerges as an analogy to the roles of the species.

The common round of time-binding in this new form of consciousness could provide the basis for a new dual sense of genealogy. When the time sense is applied to the social stream, we create kinship. But when it is applied to other species, we create natural history. Our new primate hunter experiences both, and more. He becomes aware of a natural history or theory of origins of his own species. He begins to apply the idea of kinship obligations to the interplay of other species. Although he heeds the dangers of life, the primate ancestor has only one set of relationships uppermost in his thought: relations with his fellows. Likewise, pure predators have their social side but are defined by rapt attention to other kinds. Now, our novel hunter-primate not only experiences both kinds of perception but can apprehend them as alternative expressions of a transcendent theme. By applying kin-thought to his ecology and eco-thought to his society, he doubles the modes of knowing relatedness from two to four. Natural history is articulated in a tale of origins or mythology, and thus does the explanation of one's kinship in an interspecies framework spring from the mixture of the primate's inward and the hunter's outward attention.

And the new integrating element? Speech is its instrument, music and dance its deeper expression. Anthropologists debate whether speech or song came first, as though one were the parent of the other. One may be, yet the two functions are automatically separated in left and right lobes of the cerebrum and may have had separate roles in the synthesis of primate and carnivore attention: one the voice of social harmony expressed in chant and dance, the primate fixation on social relations whose frictions threaten the cooperative necessities of the hunt; the other the voice of history, telling of myth by which clan and totem poetically incorporate the animals into society. Music is acoustic and is, like other sound stimuli, integrated temporally. Speech is linear and analytic. Unlike music, which establishes connectedness and flow in a disjointed and episodic world, speech penetrates and dissects. Its first objects were external things, animals in particular, and they were the first parts of a whole. Only insofar as it is chanted or rhetorical (and it is therefore sung) does it constitute whole melodic patterns. It is almost as though we do not trust the temporal integration of our vision that evolved in association with the old ear-mind of the nocturnal mammals squeaking under the leaves of some Mesozoic forest floor. The smell-brain, ear-brain structures may automatically make our visual experience into a continuous flow, but what's to keep the visual images that we call up from memory or imagination before the mind's eye from seeming fragmented and disjointed? They need another sound overlay, arising, like the images, from within.

In this sense poetry and music connect past, present, and future. They symbolize continuity and persistence through time. What the primate group suffers most, introverted upon its own scuffling for rank and power, where the whole of the life cycle is given to repositioning, is discontinuity. From the outside it is clearly patterned, but from the inside (and I speak as a primate) life is uncertainty, endless change, jockeying, betrayal, emotional storms, coalitions forming and breaking, ephemeral sexuality, and the lifelong wheel of growing and aging. For the human primate, song and dance counterbalance this shifting unpredictability and inconstancy. They affirm the solidarity of community over generations by articulated time-binding. Traditional music confirms the resistance of values to the erosions of human frailty. Because it does raise us above the level of individual experience, it evokes the idea of an enduring entity of which we are part. Because of it we can see the human parallel to the nonhuman species, for we can see their continuity or natural history from the outside.

Of course music does other things, too. It makes anthems. It is an archetypal frame upon which a particular group makes its own phrasing, a biological form for conveying the melodic arrangements symbolizing cohesion within a given culture. It confirms the reality of history not only universally, but directly for its members. Indeed, it serves in this way at specific points in maturation. The lullaby is a transitional connection for the infant in a world sensorially fragmented. Tunes are imprinted on the adolescent so profoundly that each generation grows into maturity nostalgic for the music of its youth. What today separates generations is precisely the process that connects those generations in traditional societies for whom there are no fashions in song or tunesmiths who manufacture new melodies.

The sentimental attachment to imprinted music extends even to our perception of the song of birds. Birds become identified with place and the particular mix of bird song of a locality evokes "home" in a way that no other assemblage of sounds can. Perhaps human singing was, in its beginnings, modeled after that of birds. But more likely there existed in human evolution a dynamic between the two, not in the sense that they serve the same purposes, but that birds were one of those nonhuman beings whose use by man was to reflect one of his own abilities, to objectify and make more manifest a trait so that it could be given a name and become available to thought. We sing and birds sing, but only we think about song.

According to anthropologist Grover S. Krantz, a threshold of brain size at about 750 cubic centimeters (a little more than half the size of the average human brain) is necessary to contain all the circuits and substance required for speech.[4] This size in prehumans could have been achieved by adding one additional round of cell divisions in embryonic growth to a chimpanzee-sized brain, and it would add slightly to the gestation time. Communication without true speech, that is, without the use of phonemes and morphemes, which distinguish it from a call system, might already have been rather advanced, as we see it now among the apes. Brains of their sizes make a very substantial mind possible, and the crossing into verbal representation would certainly not be like going from a shadowy world of reflexive animality into a reflective sunshine of humanity. The beginning of speech was a modest specialization that required perhaps as much as six or seven million years to lead on to those elaborations of conceptual thought associated with a very slow advance in brain size. Since brains also enlarge with body size, it is possible that, early in the evolution of our genus, *Homo,* only adults could speak, and the onset of speech in the individual coincided with puberty or sexual maturity rather than early childhood.

One may imagine speech in its primitive beginnings to have been entirely practical, a labeling of useful objects and acts. But it is just as likely to have been entirely composed of poetic terms with multiple meanings, what we now call metaphors, words connecting unlike things and events. To speak poetry is to illuminate and give meaning from intuition. Today, in our species, poetry and analogy are the special obsession of young adults and adolescents, perhaps because speech first appeared at puberty in our distant ancestors. Its evolution extended its practice to the years of childhood. Thus, the emergence of language and sex, at first synchronized in the life cycle, was gradually divided and separated; more precisely, the poetic part of language and the reproductive part of sexuality were initiated at puberty while the infantile and oedipal components of sexuality and the empirical vocabulary learning both shifted to the earlier years. Poetic speech was reserved for puberty, preceded by years of vocabulary learning.

The schedule of language acquisition in the individual, as we now see it, is profoundly divided into literal meaning in childhood and literal-plus-metaphorical in adulthood. Abstract usage is preceded by ten years or so of vocabulary, cataloging, and taxonomy. This separation probably emerged after a long evolution of language-using behavior during which all the phases of individual growth had become more sharply differentiated. That part of the young brain combining signals from vision, sound, and touch in the inferior parietal lobule physically matures, or becomes myelinated, with the end of childhood. Names pass through a part of it, Wernicke's area, like beasts entering Noah's Ark and, with the transitional period of puberty, the door closes on the real world, that is, on the raw materials from which a cosmos is to be created. The bridge connecting the wholly tangible past with the adult consciousness is the abstracting, poetic, metaphorical period of adolescence. The adolescent "discovers" that all those tangible things, even the creatures, signify something beyond themselves. They help to secure the polarity between self and nonself. The poetry that the older *Homo erectus* may have uttered but did not recognize as such became a synthesis not only of self and world, but also of past and present, inside and outside. Naming and classifying connected the old intuitive mind consciously with the animal world that brought it into existence. Before knowledge there was wisdom, and before facts, knowledge.

Such a view stands the old order of progress from simple to philosophical on its ear and contradicts a premise of modern education: that wisdom emerges from the contemplation of facts or data.

Language is a coding device for recall. What is recalled is attached to an image. No one knows the exact form in which millions of sense data are stored, but we do know that words retrieve some of them and that a visual picture is presented from memory, resembling that which was first offered by sight.

It is quite possible that sounds—words, even—produce mental images for educated chimpanzees. What chimpanzees cannot do is speak, transmit images by words, or construct more elaborate scenarios of visual play by speech. What the chimpanzees and other primates never needed was a vast storehouse of objects, a dictionary of otherness. What wolves and tigers had was a storehouse of diverse images—but as releasers rather than image-objects. There was no need for them to formulate models or scenarios about the world. The driving reason for those scenarios is knowledge of the self, and that was the compelling force among primates. What carnivores lacked was social fullness, one that approached the invention of abstract symbols for social categories. The carnivores had the species interest, the available symbols, but didn't need them. The human primate-omnivore brought them home to social thought.

Hypotheses about the self cannot be made in terms of the self. The self is not so easily perceived as an object; it is too fluid and close. Nor can it be easily represented. Some kind of stand-in is needed, disintegrating the person and isolating traits, making them accessible to speech and thought, and thereby to new syntheses. Complex ecosystems contained enough diversity to model the complex human individual many times over. But how was it to be got at and on what levels did it contain components that might serve as suitable analogies?

THE ZOOLOGY OF THE SELF

The most conspicuous order in nature is species membership. But how do we recognize the consistent differences that separate kinds and the similarities by which different individuals are related? All birds have wings and beaks—where do we go from there? The answer is that particular parts must be seen apart from the whole. It requires the dis-integration of individuals and the naming of those part-groups abstracted from the whole animal and whole species. Such taking apart in thought may have been preceded by taking apart in reality. It is a primate possibility because of hands; monkeys often peel and otherwise dismember the fruit they eat. But the real takers-apart of animals are the meat-eaters.

Categories are composed not only of similar entities or creatures, but similar parts. By noticing types of organs—legs, necks, livers— as well as types of animals, we give a new dimension to the imagination. Indeed, one cannot be done without the other. It extends the idea of breaking down and putting together. It enlarges the probing and scanning of the body features. Language, for mankind, directs and codes that scanning and, in speech, makes the labels that evoke similar images at the same time in different heads.

Making categories is done by classifying things or ideas with common properties as types and then repeating the operation among the types themselves. In this way the higher groupings emerge—genus, family, order, and so on. The categories are storage markers and retrieving handles. They are attention directors, too. There is an open-endedness about this approach to objects because one is never sure at first what detail may be crucial. The hunter does not know where, for certain, to look. All details are potentially significant. In this way, visual forms become objects, composed of parts, themselves in a field, not just signals or releasers, but figures in a ground.

A group or set of things with common elements is denoted by a name. It is a concept with its clutch of shared qualities recalled in naming. It is just our ability to single out similar constituents of objects or events, to group and name them, that is cognition, the source of reason. The name can become a substitute for the recollection of the experience, a term that encapsulates the past. Something happens when our attention is directed by this verbal code that is parallel to the hunt—searching, comparing, selecting, ordering, integrating.

The scrutinized object is surrounded by silently perceived data, just as the fovea centralis of the eye, the point of visual acuity, is surrounded by peripheral vision. Recollected images and the concept for which they serve as symbols move through larger contexts, whole communities of thought. Life is a hunt or search. One can only tell (or understand, or communicate) about life as a search by mastering the first hunt. One recapitulates in the linear sounds of speech the spatial events by which things are chased into order. When the events are retold, visual images march across an inner landscape. Television did not invent instant replay.

While it cannot be proven that language initially arose as an instrument for the dissection of the human personality as a means of comprehending the self, by an intensely social primate moving into a hunting ecology, it is a more interesting theory than many others, which simply take it for granted. As self-consciousness was facilitated by consciousness of the diversity of the world, our barely speaking ancestor found in animals the tangible objects he needed to embody otherwise slippery ideas.

For all animals the perceptual world is composed of a limited number of signals—some inherently recognized, some learned—which serve as releasers for behavior. In speech the word becomes a releaser that triggers an image, flashing it before the mind's eye, trailing the emotions and circumstances of something past. These images are recruited from whole animals, and parts of wholes, such as "leg" or "head," and even actions. Traits—like sluggishness, joy, nocturnality, deceit—could be dealt with in the same way so long as they could be attached to an image, an animal. The different animals not only represented usable images for social categories and sensed experience, but evoked further thought about them. The ecology of the lion produced an ecology of thought. Its anger, hunger, or motherhood bore peripheral messages carrying whole trains of connection.

Many kinds of animals learn, but few are taught. Except for man, little comes from a transmitted heritage, and even that is given by example—the migratory routes among geese, hunting techniques in tigers or wolves, for instance. The kind of learning that culture carries, however, is borne on the symbolic vehicle of speech, which denotes among other things intangible qualities, invisible events (as in the past or at a distance), spatial relations, personality traits, spiritual forces, and the whole adjectival realm of description. To the early humans and to the young human mind, these things are not perceptible; they are imageless. They cannot easily be seen in the self or even in other people. They are discoverable only as they inhere in other creatures. Friskiness, hunger, and patience can be seen respectively in pups, the searching coyote, or the waiting hawk atop a tree. Such uses of animals as various parts of speech continue now in an enormous variety of forms. A few of these are:

to buffalo	to dog it	to make a pig of
to bug	to wolf your food	yourself
to hound	to worm your way	to get his goat
to bulldog	to clam up	to be chicken
to bullshit	to crow about	(hearted)
to outfox	to horse around	to make a monkey of
to skunk	to ram home	to put on the dog
to grouse	to fish around	to duck an issue
to hawk	to bull your way	to coon apples
to crab	to be mulish	to tomcat around
to badger	to have a cowlick	to lark about
to flounder	to be dog tired	busy as a bee
to goose	to give a bear hug	in a pig's eye
to parrot	to be mousey	a lounge lizard
to rat	to be kittenish	cock-and-bull story
to duck	to be a horse's ass	quiet as a mouse
to lionize	to play leapfrog	cold turkey
to rail	to play possum	bull in a china shop
to chicken out	to turn turtle	cat got your tongue

Some of these are new, some old. Anyone can make such a list. The point is not that they persist in the language from some distant time, but that they are so rich a part of language. Joseph D. Clark's *Beastly Folklore* is a collection of about five thousand of these phrases.[5] The above examples are grouped to show that the animal term can be a noun, verb, adverb, or adjective. Not included is the simple labeling of someone as a "hawk" or a "dove"; derived terms applied directly to people, like "feline" or "dogged"; or exclamations such as "Rats!"

After perhaps as much as five hundred thousand years of human speech, it is not surprising that these terms are generally regarded only as colorful choices of wording, colloquial custom, or poetic metaphor. On the other hand, if language did begin in this way, then we could expect this animalizing to be part of its deeper structure, or of the mental apparatus that lies beneath language. If this is the case, then the intense drive of the child to learn animal names and actions may be very old and persistent, even necessary in some way to the development of speech.[6]

To summarize briefly what has been said: Speech is the means by which human intelligence developed beyond that of the apes. It was the instrument by which images could be retrieved from memory and communicated, images that made the classification of other life possible. Classification, in turn, is that order-finding analysis by which the objective world could be used to reflect the many-sided experience of being human.

Bringing time into consciousness also required tangible objects. The season, the weather, the cycle of life, the beginning, the flow of events were manifest in the coming and going and seasonal behaviors of beings other than man.

Carved and engraved animal figures could be used to transmit such ideas. A drawing or carved figure is a communal source of images synthesizing new thought. Language is a good analyzer but poor synthesizer. Its left-brain virtues fasten consciousness in linear spurts that excel in part naming but work as wholes only because words elicit pictures and song. Art makes use of pictures directly.

Hunting evolved through stages before man: goal-directed persistence, such as the crayfish following a scent through the water; interception tracking, such as the falcon aiming ahead of the flying duck; and interception by configuration, such as the wolf waiting at a rocky pass for migrating caribou. In a further—human—stage, the experience does not have to be that of the tracker himself, but a "real" experience communicated in advance. Thus do we approach reason and insight, foreshadowed in the problem-solving capacities of omnivores such as monkeys, bears, raccoons, and crows, but limited by their inability to disassemble the world and store it, with words as handles, the arts as whole-makers, and the images that words summon.

For such minding, the world is infinitely rich in clues. Nature, as Elizabeth Sewell wrote in her beautiful book, *The Orphic Voice,* becomes a language, hieroglyphic in its mystery, but subject to the scanning of the hunter's eye and the vigilance of the primate ego.[7]

We now come back for a few moments to the grasslands and the cereal world with which the chapter began. The upward spiraling of intelligence evoked in each other by predators and prey in open country made them fit tutors for our prairie hunting and escaping. Man the primate came into this milieu of mind-making after it had matured for millions of years. The prehumans who ventured into it brought a brain that was already unusual. Even the oldest known primate, *Tetonius homunculus,* whose fossil bones are fifty-five million years old, had an encephalographic quotient of .68; that is, a brain sixty-eight percent bigger than needed for physiological functions. But none of the primates in forests or quadrupedal primates in open country had a brain beyond speech-threshold size, except the one bipedal meat-eater and hunter of large mammals.

Among the routes to intelligence already mentioned (insects, birds, forest primates, and grassland large mammals), only man is both primate and open-country carnivore. Man plugged in to the running dance of wolf and deer. His primate psychology was not simply glossed over by his predatorship but synthesized with it. If one draws converging lines from chimpanzee, baboon, and wolf, their meeting point of convergence would shadow forth a glimmer of ourselves. Other primates or carnivorous mammals may be able to summon images to the mind's eye and even hold them there, but probably cannot hitch abstract qualities to visual figures or yoke them to arbitrary verbal signals.

What makes the human experience different is not simply primate origins or hunting past, but the shaping of the envisioning mind by the auditory brain, cradling imagination in time. Because of it visual thought is stretched in past and future. Like the images conjured in the head, objects seen in the terrain are never only momentary. Everything seems to take a place in memory and in anticipation as well as in the instant, a gliding triple reality. Like the linear flow of words, which is the harness of those images, objects are part of an ongoing world. The past and future are a story told, a left-brain evocation of right-brain images, order- and meaning-giving.

ART AS THE COLLECTIVE IMAGERY OF ANIMAL FORM

This recall of the past as a series of images is a public as well as a private experience. It is made public by art. The worldwide body of "primitive" art, the petroglyphs, lines cut in stone, read by eye or finger tracing their course, is such a flowing, left-brain form. Drawings or pictographs are right-brain, all-at-once messages heard by the eye. Sculpture and carved objects combine and synthesize the two, and may also be the ancestral mode, the first art, from which the etchings in stone or bone and the drawings on stone or bark are specialized developments.

This biology of art is most clearly seen in some of its oldest surviving expressions, the fabulous, worldwide cave painting and etching which span more than twenty-five thousand years. These cave and rock-shelter sanctuaries were the antecedents of temples, where the significant passages of human life were ceremonially represented. The figures in them, however, are mostly animals, a fact that misleads the modern viewer into thinking they are only about animals.

They are fossil forms of thought in which the act of imaging and symbolizing is embedded in its maternal mode, the hunt.

The drawings are virtually all large animals, hoofed and hunter, arranged in groups or individuals in significant combinations according to their kind, carefully positioned on walls, ceilings, or floors, distributed in a pattern throughout the sanctuary. Few of the drawings represent animals in motion. They are, like the visual images of memory itself, and like dream figures, stills. Their connection to a flow of events in mythical time must have been given by narration as men confronted the animal pictures. Like recollections from the personal past of our individual childhoods, they are static. Like the sleeper who scans his memory for the vestiges of his dream thoughts as though they were illustrations in a book, the cave artist presents visual images to the impressionable eyes of youthful initiates, for whom they will become the visual traces of their collective memories, not only of those awesome moments in the cave but of the time of creation and tribal beginnings. The drawings are in turn related to an even older body of carved objects carried into the sanctuaries as models. Recalled words and melodies echo in this cavern from wall to wall, like our voices in our own heads. Sounds in caves reverberate laterally as though entering from the ears. The old earth temples—and the newer—are the social ear. One crawls in to become part of a sense organ to receive messages that help explain images already there. The cave is an externalization of the head, which is in fact experienced as internal space—dark, image-laden labyrinths where we become conscious of our own thoughts, memories, history.

Numerous studies and students of this art concur that these thousands of figures signify special aspects of human life around which society was organized: marriage rules, kinship and genealogical descent, clan membership, tribal origins, the mores and myths of self-conscious beings, or at least the public instruments for asserting and affirming what is central to people. They are the tools of a cognitive and communicative process, a part of language below speech, a universal means related to thought itself. As shared and mutually stored images to which song, dance, or recitation may have been attached, they were figures of mystery except to the initiated.

Again, why formulate such central questions in the form of animals? The answer is many-sided and is not only that thought evolved in the contemplation of animals. There is also the otherness about them, which shakes us loose from ourselves, helping us to separate what is transient and personal from what endures. That about ourselves which survives us has a kind of otherness, a public aspect, part of a whole detached from individuals. Being like us and yet different, the animals manifest that invisible otherness. It is not just singular "spirit" or "soul," but as many-formed as animals themselves. Art historians have puzzled why there are so few images of men in these paintings, but we can see that the human image only reflects the puzzle of the singular and universal mixed in the one. In the animals there is a sly dissection coming between it and ourselves, a separation from which we can re-cognize those slippery abstractions.

The hunters of this transcendent otherness, whose primate blessing and curse was the relentless need to know themselves, created an art that isolated in animals constituents of the self. The cave sanctuary, like the modern temple, is a communal altar for the ceremonial attachment of collective images to myth. But religious thought is never only an explanation of the outer universe. Abbreviated and stylized as icons, beautiful mnemonic instruments of recall, these animal figures troop across the dark earth-cranium like ordered thought, the fauna of our complex self and selves.

The cave sanctuaries were probably used for facilitating passages, personal steps in certain crucial phases of individual development and, at the same time, formal social affirmation of that progress. Personality growth is marked by times of transition, intermediary stages when the individual is betwixt and between. For these episodes parents or tutors provide a special class of devices that, like a rope thrown to a floundering swimmer, connect the old self at one end and his new self at the other. These devices are known to psychiatry as "transitional objects." The animal images in the cave sanctuaries are transitional objects used to help the adolescent make a major step toward maturity. The cave ceremonies were a continuation of good mothering practices, one of the many steps by which personal identity moves from mastery of body schema and animal taxonomy toward an increasingly complex awareness of the self in the cosmos. The animals are symbols of social structure as well as recognizable species that are met with in daily life. The cave images encode a dual system in which the ecology of animals parallels the society of humans. The terrible otherness of the animals is thus approached. The drawn figures and the rituals attending them are a lifeline connecting the fragile human community with the bewildering ebullience and hidden purposes of the whole of life. In their positioning and arrangement, the mammal figures represent the human groups or clans. The animals to which they refer live in an orderly world, a visible ecosystem. Transposed to the cave walls, they bring an aura of coherence and meaning to that which they symbolize: the human community. To the eyes of the beholder they assert, with all the force of their uncanny and ravishing setting, that the human social order is part of a meaningful universe.

In its dark depth the night sky is similar to our eyes to the cavern ceiling. Like those irregular rock surfaces the spectacle of stars seems at first formless and chaotic. But it is far too large a part of the world to accept as randomly structured. Simple familiarity with its consistent patterns, even spiritualizing of the star points, has not been enough. We discern or make there organic figures. Of the forty-eight Ptolemaic constellations, all but a few are seen as organic and twenty-five are named for animals. Of the twenty-two added in the seventeenth century, nineteen have animal names. Needless to say, the choices and dispositions are arbitrary. There is nothing intrinsically animal-like (or man-like) about them, and the particular configurations seem almost playfully imposed on the stars. But it is clearly animals, and to a lesser extent our bodies and the things we make, to which we turn in order to give shape to such a haphazard spectacle.

The panoply of celestial figures contrived to give order to the sky occupies that dark vault like the figures seen in caves—not the painted ones, but the natural cracks, surfaces, and forms of the rock to which the painters responded by using them in combination with their art. Just as all tourist caves today are peopled with figures of the imagination, guided by the suggestive notions of a tour guide, perhaps Paleolithic men found in the unmodified rock what they did in the sky for centuries before they gilded those rocks with art.

The use of the imagined animal figures as an organizing nexus for subterranean amorphous rock and for the speckled night sky is also found in the daytime sky and the terrain. The attribution of creature names and likenesses to passing clouds, presumed in our civilized world to be the frivolity of children's play or poetic fancy, may be instead an important passage, a working of existential confidence, the finding of meaningful transformations in the endlessly shifting forms. On the earth's surface, colossal prehistoric earthworks, mostly in animal form, are widely found in the Americas. Some in Peru are more than a mile long. In Ohio earth sculptures form clusters occupying more than a hundred acres. Very few of them can be seen by a normal observer on the ground. Anthropologist Marlene Dobkin de Rios has developed the theory that they were designed for viewing during out-of-body trances, when the individual feels himself rising out of his own body and flying or floating upwards.[8] Whatever their ritual function or mechanics of access, such designs give form to the landscape and imply a general unifying principle underlying its seeming randomness, organizing the terrain in the truest sense.

It seems at first like childish tricks, deluding one's self and others into seeing all those fantastic animals where reality tells us is nothing but the haphazard erosion of limestone surfaces or the coincident view of distant suns. Most of those who painted the caves and made the earthworks are gone, but the Australian aborigines and Kalahari bushmen who still live with cave or rock-shelter art are anything but simpletons. They know rock from flesh; nobody is fooled about it. The "trick" is not some personifying pathetic fallacy, nor bemused, indulgent dreaming. Our modern fancy and travelers' appetite may reduce the cave figures to triviality, but that is because we think of them as spectacle and decoration.

For us the human will—the same imperious will that now creates everything around us—is our god. To it everything seems to come from within. The world is only a stage where we act out those scenarios that suit us. How could the ambience of nature be part of our physiology? How could ecology have anything to do with mind in such a view?

But another truth is that the unordered head with which we begin life has some properties of the raw rock and maze of celestial lights. We are aware of things flitting across. Our own ideas move at first through the velvet cranial spaces as unpredictably as the passage of herons or the brief flash of a startled deer at twilight. As we get to know them, we learn that their movements are not random and that they exist even when we cannot see them. If only we could hold them for a few moments and study their marvelous symmetry. . . .

In this way birds become ideas. They flit through consciousness, connecting with this twig and that branch, are attended to momentarily, and in a flash are gone. Birds are not like ideas—that is a literary simile. They are ideas. They are, each in its kind, bits of different qualities for which words heighten awareness and give control over recall. Birds are not metaphors, those analogies chosen by the private artist seeking unique expression. We do not apply this significance to the birds; it has emerged over an immense time of minding birds and being endowed with mind by them.

We may think of birds as externalizing a mental process, but it would be more accurate to say that the idea is our inward occasion of the bird's presence. Apart from the bird itself, what of the habitat through which it moves, and to which it returns unseen? If all creatures are possible ideas, relationships, emotions, feelings, the habitat is for us the outward form of the whole space of the mind. Its visible extent is like our conscious experience and its unseen distance like the unconscious. A bird flying across the sky is an idea coming from the unseen of the preconscious and disappearing again into the realm of dreams.

We have surrounded ourselves with geometrized, humanized landscapes cut from an ancient wilderness. Most of the animals in our daily lives are tame. Our man-made landscapes are caricatures of the rational mind, the external extension of civilized thought. Here and there in them we have put little lessons in meaning, intended to relieve the terrain made by the implacable economics of the state and detritus of our mastery. These are gardens, and garden style is a continuing expression of the changing idea of the universe. In medieval Europe it was a distant, perfect Paradise, a stark contrast to the sullied and soiled nature that had fallen with Adam. For the Renaissance in Italy it was a private domain, complexly ordered like aristocratic society. In Isaac Newton's day it was shaped by the laws of cosmic geometry, a vast mathematical diagram. And for romantic England it was a dream of pastoral peace in which the tame and wild worlds merged at the boundaries. But such formal statements are few. The countryside everywhere is an embodiment of the cultural perspective, economic imperatives, and historical preoccupations of its modern human occupants.

It is easy to misinterpret the point in this. The terrain is not something we dream up; no mind-is-all solipsism is intended. What is perceived is not "our" creation. The older Berkeleyan and the post-modern existentialist would have us believe that the world is the product of human imagination. Having discovered psychology, we proceeded to try to make it the only reality. What is meant here is something more mutually and functionally interdependent between mind and terrain, an organic relationship between the environment and the unconscious, the visible space and the conscious, the ideas and the creatures. In the forest visible space was sharply limited; in the prairie things opened up and we awoke.

Inner and outer terrains vary, just as do the choice of animals as analogues of qualities. The man-made domestic landscape is the extension of those deliberate and intensive acts of domination with castrated and coralled animals. But they are only a few thousand years old and are not the environment in which the terrain of human thought emerged, with its peaks of achievement, depressions, streams of ideas, areas and fields of work, its paths and information pools.

The man-made habitat and domestic animals are related to each other just as wilderness is related to wild animals. If the mind discovers structure in nature because its own structure is a product of the order of nature, then such comparison is not a discovery or an original insight, but is inevitable. We know that the brain has a projection area to which the visual tracts lead in the occipital lobe, which has real space in neural tissue, where the firing of neurons in some sense duplicates the three-dimensional space perceived by the eye. Things move through the brain as they do through the field of vision, giving off sounds, reflected light, and odors that carry into the distance. As geopsychist Dewey Moore says, "Any of the aspects of intelligence we have are developed from modeling or association with the environment. As we look at nature we always unconsciously recognize the source of our mental function. That feeling of 'experiencing the wilderness' from which we have come is an operational definition of the basis for nature mysticism."[9]

The individual may project his psychic events into the external world, fastening his unconscious thoughts symbolically onto objects there, but only because those external forms shaped his psyche in the first place. The inner and outer counterparts have living as well as past meaning, a continuing, necessary relationship. As primates we are obliged by our nature to persistently examine the social contract, but not only in the field of action as other primates do. The leap in mind that made us human was a result of the synthesis of that inward scrutiny with an external means, the carnivore's scrutiny of other animals. Nor has that redirection of attention to the nonhuman ever lost its social context. Consciousness for us signifies duality, the poetry of marriage and diet, the rules of eating and kinship, the rites of food-sharing and exogamy, the adventure of hunting and courting, the figures of love and death. Through language, common terms appear for relatedness (sex and nutrition), history (genealogy and the animal life cycle), membership (clan and species), individuality (personality and species behavior), role (gender and age and niche), drawing simultaneously from within the society and from the ecology without. Each of these is incomplete without the other.

Of a generation reared on introspection, analysis, dream study, and group dynamics, exploring the affluence produced by its Faustian drive modeled after a Creator whose prominent feature is His will, the inheritors of Jewish inward vision and Greek narcissism, little else could be expected than a loss of the ecological roots of mind. The roles of flowers, pollinating insects, soil, seeds and cereals, fruits, the grasslands, the ballets of predator and prey, the intense interpersonality of monkeys and apes are all foreign to the overriding premise of thought that human identity is a matter of mirrors and self-determination. Our reflections on how the mind works must now carry us beyond ourselves, pursuing the nature of thought as the thought of nature.

THREE

The Mental Menagerie

As I have suggested, the human brain is an evolutionary experiment made possible by primate society and predator ecology. Its most unique feature is the opening of mind and thought to the whole of experience. The strategy by which natural selection created such a brain was the infantilizing of the individual—that is, the extension of immaturity and specialization of the psychological processes of development.

Brains are screening and shunting devices for translating incoming data into action. An animal needs an efficient, coordinated relay system hooked to sensors at one end and to glands and muscles at the other. Typically, improvements of such an organ increase its sensitivity to specific stimuli and thus modulate behavior more delicately. For most mammals it is enough for the brain to administer the body's internal complexity and adjust to one's fellows, foods, enemies, and habitat without building a world picture. While there could be some advantage to storing information, there would be little in removing those filters which admit only usable input and screen out a flood of unusable stimuli.

As any trip to the zoo will show, however, evolution seems to try everything. An exception to the limited role for brains is found where cunning has high priority, where there is challenge and competition. But there is no advantage to cunning creatures without cunning antagonists. No need for a highly intelligent predator if his food is all bumbling sluggards or predictable automatons. No point in having intelligent deer if the wolves are mere random searchers, no point in sniffing political nuance or craftily imposing one's will except in a society rich in graded and complex relationships and fine shades of status.

But even among animals with progressive, predator-prey intelligence, new limitations appear. At how many removes could information remain pertinent? Whether to cross an open field or to skirt it was not a problem for the old archaic forms with brains prewired for such decisions, but for the new brains, seeking insight from a whole new range of experience, how would they know when they had enough information or what they should attend to? A single lifetime was too short a period in which to answer this question. The kind of integrated information needed could be got only from the pooled experience of others. The limited utility of personal experience is that death is a poor teacher. What one needed was a view into the possibilities beyond personal horizons.

This is the level at which the predator-prey and primate brains reached their limits. The wolf and caribou and all other modern hoofed animals and their pursuers, as well as the monkeys and apes, were admirably advanced beyond their duller ancestors. They were great experiments that worked without a means of encapsulating units of experience and referring to them. There was no way to label, package, store, retrieve, and transmit these data bundles between individuals except by example or calls with fixed meaning.

As I have mentioned, the breakthrough required speech. Today one can imagine all sorts of advantages in the human departure from the primate social frenzy and the preoccupation with catch-or-escape. But all the benefits reflect the bias of retrospect. Speech has enabled us to solve problems, think philosophically, know love, consider the stars, make art, cherish ideas, keep history. The trouble is that none explains why or how our prehuman ancestor should have developed the capacity for attending to the irrelevant as well as the relevant, with its almost certain danger of making wrong decisions. There is a sense in which speech and the perceptual world of objects put a barrier between ourselves and the world that was not there before. The image-world could be an illusion-world.

For a time some anthropologists proposed that the early prehumans were "forced" into the human realm because of weakness and vulnerability. But the Reject Ape theory of human evolution conflicts with everything we know about the history of life and of species evolution. No creature lives without a home; none is kicked out (of the forest) and wanders nicheless and nomadic; none is unadapted to the environment in which it lives. And the evidence now is, in any case, that our ancestors, like ourselves, were never fragile or at the mercy of other animals.[1]

This is related to another troublesome side of the evolution of the human psyche. Opponents of the theory of evolution have argued that such marvelous organs as the human eye could not have come slowly into existence because any imperfection would render it inoperable, like taking a part out of a fine watch. Whatever our theory about eyes, brains, and other organs of human emergence, they indeed worked at all stages. Eyes, as seen in different species, represent varying degrees of resolving power, binocularity, light/dark adaptation, conjugated movement, optical brain specialization, and so on. Likewise, speech, however primitive, must have "always" worked.

The enlargement of human attention from a small, genetically determined segment of the surroundings to the whole of it was surely achieved slowly and by degrees, probably beginning with an intelligence very similar to that of a chimpanzee. Anthropologists have speculated that primate calls had the potential for becoming words, and words are the labeling instrument by which an enormously complicated world could be systematically presented to the mind and to other minds. Words very likely were applied to tangible objects before they were applied to abstract things. From the beginning, words probably evoked fleeting mental images similar to the visual experience of the objects they represented.

LANGUAGE AND TAXONOMY

The evolution of the noun opened a door beyond the point to which primates and predation had brought the brain. As a word spoken to the self, the noun evokes a surrogate image; as a sound it communicates that image to another. A system of purely additive nouns and images runs into the thousands before it even begins to make possible landscapes of the mind that simulate an ongoing visual reality.

Consciousness, according to Harry Jerison, author of *The Evolution of the Brain and Intelligence,* is the ability to summon images. To do so requires that they be named. Naming is not arbitrary, but follows a logic of similarity and the rules of category-making. It is a sequence of alternatives, of simple binary choices. For example:

1. *A thing is alive or not alive.*
2. *If alive, it moves about or is anchored in place.*
3. *If it moves, it has four legs or it does not.*
4. *If it has four legs, it has fur or is covered with something else.*
5. *If it has fur, it is small and lives in trees or is otherwise.*
6. *If it lives in trees, it has a furry tail and scampers or does not.*
7. *If it has a furry tail, scampers, and has large incisor teeth, it is a squirrel.*

At each of the alternatives to these seven steps one may be led to other series. If it does not have four legs it may have wings, in which case one shifts to a different set of alternatives. The procedure is familiar to anyone who has ever used a plant or animal key.

Descent and kinship form a master model. The *visible* difference between different species of birds, for instance, is in part due to the evolution of adaptive size and structure, but also in part to distinct features that make it easy for the birds themselves to know their own kind at a glance. Crows and ravens differ because they are adapted to different ecological niches, but also because they themselves must keep identities clear. If birds were nose- rather than eye-oriented, their appearances to us might not clearly separate kinds. It is fortunate for us that they are visual, and this may even have been crucial for our own intelligence, insofar as it depends on categorization. We also use the mammals for models of classification. They are not primarily visual but, luckily, are so few in kinds that we can easily see the differences, even though they are based almost entirely on function in food chains and other ecological systems. Like the birds, the butterflies are, as Adolf Portmann says, "designed to be seen" and recognized by one another, and therefore serve as compelling yet discrete species to our own eyes.[2]

Classifying by arranging things in pairs of opposites is our way of thought, its utility based on the physical reality of species. Dividing everything into opposites is the most logical way of coping with an extended, chaotic world—like that of the child.

Keys to the species of plants or animals do not require a formal understanding of the logic of binary sequencing, which is tacit. Their structure was not invented by institutional science. The structure is human logic, cognition itself. It is the way each of us brings order into his world, however carelessly or with whatever contradictions we exercise it.

It is innately human, and yet it does not operate in a social vacuum. The details of anatomy or behavior by which such distinctions are made differ among different groups of people. The names of the animal groups, or taxa, are part of a particular language, which is part of a culture. As anthropologists are quick to assert, the cultural variations for classifying are numerous. Indeed, much of anthropology has been preoccupied with those differences. The universality of this taxonomic sorting process lies at the root of our humanity and our consciousness, our ability to name and recall, to review experience, to plan, to investigate, to imagine. While its style and content are endowed by our particular group, the process itself is intrinsic to every child.

In building up and employing this model, the individual may learn a great deal about animals, but it is unlikely that this was ever the primary function or "purpose" of such a laborious and difficult activity. It is not even clear that this activity improves our efficiency as material users of nature. The requirements of hunting and gathering were never that difficult, as thousands of other species, no better endowed than ourselves, will attest. As a naturalist, I do not doubt that natural selection is the agency by which categorical language came into being and grew, and therefore had some benefit in terms of the early human niche and in the advantage that some offspring had over others. But that advantage may have operated at several removes from the actual causes of death or of the differential success in leaving one's genes in the living stream.

In any case, the logic that the child exercises as the core of the maturing skills of intelligence is certainly not applied by him to daily needs. The whole of his capacity for insight is involved. Its application is not only to animals and plants, but to his interpersonal life, to the elements material and immaterial of the cultus, to the realm of man-made things, and to nature in its broadest sense.

The vast preponderance of the earth's surface is *not* made up of such pellucid memberships and discontinuities as the species system. The terrain, weather, land forms, and sky are distressingly continuous and blended. The total physical space occupied by conspicuous plants and animals is extremely small. Yet the perceptual space that they occupy cannot be underestimated. It can be truly said that we are "naturally" interested in nonhuman life, but that is not simply because it is alive like us or because it is useful, but because creatures are consistent in their likenesses and differences, species patterns linking them into larger orders. That is exactly the instrument that conceptualizing required in order to store the world's diversity into word-images that did not simply pile up like objects at the city dump.

Words are themselves abstractions, but there is a difference between words that stand for a discrete object and those that refer to things intangible and invisible. Abstract category-making must have been a later step in human cognition, made possible because of speech on the one hand and a tangible model on the other. The opening-out of attention to the world at large would have otherwise been a fruitless experiment in sensory flooding and psychological overloading. Language is a coding system, needing an objective schema in order to work.

Apart from the design limitations of a data-bank system without hierarchic classification, one may, however, still ask, "Why the taxonomy of animals?" The prehuman hunter-gatherer primate brought speech to bear on his two principal concerns: the social drama and the food quest. Relationships in both realms were bound up with kinship—simply in the sense of birth and family as the source of closeness and the basis of sharing. It is not surprising that language should have brought food and family into an electric conjunction that would permanently mark the conception of each with qualities of the other. What we eat—the animals—are descended one from another and related, one species to another, just as the infant is related to the mother, whose nipple he "eats." Here is the oral-centeredness of the infant as described by psychoanalysis, where eating and kinship are one, its symbols uniting the maternal with the nonhuman through the instrument of speech. Eating or being eaten are the shaping constraints on the lives of all predators and prey, but, except for man the predator, none of them ever got around to the practice of engulfing the world in order to project it, of interiorizing the environment before it can be found out there.

The social and ecological aspects of life were the real polarity stamped upon the world of thought. Language administered the dualities of experience: inside and outside, male and female, social and ecological. Such category-making is the basic act of cognition, a sequence of binary choices by which classification and taxonomy are carried on. One term, like a family name, is the means for re-calling its members. Humans internalized the species system as an instrument by which ideas could be stored in memory, retrieved, pre-sented to the self and others, sorted, retried, and manipulated. As primate hunters, men probed the guts and muscles of birds and mammals, noticing the orderly arrangement of the organs and the unity in diversity of patterns reflecting the species themselves. A monkey-like omnivore with no real interest in the insides of animals had bequeathed to its meat-eating descendants a flair for social nu-ance for thinking about the relationship of the liver to the gall blad-der, as well as the crow to the raven.

To the question "Why the taxonomy of animals?" we might ten-tatively answer that animals have conspicuous living organs inside that make up the whole like a small community. They correspond to parts in other animals like species in a genus, since all mammals have livers, lungs, heart, blood, and so on. They are related to the body like members of a social hierarchy. The society of the insides confirms objectively what consciousness, thought, introspection, and dream-ing tell us subjectively: that there is an orderly arrangement within and without, that the beings within have a life of their own which in some inscrutable way is a transformation of the life without. Lan-guage clumps these inner and outer domains and makes their parts and the relationships of parts memorable. It presents details to con-sciousness by linking to them an architecture of sounds. Speech is limited in vocal elements, but their combinations enable us to in-ventory the world and explore the imagination by using a code mod-eled by the species system, the touchstone of the intangible and abstract.

THE VOCAL OBLIGATIONS OF INFANCY

At this point the reader may feel that there may be some validity in what has been said, but that it all belongs to the very distant past. As a guess about things that may have happened long ago in prehuman evolution it is all right, but, beyond that, so what? The universal membership of plants and animals in species and the membership of groups of species in higher orders may have been the key that unlocked Pandora's Box, releasing the natural world potentially into human mental grasp as a means of analyzing and sharing ideas, but having achieved that breakthrough in perception and intelligence, the whole matter would seem to be as distant from us as the Neanderthals.

The seeming irrelevance of these events to the present is due largely to our tendency to think that an organ is independent of its origin. We confuse the products of evolution with inventions, with made objects. We take the brain as given and try to think what we can do with it in the same way we think about an electric generator. The genius of our creative and inventive style is itself seen as an invention, like an idiosyncratic piece of art. But the organic realm and evolutionary process are not like that. Instead of means and ends, there are only means. What we achieved as hunter-primates was a means of learning. We did not graduate from thinking animal classification to thinking philosophy, but continue to emerge in a mode of individual development.

In many ways, the evolution of *Homo sapiens* seems to have freed us from the rigidities of animal behavior, to have enlarged human freedom—a point widely and mistakenly celebrated in modern humanism. But freedom is part of some organic processes which are not free; it is the understanding and affirmation of one's limitations, such as the developmental procession of each individual life.

Human ontogeny is the most complex of any we know. It is spread across more years and is so vulnerable that it includes mending that can, to a degree, heal the inevitable errors of infancy. This genetically blueprinted timetable of needs, behaviors, and dependencies begins before we are born and lasts at least a quarter century—perhaps for life. Nurturing and nutrition, physical growth, sibling relationships, play, learning, and other maturational events reveal the biological unfolding of episodes. Our understanding of what it means to be human has come a long way from the view espoused by John Locke that the mind begins as a blank sheet and the body as a bit of new clay. When the hunter-primate emerged from the blinders of the older lock-and-key vision, the new human sensibility to the multiplicity of the world did not free us from the physical world but increased our dependence on it by extending our perceptual needs. The new mind had a prodigious appetite for diversity. Its development sets off the phases of individual growth distinctly, giving each its own environmental requirements.

One of the most astonishing aspects of language is its ties to the personal calendar. The unfolding process, starting with the yearling, is as tightly regimented as a fire drill: cooing, lallation, babbling, single nouns, adverbs, conjunctions, all in their time as though a Chinese scroll were unrolled bit by bit at the striking of a gong. Primary language learning is scheduled to be basically complete in the individual by the age of four. Yet the kind and amount of communication in speech done by four-year-olds hardly seems to demand language at all. We are likely to assume too quickly that the more talking we do the better. As adults we live under a verbal waterfall and are seldom dried out by silence. Whatever could evolution have been thinking of, to rig our personal timetables so as to put words into the mouths of babes?

In the nineteenth century, biologists noticed that human embryological development was first invertebrate, then fish- and amphibian-like, followed by quadrupedal mammalian and finally monkey-like features, a minute simulation of the whole evolutionary series of our ancestry. The idea was adopted by some anthropologists and other social scientists who thought they could see each child transiting the stages of human history from primitive hunters through simple pastoralists and planters on their way to urban adulthood.

Closer examination revealed that the human embryo was never a fish, but something like a fish embryo. As for children passing through the stages of primitive man, what they really went through was a phase resembling that of hunters' children. The corrected idea, that "Ontogeny recapitulates Ontogeny," was more to the point. When we apply it to the emergence of speech in the child, we get a clue as to what evolution had in mind. From its very beginning in human prehistory, perhaps a million years ago, speech in childhood, even though derived from sound communication among adults (a particular language) had to do with the development of cognition in the human suckling, not communication.

It is generally recognized in psychiatry that the more profound pathologies are traceable to the patient's childhood. The deeper the character flaw, the earlier it began in the individual's past. Although somewhat too sweeping to be exactly true, this generalization inversely says that *normal* adult behavior of the healthy individual has infantile antecedents. The earliness of speech in the individual speaks to its depth in the matrix of adult behavior, and to its place in the life of the unconscious. Nothing so superficial and adult as philosophy, science, political ideas, theology, aesthetic theory, or literature is the purpose of language beginnings, though speech makes them all possible later in life.

What evolution had in mind was as much characteristic of the two-to-four age group as drinking milk. Before it could become communication, speech provided an "external" link between the sound brain, with its age-old ability to make sense of sequential input, and the newer visual perception that gave a Big Picture, at which the primates excelled.

Speech is the means by which category making proceeds, representing things that could be pyramided and stacked in memory by classifying. If memory was analogous to a great electric vault whose records are hidden from view, at least some of its circuits were accessible to the waking mind directly through the speech apparatus. Thinking is, of course, far more than naming, categorizing, and recalling, but these are basic to it. The meaning of words is straightforward for the child. The subtleties of symbolism, serendipities of insight, and the permutations of ideas are of great value, but they are only potential for the individual if he has a proper infancy of mundane name learning.

As surely as he "learns" to walk, the two-year-old begins to demand the names of things.[3] By vocal imitation and repetition, he begins a compulsive collecting of kinds that will go on for a decade. The process has that inexorable quality of the growth of plant tendrils, and one can almost feel the neural cells putting down rootlets that organize the soil spaces beneath them. No imaginary animals at this age are of interest as such. The lust for seeing the creature is as strong as that for naming it. Imagining is obviously something that needs practice, a skill which, like much of our behaving, from walking to religious speculation, is initiated by genetic timers but achieved through practice.

The answer to the question of "So what?" has at least three parts.

First, what evolved in us was not intelligence, but a developmental process. The process, like the embryology of the eye, is prefigured by a genetic program but not completed by it. If a patch is put over the eye of a newborn animal, it fails to develop those final nerve connections in the absence of light and the creature remains blind, even after the patch is removed. If children do not learn the names of visual images early in life (because of congenital lack of sight), they may do so later (after the restoration of sight by surgery) only with enormous difficulty or not at all. The permanently blind substitute tactile schemata for images, but also associate them with a spoken terminology. The blind and deaf must learn a tactile language or lose the capacity for intelligent thought with which they are born. Helen Keller's autobiography speaks of the enormous importance to her of the "discovery" that everything has a name. The use of the natural species system as the model of universal coherence was not a catalyst that set in motion, once and for all, the abstracting and ordering human mind. It became, rather, a part of the process.

Second, what natural selection did was not produce a higher cognitive instrument that could assimilate an infinitely complex world like a stomach digesting meat, but instead a linking device. Timed to the appropriate stage of individual development, this device, coordinated with speech, visual consciousness, and instinctual drive behavior, took an imprint of order from natural creation. The clever brain employed the existing composition of plants and animals of the ecosystem itself as a master model. The price was that it had to become part of the ontogeny of each individual, to be done again with each new human life. But that had its advantages, too, perhaps even a saving grace in its adaptability to a specific region.

Third, by not fixing the order making independent of the actual surroundings, the system was highly adaptable to differences both of environment and of human cultures. Apart from its cognition function, speech lent itself from the beginning to this differentiation of human groups and the in-focusing and cohesion that are part of belonging and loyalty. Consciousness, newly opened up to the world's enormity, otherness, and diversity, gave membership new intellectual dimensions and new emotional intensity. For a frog or a cat, most otherness is largely invisible; when the whole world was taken as an object of thought, the breaking of those old filters required new kinds of protection. If the world's diversity was not to be a maddening chaos, new forms of order making were necessary. One of these was extended kinship, the extension of belonging beyond the resident group to other groups, connections reflecting the organization of nature itself.

From an ecological point of view, basing the cognitive process on learning to classify real species instead of a totally self-winding model enabled our ancestors to spread out across the world. The ecosystems they invaded were already occupied by different groups of plants and animals. They moved into lacustrine basins, river valleys, tundra, desert scrubland, spruce-moose communities, cold steppes, and so on across the continents. A main purpose of thought is to make sense of one's environment, ecological as well as social. Suppose the primate hunter had evolved a set of fixed relationships to certain species during protohuman inhabitation of tropical savannas. Such brain machinery might be maladaptive in equatorial rain forests or on high plateaus. Moreover, half the species of large animals present during the early evolution of our genus, *Homo,* when all this began, have since become extinct and their places taken by newer forms with different behaviors. With fixed, autonomous minding, unrelated in its genesis to personal experience in the natural world, human thought would have been cut loose from the reflex system of the older primates only to flounder in an alien, changing world. There would have ceased to be any connection between idea and reality or means of testing the rationality of a plan or the significance of an idea. Grouping and categorizing are not something done by children simply because their biology requires it, but because the real animal world of each child is to be his concrete model of reality.

It is this notion of coding our ideas to the visible order that leads to the next consideration: that every child should have to initiate his cognitive training by reference to the images and names of real creatures. The laboratory science teacher, the naturalist guide, and the art critic struggle to make people look carefully, to see what is there, to scrutinize what they have already glanced at. The taxonomic job into which the small child plunges like a fledgling penguin leaping into the Antarctic Sea is not one of mere recognition but of intense examination.

Reflexively, visual animals need only a simple signal for recognition: a robin defends its territory not against another robin but against a red patch—cloth, feathers, any material—as long as it is about the right size and has two legs. People still behave this way in our use of emblems, insignia, logos, icons, and other simple signals, as well as toward a host of innate releasers. But the quest of the ordering mind was toward the thousands of forms that had no given meaning, and the quest of each new human mind is a renewal of that open-ended venture toward the meaning of meaning.

Roger Fry, the art historian, once pointed out that emblemizing things reduces their visual demands; it has just the opposite effect of the rigorous visual work required to discover precisely those details which all oak leaves or all finches have in common and the other details in which each kind differs.[4] The individual differences, to which primates are by nature supersensitive among their own kind, attract the knowing eye. Butchers, ethologists, still-life painters, veterinarians, and zookeepers extend to members of other species that attention to "character" which surgeons, portrait painters, psychiatrists, and others extend within the species. What all these people are doing is confirming the shared traits by discerning the particular, struggling against the tendency to tag and thereafter not to see but merely, as Fry said, to glance at the tags around them.

Such is the pitfall of taxonomy as an end in itself. Does it draw and focus the attention of an eye looking to see how the individuals depart from the norms of the tribe and so speak silently about the peculiarities of the particular environment and the scars of history, or does it become an exercise in overlooking? Is this not the same paradox that confronts democracy with its concern for the individual, which a manipulating power can transform into mass-man? Isn't it the same set of alternatives among the giant redwoods, of which one version is that if you've "seen one redwood you've seen 'em all"?[5]

We have wandered away from the child, but my point is that the differences in these two positions grow directly from early experience and from our categorizing capacities. Taxonomy is not a two-edged sword. It has a sharp front and a blunt back. It is incisive and opens things to their inner order, or it merely names. It is either the most exciting or the dullest subject in the whole realm of the arts and sciences, either a Russian novel or the telephone book. It is the instinctive approach to the world by every human child, the key to a lifelong series of ever more elegant refinements in perception of the mystery of life, slicing surprisingly across the conventional perception, a key that makes the intelligence—or it is monotonous rote that dulls instead of educates. It is employed to enlarge our individual human power because our species knows that the natural world holds clues to meaning and life, an eternal hunt among kinds. Without the assumption of the hunt, we lock ourselves in our primate half by creating a world of mirrors.

■

The widespread observation among anthropologists that tribal peoples throughout the world develop elaborate taxonomies of the natural world was recognized by Claude Lévi-Strauss as a universal inquiry into order. Nature's differentiating features are more important than content—that is, the purpose was not utilitarian, aimed only at exploiting creatures as food or raw materials or avoiding them as dangerous. "There are probably no human societies," says Lévi-Strauss, "which have not made a very extensive inventory of their zoological and botanical environment and described it in specific terms."[6] Such terminologies often run into the thousands. The lexical systems include species and higher groupings, organs, body parts, diseases, habitats, modes of travel, and virtually any and all characteristics by which one can compare kinds of living forms. It is his genius to see beyond the order-giving symbolic function of these systems in themselves to the sets of oppositions generated when two such series were envisioned on the axes of a grid, and to proceed in *The Savage Mind* and elsewhere to examine human social structure and mythology as they are influenced by the social analogies to these arrays of natural forms.

As Lévi-Strauss points out, "the savage mind" is not only a property of savages, but an aspect of all human minds. Among those human groups not yet buried in their own effluvia he found "a consuming symbolic ambition such as humanity has never again seen rivaled." His concern is the "passage between images and ideas." In discussing the way in which nature is used as the language of myth, he emphasizes the inexorable taxonomic training in the young.

The animal totem, because of anthropologists like Lévi-Strauss, has ceased to be disdained in social theory as a magic idol to which childish savages bowed in superstitious worship. It is now seen as a conceptual tool. Like other conceptual tools, it did not spring finished into the human head, nor is it simply inculcated in the young. It emerges in the maturing of the brain's own timetable, nourished by cultural care. These taxonomic enterprises, to borrow a phrase from Gregory Bateson, are personal "steps toward an ecology of mind."

Like the rooms in a house that may be used for different purposes, the mythopoetic meaning of the species system rests on an utterly banal foundation that has no metaphor. The child mason stacks rocks whose surfaces no more tell him what is to come than does his infantile sexuality reveal mature love. The naked realism in which all things are what they seem, and in which they seem to be ends rather than means, is part of that halcyon Paradise that every youth must lose when all its creatures are pure, the luster of creation is perfect, and nothing seems concealed.

A FAUNA AS HOME

For each society the intensity of this primordial radiance is focused upon a particular set of animals. The imprinting of a particular group of animals has its significance as "the originals." The question was posed earlier: why should each child have to develop the order-making, classifying process by studying the kinds of creatures instead of receiving it as an automatic, built-in mode of behavior? It was suggested that there must be something crucial in knowing the particular group of creatures that belongs to one's personal youth. Its sentimental and nostalgic value is that it means home. The heartache of being a stranger in a strange land is the uncanny displacement of its creatures. To the displaced person the whole arrangement is there, the landscape with plant and animal inhabitants, yet all are unfamiliar in kind. Immigrants to a new country often find that they are never able to accept this slightly skewed creation as the real one, because of the branding effect of the singular truth of one's first fauna.

The original set bonds the individual to place by rootedness of images and protects reality from the intellectual abuses to which we can put the species system as adults. The human primate is a shameless exploiter of this system by analogy. A lifelong builder of fantasy castles, myths, metaphors, symbols, parables, and caricatures might very easily mix up the original order with his homological creations and confuse the derivatives with the original. Nature is in constant danger of becoming a paradigm or some other abstraction. Intoxicated by his own mind, the human animal may need to be reminded by that first deep imprint that animal drawings are not animals and that there is a concrete reality he did not invent, whose velvet glove will deliver the final verdict on the validity of his imagination.

CONCEALED CREATURES

All animals are prompted by their own nervous system to seek those signals in nature that will trigger feeding or fleeing or mating. Humans too seek such sensible figures. For us, however, they mean not only a meal or danger, but clues, indirect signs, that are parts of a puzzle. In loosening the locked-in meanings of fixed signal/response behavior, our species did not escape nature and its constraints, but turned the whole of it into a language. Like any good carnivorous predator, man continued to separate figure from ground, searching out the living forms in the terrain.

Evidence for this is seen in an unusual experiment reported in *Science* magazine in which the subject was given a brief glimpse of the drawing of a tree, some of whose limbs formed the profile of a duck. Asked to describe what he saw, the observer revealed that he was not conscious of the duck outline. He was then asked to tell a story. The details of the story include a highly improbable number of references to feathers, nests, flight, ponds, and other phenomena related to ducks. The examiners concluded that the duck had been perceived subliminally or unconsciously. The conclusions of the researchers went no further, but the implication is inescapable that this perceptual activity goes on all the time, that, as adults, we see creatures to which we do not consciously attend, and that we weave them continuously into the flow of thought, from which they shed telltale signs into our conscious life.

A curious aspect of these "embedded figures" is that people suffering from some forms of schizophrenia are especially keen at spotting them. Schizophrenics tend to withdraw from the world, to dichotomize it irreparably. Some make ingenious neologisms or new words for parts of their separate, lost reality. They have an aura of overdetermined existentialism and seem to represent the breaking point of a culture too reliant on left-brain functions, unable to put masses of data together into wholes. They are at the opposite pole from the traditional, rhetorical, polemic society that can get overcharged with structure and starved for information, whose psychosis is to run amok rather than to withdraw.

One is reminded of color-blind artillery spotters who can better see camouflaged enemy gun installations than spotters with normal vision. When a pathology makes some organic function such as this more efficient, we might wonder if some opposing function is impaired. The advantage of color vision is that objects intended to be seen (such as flowers and fruits, eye color and stoplights) are more easily located and attended to at the price of seeing the whole, of which those objects are but a small part. We are eternally caught in a bind—to see parts or to see wholes. Discerning cryptic patterns in a maze of lines may be less advantageous to an "open-minded" species than recognizing wholes. The tests with the concealed duck figure suggest that we keep both abilities, but as healthy individuals we relegate the perception of subordinate forms to the unconscious in order that we may perceive overall design. Perhaps there is a set of triggers or templates in the unconscious that fit animal forms and that communicate mood and motivation to the searcher or hunter by saying, "Keep the big picture in mind if you must, but *keep looking, there is a duck there*," or, alternatively, "Of course you see the duck, but file it away where it won't interfere with your sense of the whole."

The researchers did not say why they chose a duck and not a shaving mug. If this were an isolated instance in psychological research we might dismiss it as an accident. But the use of the animal figure is widespread in intelligence tests, personality studies, psychological therapy, and perceptual research. The whole realm of visual figure use in psychology, especially in the study of children, is shot through with animals. Clinical interpretations seek to sort out the symbolic meanings of animals in terms of the child's relationships to other people. The most extraordinary aspect of all such studies is that the researchers never raise the question of the reason for using animals at all, except to say that children "identify more readily" with animals and that animals offer better disguises for the people whom they "represent."

One could say, perhaps unfairly, that psychology traditionally addresses itself to aspects of human behavior related to personal experience and not to species experience. Its professional heritage, though now changing, regards as unfashionable that about ourselves which cannot be modified by therapy.

A whole subdiscipline, based on the Rorschach test, in which the subject interprets bilateral "ink blots" is another example. The blots are usually seen as animals, yet the journals, books, and papers on Rorschach theory devote little attention to the most fundamental question that it raises. That otherwise meaningless shapes are perceived as the bodies of organisms is simply accepted, perhaps regarded as innate or due to conditioned experience, but it is not seen as evidence in the genesis of thought itself. To the question "Why do we use animal pictures to elicit information about a child's relationship to parents, siblings, friends, strangers, old people, or babies?" it merely begs the issue to say, "Why, because animal figures have 'high stimulus value' or 'symbolic proximity,'" or that "In dreams and imagination humans are symbolically represented by animals."

We must go beyond the explanation that assumes that the child chooses animals as surrogates in the same spirit that writers choose metaphors, or the alternative, that it is an innate mechanism invented by fairies at the boundary between the id and the ego. We do not come into the world with brains that we learn to use any more than our distant forefathers evolved brains and then learned to be intelligent. Brain and thought process evolved together and they develop together.

ANIMAL PROTAGONISTS

Literary studies also deal with animals, but, like the psychologists, the analysts of contemporary literature usually seem to assume that their use is arbitrary. In *Animal Land,* for example, Margaret Blount's examination of the animals in children's stories, the author asks why so many stories are about animals if their purpose is to shape the child's understanding of people. Her answer, that some authors are so inclined, and animal stories signify a return to Paradise or Eden, may be right as far as it goes, but her first response starts at the wrong end. While it is true that some writers write about animals and some do not, *all* children tell and listen to stories about them. Blount's book is about children's stories, but her reference to Paradise would seem to apply better to adults than to children.[7]

The anthropological view is that stories establish cultural moods or attitudes and formulate ideas of a general order of existence. Life is very complicated even for adults, and children are excluded from much of the information that enables adults to make sense of things. Stories remedy this by clothing in simple, dramatic episodes the mood or cultural mode of thought. They convey the gist of what is valued and what is tabooed.

If it seems strange that animal figures should be chosen to simplify human relations, we must realize that the strangeness comes largely from our adult attitudes in a culture that emphasizes the gap between the human and nonhuman. The demand by children for animals in these stories and the silent affirmation of this wisdom by the consenting adult suggest that their purpose endures even in conflict with the prevailing mood of modern society, which rewards heroic, eccentric art and which places contemporary human problems in political rather than organic or natural perspective.

If one were trying to guess how to invent such a complicated thinking being as a human from parts inherited from the hypersocial primates, it might seem more logical to develop each individual first socially and then ecologically. Indeed, such a view of human development is widely held. Born an animal and made human by culture and experience, the argument runs, the infant and child live in a social cocoon, taking a playful interest in the nonhuman, shaped from a kind of vegetative, glandular blobness primarily by human example and instruction. The shaping of attention is set in a human context, growing through layers of parental, family, and communal cultural surroundings, outward toward the nonhuman, which it reaches at the end of a long maturing process. As one historian put this development in terms of ethical stages, one becomes aware of "the rights of rocks" only at the end of a long human-centered preoccupation.[8]

But the truth is that no such simple progression to the more distant animal world occurs. There is an early, intense embryonic and maternal relationship, more organic and more chemical than personal. The first decade of life oscillates between attention to the human *and* to the nonhuman, in which the latter can now be seen to be both an end in itself and an instrument in human socialization.

The growing child quickly learns to separate people from four-legged animals, to perceive general types in fish, birds, and insects. For a decade his principal task is to refine these differentiations. He is gaining an ecological education, but equally important, he is gaining the forms of an inner as well as outer taxonomy, the threads from which the whole tapestry of his feelings are prefigured.

Mother Goose, the animal fable, the fairy tale, and the myth differ from one another in the nature of the communication. Some deal with human social relations, some with moral precautions, some with psychic dilemmas of the personality, but all use animals because their variety of form offers holding ground for otherwise intractable and transient experiences.

This is not to say that the content of such tales and rhymes is always good, for they can be badly used—to repress, to frighten, to impose rigid moral order. The whole process can be perverted. Unresolved fears, given the forms of animals, attach themselves to the real creatures. The adult whose phobias are triggered by a spider, snake, or bat had failed to cope with the inner problems for which these animals once served as objective vessels and will hate real snakes and bats. The unconscious remains chaotic and the world becomes a jungle. Monsters too have a real place in the child's fantasy: they signify the danger of inner ambiguity, of things run together. The psychologically arrested adult will fear them in the real woods and fields.

Thus we learn two lessons early in life: there is no limit to the degree by which inner and outer fauna can be differentiated; and each kind of animal is sticky and will carry some train of connections. And no matter how long we live or how intelligent we become, this rule continues to apply. Books like J. R. R. Tolkien's *Lord of the Rings* in the 1960s and Richard Adams's *Watership Down* in the 1970s are examples of this continuing process in adult life. One moves along the frontier of one's uncertainties from Goosey Gander and Chicken Little through the Three Bears to dragons and orcs and societies of rabbits as complex as a Dickens novel. These stories constrain the slippery parts of reality by temporarily harnessing them to the net of animal systematics and ecology.

Many of these, from simple small-child ditties like the "Three Little Pigs" to the preadolescent dramatized natural history of otters, wolves, and eagles, are ostensibly about animals. But in our hearts we know it is not so. Beginning to think depends on these animal instruments that make our mental lives possible. It is not only that each species occupies a taxonomic space that serves to model categorizing, but each is framed in relationship to others by behavior and personality, animal nouns carrying the whole of the verb and adjectival world with them.

This connection building between animals and qualities is done partly in sleep: why are animals in dreams? Freudian psychology holds them to be part of the body of symbols acceptable to the dreaming mind by which otherwise repressed ideas are allowed to ascend to thought. But why should the mind use animals and not something else? What makes them universally suitable for representing repulsive people, fearful feelings, contradictory attitudes, or danger? The unconscious is that memory to which much of our early experience descends, not only as fact, but to be organized. All cataloging is in some mysterious but dynamic way an extension of the dominant logical classificatory system available to us as children: the system of creatures. There are also systems of things (people are symbolized in dreams by machines or houses or stones) and systems of heroic figures, but they are apparently not as satisfactory. Perhaps it is a matter of access, the more formal animal classification being more precise and efficient as a storing, retrieving, and coupling device. Animal images link more easily into the analogical systems of the fairy tale, myth, fable, or folktale. For the child, action can replace understanding, and animals are characterized by their actions. The will, ideas, feelings all seem to "move" us and are imagined as things that move.

Animals are like an infinite company of sign bearers. By the time the child is eleven years old we may give him a book on the life of the salmon, written by an ichthyologist, which carries the National Academy of Science's stamp of approval, but the child can no more read it only for "data" than he can fly. For the preadolescent there is no such thing as pure natural history. Science fairs, natural history books, academic courses, and other extensions of scientific objectivity grant him a formal mode for his public demeanor, but the sensory channels into his brain can never be completely unhinged from that system that is the stuff of his perception.

THE INTELLECTUAL ABUSE OF ANIMALS

At the other extreme, the modern literary child's enmeshment in a warm and cozy world of little furry creatures is often merely sentimental. Since the purpose of animal stories is to bear cultural loads (and to bare cultural lodes), they can be made to shape the responding mind, to create and tone moral and conceptual frameworks. One reaction to human callousness is to hide it, to minimize the disagreeable—masking death and pain, padding the child's not-so-tender mind in the same way that female adolescents in middle-class society were "protected" in the past from those facts of life for which their constitution was believed too weak. That animals live by eating other creatures, that more than 50 percent of the newborns will not

live a year, that predators and scavengers are good and necessary—
this is incompatible with the sentimental cloak that characterizes
the nineteenth- and twentieth-century animal story, the Walt Disney view.[9]

Thinking animals makes possible an unlimited means of self-
understanding and of appreciating the qualities of others in minute
detail. But animal images can be misused to protect the person from
unwelcome reality, too. Examples of such abuse of the animal tale
that panders to the overprotective attitudes of parents are Hans
Christian Andersen's "The Ugly Duckling" and Richard Bach's *Jon-
athan Livingston Seagull.*

Both are idealized from the Adlerian-Watsonian psychology of the
self as the willful fabricator of one's own nature. "The Ugly Duckling" encourages the child to think that his problems are due to the
fault of others and that he can be transformed by the unfolding of
his superior destiny. In the popular book on the sea gull, the young
bird is led to reject not only the qualities of his own kind before he
can know them, but to aspire beyond all limitations and to repudiate
the idea of kind. Both lead to the belief that the given world is only
dross upon which the correcting and striving of the ego or the intrinsic superiority of the self will make a better reality. Because of
their mangling of inner truth and the outer world, they can lead their
readers in time only to deep resentment and rejection of the world.

The error of the sugared view is to assume that the correlation
between interspecies behavior and interpersonal behavior is literal,
merely scaled up or down. For example, in hiding the killing of some
animals by others we suppose we are simply reducing the volume of
violent death and that the child will be less inclined to solve his personal and social problems by resorting to murder or war. What actually happens is much more complicated and is likely to have the
opposite results than those which we wish. Since death is a fundamental component in the cycle of animal life, it cannot be abolished;

it can only be censored. Knowing it is there, but deprived of all those strands of connectedness by which death helps hold a comprehensible world together, the child is likely to become obsessed, misinformed, and guilty. The whole transformational process by which animal food chains are assimilated as social analogies may break down. Shielded from killing among animals (seen as struggle for power, increase in disorder), as well as from any understanding of war in human society, the child may even reverse the order-making analogical series as an adult by "explaining" nature according to his social and political comprehension of war.

The human analogy of the repudiation of death can be seen in the "historicizing" of predation. One yearns for the escape of the innocent rabbit from the wily fox in the same context with which we seek the protection of peoples from tyrannical persecution or slaughter by aggressors. The Bible sees the fall of man and the fall of nature as joint consequences of Evil. It asserts that before the fall there was no predation, no killing, no meat-eating by animals of one another, between men and animals, or among men. Deprivation of death and monsters in the tales gives the child's inner monsters or his nascent affirmation of death no outer connection. Denied as real in the shared fantasy of myth or fairy tale, they can only be repressed by the child, who rejects the messages from his intuitive grasp, his unconscious, and his own observations of the world. The cycle of his anxiety is perpetuated across generations. If an adult is convinced that predation in nature is the analogical equivalent of murder and war, he will translate this attitude in his telling of fairy tales and fables. A falseness of outer reality leads to falsification of the inner. The child is perverted by the mechanics of his own perception, and an individual psychopathic trap is laid that will favor an ideological expression when he becomes a young adult, and as an adult he will perpetuate the process on his own children.[10]

In Bruno Bettelheim's analysis of the role of animals in fairy stories, the problems of the id ("animal nature" or "instinctive drive" in each of us) are often represented as animals. Our task is to master and to overcome these forces.[11] One might suppose from this that animals represent only the dangerous and troublesome aspects of the psyche, to be replaced by more humanistic symbols as we become mature. But Bettelheim assures us that this is not the case. The wolf does indeed represent our unconscious asocial tendencies, but the owl and dove signify wisdom and love. More important, the animal is not only the gross beast, but the vital potential for renewal and transformation. Like the body, it is a fundamental resource from which new energy and new beginnings come.

ORGANS AS CREATURES

Small children are as deeply curious about the insides of things as they are about kinds of creatures. As long as the child is uninhibited by adult disapproval or repugnance for squishy things, he is a keen student of insides, which are a kind of fauna. His own body is also a collection of soft parts, and he connects his perception of the insides of other creatures to his own insides. His primary apprehension of both orders is through taxonomy. But the connection is not simply one of parallel patterns. The terrain contains creatures whose bodies are, in turn, landscapes—that is, a terrain of body parts. Creatures are geographies within geographies. They are like social entities within larger groups, all giving meaning and definition to the spaces they occupy.

In time, the adult comes to think of the total community of life in a meaningful space. Euclidian/Newtonian space, as Jean Piaget has shown, is a normal part of late childhood, and our culture strongly encourages that view of space as fixed by geometry. But long before he has images of such rigidly proportioned and mathematically definable volumes, the child is alert to an Einsteinian inner world governed by the relativity of species and the skewing of proportion by feeling. The sensuousness of eating, defecating, or pain such as toothaches or stomachaches modifies the "size" of body parts. This variability is confirmed by seeing how small the stomach of a lizard can be and how big the stomach of a caribou. The variations on a theme are very similar, psychologically, to the systems of difference in similarity by which taxonomy proceeds to sort out species. In spite of their differences in different animals, stomachs are all a kind of being. Indeed, each of the types of organs is a kind of species. This grouping of like parts from different animals is complementary to that which separates species, for it reunites them at new integrative levels. In a sense it brings together what species naming has put apart.

As the child becomes increasingly aware of the diversity and spatial extent of his own body, he is simultaneously growing in sensitivity to the terrain. What we call landscape, but which might more usefully be understood as habitat, has boundaries, structure, parts, dynamic qualities, and even analogous features to the human body: streams like blood, vegetation like hair, caves like body openings, and so on.

In the modern world we are inclined to regard those analogies as poetic and to credit fantasy with a play of language that is entertaining, aesthetic, and somewhat frivolous. We have a catch-all term, "anthropomorphism," for analogies like that between the earth and the torso, or in which animals seem to behave as though they had plans, ideas, or feelings that are human.[12] No doubt there are many literary applications of such ideas and expressions of them in the visual arts just as arbitrary. Like conventions, they become hackneyed with overuse.

THE DIALOGUE OF INSIDE-OUTSIDE

When a good poet calls an adult's attention by way of a metaphor, it is to evoke our capacity for feedback between the members of a homology, and the next step of discovering diversity in unity. When

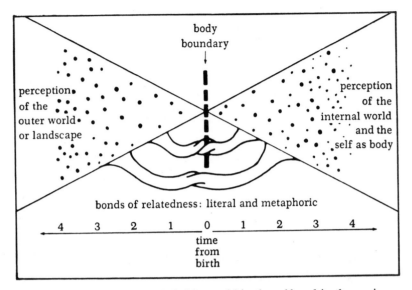

perception of the outer world or landscape

body boundary

perception of the internal world and the self as body

bonds of relatedness: literal and metaphoric

4   3   2   1   0   1   2   3   4

time from birth

The density of things and definitions within the self and in the environment increase proportionally and simultaneously. As the individual ages, the inner and outer worlds are pushed farther apart, however, unless their relationship is progressively affirmed by concepts and intuitions of relatedness.

a bad poet does so, one thing is simply defined in terms of the other and we are left with a bad pun that simply lumps things together and tends to isolate us from our own inner past. The inner past is a progressive detailing going on simultaneously, creating vision on either side of our body-boundary, our skin, inside and outside. At the center of each individual is the mind's eye, looking outward at the space of the world and inward at the body parts. It is, so to speak, a single eye whose healthy function depends on its looking at our inner visceral landscape and at the bright countryside in rapid order.

Early in life the detail on either side is limited and sparse. As vision grows, details increase in density, inside and outside, always named. This process of further resolution continues as new things, events, actions are recognized, along with the spatial networks they form.

A danger in this is that the things discovered are increasingly far apart from the skin boundary, which separates. Something more is necessary, which must relate and integrate the increasing detail on the two sides; otherwise they become first separate, then isolated, and finally alienated realms. Without some kind of developing bonds of such relatedness, the inner and outer realities become exclusive, as the skin gets to be more like a barrier than like a transmitter. Such connecting bonds work like the world currents of air or its magnetic fields, giving the poles definition by their relationship to each other.

No doubt the theory here is too simple and primitive. But the pictures children draw show an equilibrium of parts inside and outside. Those with a weak sense of the origins of bodily sensation and of the location of body parts have an equally impoverished concept of the proportions, appearance, and diversity of the objects and events in the outer world. When there is no firm boundary between inner and outer, the child slips toward schizophrenia; when the body boundary rigidifies, he perceives himself encased in a protective shell and is neurotically frightened by threats to penetrate it.

In pretending in play to be different creatures, the child is preparing to accept his own transformations. He will move through a series of changes as he grows up that alter his appearance, feelings, relationship to others, and the quality of his experience so dramatically that he can be likened to different beings. This sequence follows an orderly growth pattern. The location of inside and outside, the places where bodily sensations arise, the outlining of the body with one's hands, tension where skin is stretched over bone joints, reflected images, observation of other bodies, living and dead, as containers, the rise and fall of libidinal energy around body openings—these are but a few of the experiences that contribute to the development of a phantom figure in our own minds, the body image. These formative events are enhanced in childhood by getting out of one's skin vicariously, mimicking animals, dressing up or masquerading. The capacity to go in and out subjectively helps him resist the overhardening of the maturing image. The idea of what we are can get too brittle and our identity making, utterly dependent on the body image, varies between a hard and a soft exterior. The dramatic mimicry in dance, games, and ceremony is an essential ingredient in this slow molding, keeping it from setting too hard too quickly, preventing it from becoming a shell.

And what has all this to do with animals? The child's first and most powerful attention to the surroundings, apart from his human family, is riveted upon animals. Their names give access to the model for order that can be understood internally as anatomical arrangement. Their movement in the terrain makes traces that are a network of lines giving space depth and interconnectedness. A land with no creatures running across it, flying over it, hopping, slithering, or walking is a static, two-dimensional, dead world. Great herds in motion across open land and vast flocks of waterfowl are among the most exhilarating sights and sounds on earth and imbue the setting with special significance.

The interior terrain also has its creatures with their own kinds of movement. Most of our internal organs have the same shimmering, organic vitality. Seen in the newly opened body, the organs are clearly palpitating, vibrant beings. They compare to similar organs in the bodies of the animals, hence constitute the living animal. We eat those corresponding parts of the animals; they travel down our throats and occupy us and meet our muscles and livers with the gift of life and in part pass on through us. When we eat the brain of an animal we initiate a kind of courtship resulting in a mating of its brain and ours. This conception of brains as species is one of those "bonds of relatedness" that connect inside and outside. In being eaten, the tissue enters through an opening in the skin, the mouth, which is where the word "brain" seems to come from. It is a taste and a texture and a smell as well as—or as part of—an image.

Eating different animals joins us in a kind of unity with them. But there are always parts that we do not eat, and this exclusion prevents unity. A total melting coalescence would bring everything together in a kind of lump, making the world poorer, not richer, in kinds.

Of course, plants play a further role in this. They remind us that our organs can be alive though stationary. They create the points of reference and habitat through which movement takes on significance. Like animals, they pass into us from the outside, and the words that are their names pass out into the world. That their internal anatomy does not correspond to our own is a lesson in otherness, perhaps a more advanced kind; a lesson for older minds, a more subtle kingdom in the mental menagerie.

Brain asymmetry is that peculiarity found in the heads of people and birds in which right and left cerebral hemispheres develop differently (in humans, during the third to eighth year of life). The left, "propositional" set of centers and their association tracts function in analysis, mathematics, and speech, while the right, "appositional" brain is the center for the perception of the body, space, and music, and may be said to be synthesis-directed in the sense of making wholes. There is as much as a 30-percent difference in the volumes of the two areas.

The growth of these two areas marks off childhood, and the maturing or myelination of their neurons corresponds in one side to the learning of faunal nomenclature and vocabulary. Simultaneously, on the other side, there is an imprinting of place, a human juvenile home range, which will be the original model for the idea of "home terrain." This division of brain is the primary model and organ of the perceptual disjunction of reality. One attends progressively throughout life to distinctions that separate and make a diverse world and to clues that keep it whole.

This bilateral brain is not totally divided but is joined by a tissue bridge (the *corpus callosum*). In a sense these two halves are not doing different things but working in different directions along a single axis from a common center toward a richer perceptual world. Indeed, the differences in function tend to be largely quantitative, as some of the work of one side can be assumed by the other if the brain is injured early in life.

The view of the world as having a dual aspect, progressively fine-grained and yet variable and increasingly organized, is not, therefore, an invention of philosophers but a description of the way the mind works. Parents and society facilitate this activity. The system of plant and animal species is the most conspicuous place for it to start, the archetype of all such two-part order making throughout life.

There is a curious relationship between naming and the structure of myth. According to structural anthropologists the latter is composed of "intuitively selected pairs of opposed elements. These binary opponents are the basis of our elaborate structure of symmetries and isomorphisms which frequently repeat themselves as they undergo various logical transformations."[13] In short, the mythical tale begins with a dual set and goes on to play with the two parts in a fictional story. In both identifying animals and hearing stories, the child is singularly demanding and is happy with repetition. It seems that the use we make of our classifying is a first step in myth making, which in turn amplifies and extends that initial dividing and opposing of things into sets of opposing pair members.

The myth may refer to animal totems, give directions for growing up, deal with social and ecological problems, incorporate historical events, or rationalize taboos. But it contains an information code whose basic form is binary, like that of animal classification or taxonomic keys. It relays a mode of thought from one domain (animal identification) to another (human affairs) and establishes a framework for thought and feeling within the culture.

Stages in the maturing of both sides of the brain are undoubtedly integrated with other parts of normal growth or ontogeny. The way in which the polar system divides attention probably creates some competition between analysis and synthesis that different individuals resolve in different measure. In clinical experiments in which the subject is exposed competitively to speech and music at the same time, music, the pattern synthesis, dominates. Order making has priority over getting more details. Facts are useless without theory, figures are lost without a ground. The dominance of music over visual data is even more pronounced, related perhaps to the more complex pathways between ear and brain than to those between eye and brain, and to the evolutionary antecedence of hearing as a deep-brain complex, already complex when our ancestral primates were just coming out of the dark of nocturnal existence.

Even within the right or synthesis brain, music is the most important input. This is the reason why no picture ever became a national anthem. Song is unifying for us and for our perception of birds, whose songs are the anthems of their respective races, as we have seen. Human music may even have evolved by reference to the avian example as prehuman groups moved toward group consciousness and cultural diversity. In much of the world bird melody is still available during many hours of each day during the first year of life and we should not discount its importance out of hand.

Deeply attuned to his mother's lullaby, the infant surely cannot miss the similarity of melodic phrasing and repetitive chorusing. No one who has cared for babies can doubt the importance of the lullaby, whose social purposes may parallel the ecological purposes of birdsong.

Song is produced by air moving across the ligaments of the human larynx or bird syrinx. Sung music is the patterned movement of air over surfaces. We are all familiar with the literary imagery of the "song of the wind in the pines" and the haunting voice-like effects of desert and plains winds. One thinks of titles such as Joseph Wood

Krutch's *Voice of the Desert* or Guy Murchie's *Song of the Sky.* Lying on the ground at night in a Mexican wilderness, I have been filled with a sense that the hills around me seemed to be humming, and yet I knew it was not the calls of insects. The celestial "music of the spheres" is the hackneyed expression of a widespread notion of a pervasive harmony, to which our earth and we ourselves contribute.

These musical landscapes have in common a joyousness that is more immediate than the satisfactions from pictorial landscapes, the more staid pleasures of scenery. I know of no other mode by which a sense of the goodness, order, and purposefulness of life is so clearly perceived. It may seem rash to credit birdsong as the first integrating experience. But why should not the idea of a joyous cosmos come to us unbidden from a singer "up there" unseen, an evocation of the first iridescent pleasure of sheer being? Rachel Carson's widely read book of the 1960s, *Silent Spring,* was only ostensibly about the death of birds from insecticide poisoning. Surely she referred to all those larger rhythms in which our first and most dear sense of coherence is sheltered.

FOUR

The Metaphysical Bear

THE BEAR TEACHER

THERE WAS ONCE A MAN who lived deep in the forest where he was perfectly content. Everything he wanted was at hand, and he had only to reach out for all the fruits the forest had to offer. He was safe and comfortable. He noticed the other animals hardly at all, but they too seemed to lack nothing.

But slowly things changed. The forest became sparse and the foods more scattered and hidden. The weather shifted, turning seasonal. Danger appeared, so that nothing was so simple and easy as it had been. The man had many needs—foods of all kinds, herbs for his health, healing substances, materials for his bed, and so on. As an omnivorous, traveling animal, his needs were flexible yet demanding, and it was hard work just to learn everything he had to know to survive. Gradually he saw with a growing sense of respect how the other animals succeeded, each in some particular way beyond his own ability: the wolf pursued prey with supreme endurance, the horse was strong and swift, the caterpillar wove and the marmot dug expertly, the otter was a master of swimming and the squirrel of climbing; and it dawned on him that he might learn from them. So he studied them all, admiring each for its gift and revering the wisdom that such skills showed. It was as though every animal was a piece of the whole of nature, and at the same time a tutor or teacher to the man. He saw that each was an aspect of himself, the beaver reflecting one thing, the snake another, and he learned from them all.

But one problem remained: how to put all the skills together as parts of himself in proper proportion, and to use each in its right moment in the course of the day or the year. Keeping the different talents tuned to the seasonal rhythm was the most difficult task of all, and the man wondered who, like himself, had so many things to remember. At first there seemed to be no animal who had mastered this. Then he noticed that the bear looked a little like himself and attended all things. The bear could swim and climb and dig; it could play and make love and make a bed on which to sleep; it knew where to find the early spring greens and when the salmon would come; it knew not only the habits of the elk but when to look for the grouse's nest and when the acorns would be ready. The bear was brave and strong, yet also a tender mother. It seemed to know even more than the man could learn—to sense the coming season and to understand the art of living underground without eating.

So the bear became the man's special guide in shaping all the separate acts of life into a harmonious whole, fostering in the man's mind the idea of coherence and sequence and even transcendence. Further, in its assured and solitary way the bear seemed to know something that was not enacted, perhaps to have a secret. The man watched the bear for many years and finally he understood: the bear, knowing what was to come from what was, was himself the eye of the future watching the present. His gift of revelation, unlike those skills which man could learn from the other animals once and for all, was continuous. His message was the health of the wilderness, which was always changing. The bear was the voice of the earth itself. Then the man, remembering that the bear was his mentor, realized that he himself had that voice, if only he could learn to sing as sweetly as the bear.

THE COSMIC HUNT

To realize what a great part of the northern sky was dominated by the great hunt, one needs to watch all night. Ursa Minor, Ursa Major, and Boötes, who make up the prey and pursuer, pivot around the North Star in the course of the night. The sky is swept by this great arm of lights, the drama of the chase from horizon to zenith, circling from right to left, dominating the visual field, awesome in its energy. In the Paleolithic era it was not Polaris but another "north star" that was hub of the revolving universe. The "pursuit" was like a great gear on an invisible axis, driving the whole stellar panorama through the night, bringing the rising sun, whose brightness was therefore also the bear's doing: the ultimate food chain. Hunters have always known that the chase liberates the energy that turns the world.

Although they agree on the nature of the spectacle, different peoples identify the players somewhat differently. Three examples follow:

1. *In the archaic myth the "big bear" and "little bear" are the cosmic elk, Kheglen, pursued by Mangi, the bear spirit (Boötes).*
2. *In Europe the bear is not the hunter but the hunted. Along with the little bear, she is chased by the human hunter in the constellation Boötes.*
3. *To Algonkian Indians, the stars near the pole are the bear's den, the four stars of the bowl of the Big Dipper are the bear, and the seven hunters trail out behind.*

Thus we have worked back from the Greeks, Finns, and Hindus toward an older, Paleolithic substrate, framed in notions of the hunt that nightly crosses the sky. The hunt is not a frenzied pursuit but the stately procession of final things, energy gained and spent, transferred, assimilated, and dissipated, only to be renewed again by the holy sun. Who knew better than those Paleolithic peoples (and bears) that food chains or some cosmic equivalent turn with their energy the great wheel of the universe? The bear dominating the northern sky as predator in one view, prey in the other, reminds us of its high place in the food chains on earth, hunted by men and yet an avatar of the forces that rule all life.

DEMETER AND ARTEMIS:
THE BEAR GODDESSES

In the Bronze Age twilight of Neolithic religions, as many of the old animal divinities faded in popularity, the rich figure of the legendary bear spread itself across the conclave of Mediterranean gods. Among these the Greek goddess Demeter was the most important. Literally, Demeter means "the grain of the bear mother"—that is, "barley mother." Older than Artemis, she was sometimes spoken of as Artemis's mother. Demeter was called "the broad-faced one" and, by Euripides, "the mountain-ranging mother of the gods." As a form of Rhea, she turned the spindle of the celestial universe, its energy focused nightly in the master figure of the Great Bear. Demeter was also a form of Gaia, "a great goddess of the lower world," a supreme chthonian power of the Greek cosmos.

Demeter's underworld associations are multifold. She was the nurse of Trophonios, the cave-dwelling oracle and master of initiation rites. A temple in her honor stood in the Grove of Trophonios at Lebadea. Demeter's ceremonies at Phigaleia and elsewhere took place in a cavern, sometimes referred to as an "underground sleeping room" or sanctuary. The myth of her descent into and return from the underworld precedes the tales of later Olympian heroes who embodied dramatic elaborations of the metaphors of rebirth. Among the most famous Greek ceremonies, the Eleusinian mysteries, performed at Eleusis, which means a "place of birth," were Demeter's rites. They were celebrated with a barley water–mint drink, *kykem,* and a torchlight parade reflecting on earth the seasonal march of stars across the heavens. As the mistress of renewal, Demeter came in time to oversee fruition in agriculture, but in her origins there were no farms, only, says Lewis Farnell, "the shadowy form of an aboriginal earth spirit."[1]

■

Artemis, whose name means "bear," is the goddess who absorbs some of the sacred bear's ultimate qualities as the animal image itself disappears, Cheshire-cat-like, in the anthropomorphism of the Classical gods. It is she who is most other and wild. Artemis is a vital spirit in both the mythical tale and the human spirit. Observed as an aspect of her own psyche by Christine Downing in her book *The Goddess,* the Artemis-bear lives not only in the polar realms of sky and underworld but in both the landscape and the heartscape. For Downing, Artemis represents three things: "she who slays, she who is other, she who comes from afar." Least of all the divinities in the Greek pantheon is she at home on Olympus. "Artemis embodies," says Downing, "a profound denial of the world of patriarchy, the world where some persons have power over others, the world of dominance and submission, where one can be hunter or hunted."[2]

The Classical Greeks stripped the goddess still further of her traits. In Ovid's *Metamorphoses,* Callisto, a "companion" or form of Artemis, was in myth punished for pregnancy, demoted from her human form back into that of the bear, and turned into stars, leaving to Artemis the pure, final aloofness of virginal wildness, not a sentimental shepherdess but a solitary *anima* who will never be tamed, removed from the civilized world.

In her votary power as protectress of mothers in childbirth, Artemis is closer to her fecund spiritual mother, Demeter. She is, continues Downing, the one who "knows each tree by its bark or leaf or fruit, each beast by its footprint or spoor, each bird by its plumage or call or nest . . . each tree, laurel or myrrh, oak or ash . . . each brook or stream," a maternal source beyond motherhood. For all her wildness, Artemis is not transcended in consciousness. She is the "recreation (or recovery) of a world within which we live as a realm of souls, of living, meaningful-in-themselves beings." She is not the past, but, as Hippolytus says, "Artemis seems to beckon from the future, to call me toward who I am now to become."

RESURRECTION, THE MADONNA, AND THE DIVINE CHILD

Writing in the *Journal of American Folklore* in 1946, Marius Barbeau summarized the Eurasian and American mythology of the bear as having the following motifs: a mystic union between a human and a divinity, producing offspring who became intermediaries between men and a powerful god; the self-sacrifice and immolation of the supernatural Bear Father in order to benefit humans; a tradition of a sacramental feast on the flesh of the divine animal; and atonement, rituals, offerings, and prayers to the spirit of the sacred animal. He notes that the Laplanders called the male bear the "sacred man" and the female the "sacred virgin."[3]

The classical scholar Lewis Farnell, writing of the Thracian/Greek oracles Zalmoxis and Trophonios, says, "A vegetation god was likely to have his annual appearances and disappearances, and one who lives in the dark beneath the earth might come at times to be regarded as dead or sleeping, at other times as awakened or revived. . . . The death of the god, followed no doubt by his resurrection, was an idea expressed in genuine Thracian ritual." Such a vegetation god was the sun king, accompanied by a mother-consort, the central theme of Frazer's *The Golden Bough*.

One may see in this widespread and diverse mythology a history of ideas and consciousness leading from the bear toward the divinities of the Mediterranean world, including the sacred mother and the son king of the Near and Middle East, the genetrix whose son's inevitable death was a resonance of the two-season Mediterranean year. Just as in Bohemia, where the shrovetide bear is, says Frazer, a "corn spirit" in animal shape, a vegetation god, as suggested by Farnell, reflects the work of a deeper, seasonal power, a weather prophet associated with the sky, where the bear's great might was exercised. Perhaps the transition to a plant spirit is easily made from the bear because it is a plant-eater that is closely and seasonally linked to the calendar of plant growth and fruiting. Does the bear furnish the agricultural peoples with their earliest intuitions of the Great Mother Earth, first worshiped in caves, whose sons must die like the withering grasses and whose daughters must be lost to the underworld with Persephone, like grain planted but not yet germinated? Perhaps the half-human, half-bear figurines venerated in Yugoslavia seven thousand years ago are tracks of the shift from animal to human images in human thought (allowing that the same process may have been in different stages at the same time in different parts of the world). Greek gods of non-Greek origin—Hecate, Cybele, Ishtar, and, notably, Artemis—each kept some bearish quality or power of the shadowy ancestor. Apollo the healer and "shining one," Demeter the "barley mother," Hermes the fertility and underworld guide, Themis the oracle of the sacred seasons, and many others absorbed and inherited different powers of the ancestral bear.

A long interval of complex and often obscure history separates the primordial bear, even the Bear Son, from later concepts of the god's resurrection. Even so, the Christian Madonna still occupies her cave in the sculpted grottoes of a thousand churchyards. A Byzantine illustration shows the ascent of Christ, his sarcophagus supported by bears. We cannot know whether these are the same bears with glowing eyes that Jung said were the renewing force of the deepest self, or those the Algonkians associated with the four points of the compass, or the four corners of Ursa Major. Perhaps the idea of eternally renewed life, alternating with death and descent into the lower world, is not *derived* from the example of the bear, but, because it is expressed in so many different cultures and languages, the example of the bear releases the concept from its culture bonds. The bear's example precedes all specific man-made ceremonies and stories of the perennial but transformed being who unites the poles of life and death. As Jung's associate C. Kerenyi says, "In the domain of myth is to be found not ordinary truth but a higher truth, which permits approaches to itself from the domain of *bios*."[4]

LEARNING ABOUT OURSELVES
FROM BEARS

Ever since ancient times, says anthropologist William S. Laughlin, men have argued "from animals to men and back again with sophistication and success."[5] But what do animals tell us most about ourselves? Since man "rediscovered" that he was an animal with the publication of Darwin's *Origin of Species* in 1859, three kinds of animals have stood above all others in this regard. The first is the rat, especially in its white or laboratory form. In hundreds of ways the rat has predicted human reaction to stress, environmental poisons, nutritional deprivations, overcrowding, organ transplants, alcoholism, and so on. Thanks to rats, we understand much about cancer and conditioned reflexes. The second is the primate, especially monkeys and apes. Anyone familiar with Harry Harlow's experiments with mother-deprived monkeys or Jane Goodall's and Richard Lee's observations of chimpanzee and wild baboon societies is aware of this. Finally, Farley Mowat, George Schaller, and others have shown that we owe much to the study of wolves, wild dogs, and lions in understanding sex roles, group hunting, and cooperation in evolution, human and otherwise.

But none of the above animals is a large omnivore. None tells us about the speculative range of mind over possibilities, the choosing of alternatives in a strongly seasonal climate. Stuck perpetually with pack life, monkeys, rats, and wolves hardly know true solitude or the needs and joys of independence. The individual counts little among them. What more do we cherish as humans than these things that the bear can perhaps illuminate—the freedom and capacity for personal decisions and individual idiosyncrasies that decide our fate?

In their social interactions bears seem more like humans, whose life is always on the knife-edge between the soliloquy of the self and the chorus of the group. Evolving man moved toward individual uniqueness, liberation from group-think, away from the invisibility of the one in the many, or the final tyranny like that of the ant colony. Who better to demonstrate to us autonomy and its special style of attention and introspection than the social yet irascible, supreme recusant, *Arctos*?

In the third stanza of her poem "Many Winters," Nancy Wood speaks of this lesson from the bear:

> *There is the young girl in me traveling west*
> *With the bear which taught me to look inside.*
> *The bear stood by himself and said,*
> *There is a time for being alone*
> *So that you do not take on*
> *The appearance of your friends.*
> *There is a time for being at home with yourself.*[6]

FIVE

On the Significance
of Being Shaped
by the Past

THE ELEGANT REFINEMENTS OF SOCIAL CARNIVOROUSNESS

THE POPULAR CONCEPT OF "man's rise to civilization" projects for the mind's eye a dark struggle with a primordial past, in which men were constantly threatened by a hostile world, followed by the greater margin of safety and enlightened institutions of civilization. Prehistoric man stands sentenced to the limbo of savagery by a conventional historical view that is seldom questioned. Briefly, this view holds that the development of agriculture made it possible for people to abandon the nomadic and uncertain life of hunting and gathering, and that they gladly did so, becoming sedentary. Human well-being was improved and society was stabilized by increasing man's security from starvation, disease, poverty, uncertainty about the future, and the danger of wild animals, storms, and other natural forces. Because food growing supported more people, the population rapidly increased. The agricultural revolution, it is said, made civilized institutions such as art and religion possible, framed ethical and moral principles, and forged relations among men based on compassion and respect for the rights of the individual.

My objection to these statements is simple: they are not true. For every man whose life was improved by that momentous Neolithic revolution, hundreds lost health, freedom, and social dignity. Because a fortunate few controlled the recording of history, civilized culture became a propaganda machine for itself, which easily manipulated the resentments of peasants and, by redirecting their distorted lives, helped rationalize the genocide of hunter-gatherers on agriculture's enlarging frontier. It is a tragedy euphemistically called historical destiny, economic progress, or the inexorable surge of the political state. Yet, from the beginning, agriculture failed our species, and now, after fifty centuries with scarcely a word raised against its mythology of virtue and security, it is failing the modern world, failing to nourish it both physically and spiritually.

Important to our ecological reawakening is an understanding of the hunting-gathering people: first, as forebears who have constituted more than 99 percent of all human time and all human lives; second, as people who still live today in remote parts of the world according to preagricultural traditions; and third, as profound aspects of ourselves.

On Being Well and Well Fed

The most authoritative estimates of the history of the human population show some increase in human numbers from forty thousand years ago until about five thousand years ago, then the fearful exponential curve whose thrust still rushes upward like a rocket. Because the start of this upswing coincided with the beginning of centralized agriculture, it has generally been supposed that it was the result of increased food production. The logic is that of the pig-breeder who assumes that the fruit of his sty will be limited only by the amount of corn he puts into it.

If this were true, then the quantity of food must have been the factor that limited the population of all preagricultural people. Yet the study of living hunter-gatherer societies shows that some of them have times of hunger but that starvation is uncommon and that their environment can support more people than inhabit it. Of more than a score of such societies whose foods and nutrition have been studied, all use more than fifty kinds of plants and twenty kinds of animals. From such a broad base something is always available. The living hunters who are most vulnerable to starvation inhabit the most difficult environments, the Australian deserts and the Arctic North. They are certainly not typical of Pleistocene men. Even there, hunter-gatherers are vastly more secure and competent than one is led to believe from the hungry, hapless wanderers described in film and fiction. Desert aborigines consume a surprising variety of plants, and Eskimos, who seem to have nothing but blubber and snow, get salads from the guts of slain herbivores, such as the caribou. Of course, certain foods are preferred to others, and the least liked are used only when others are unavailable. Like all omnivores, such people can readily turn to alternatives as the season or other conditions affect availability.

Nor does the evidence from paleoanthropology support the view that food was the bung in the barrel of human population growth before the dawn of agriculture. Had it been, fossil teeth and skeletons would show the deformities of starvation, and campsites would not be littered with the remains of marginal food plants and animals. Except for local vitamin deficiencies there is little evidence of deprivation or the kind of environmental pillaging seen among starving people today—consumption of leaves, leather, and each other.

Most populations of hunters were not and are not limited by food supply. Studies of living hunters not only refute starvation but reveal that food getting requires a relatively modest investment of time and energy. By African Bushman standards, the "work" of a typical hunter requires no more than about three hours per day or three days per week. Hunter-gatherers show a lack of concern about finding food, since they seldom fail. They are characteristically neither anxious nor future-oriented. When these people were first encountered by Europeans, this nonchalance was sometimes interpreted as defective lack of foresight and intelligence. Modern men could not at first comprehend that people could exist who did not worry about tomorrow unless there was something wrong with them.

That famine was uncommon—and often unknown during the lifetime of an individual—is consistent with the general principle of ecology relating size to population density and stability. In general, large animals are found in numbers below what is possible in terms of the food supplies; while smaller and shorter-lived forms occur in densities approaching whatever the productivity of the habitat will allow. Among many large herbivorous mammals, such as the deer, antelope, and rhinoceros, the available habitat is divided by them into territories, which are in turn related by courtship and mating behavior to reproduction in such a way that the number of young each year is related to the number of territories. Large predators, like wolves, lions, and tigers, are characteristically fewer in number than the potential of the environment without establishing defended territories. Their very low birth rates—or, more correctly, replacement rates—seem tuned to keeping each species rare rather than to "maximizing" its numbers. Some biologists believe that, while the quantity of food may not limit these larger species from year to year, the population size and replacement rates are set genetically by the worst food years that occur over a long time. Long-lived animals, whose behavior is guided by social learning and who require stable and dependable interindividual relations, would be disastrously affected by sudden high death rates.

Modern man sees hunger and starvation as a stage on a scale of diminishing food supply, of which continuous satiation is the opposite. Satiation is the ideal and norm for the herbivore or potato-eater, who must take in massive amounts of carbohydrate foods to get enough nourishment. Hunger, however, is a normal state for carnivores, who have empty stomachs most of the time. In spite of men's food habits, which are not entirely carnivorous, they behave demographically like carnivores. Insofar as man is a carnivore, he is healthier when he does not eat much. Medically, people who eat less—even who border on malnourishment—feel better, have less organic failure, and live longer.

The anomalous position of man in the ecological community is that, physiologically, from the neck down, so to speak, he is an omnivore whose diet is about three-quarters plant products, like a bear or boar. By looking only at his gut one might predict that he is a kind of oversized raccoon. Yet the patterns of life set by hunting-gathering peoples are centered on the spiritual and ceremonial eating of large mammals. Behavior and culture are more wolflike than bearlike. No other omnivore engages in the group hunting of large, dangerous prey.

On Birth Rates and Death Rates

The carnivorelike traits of hunter-gatherers carried over into population size and density: few and stable in number, unaffected for years at a time by weather, disease, predation, or other fluctations in the environment. This means that in the past the number of humans was limited by the birth rate, not the death rate. Humans did not—and living hunters do not—reproduce at their maximum possible rate or live in saturation densities. It is not clear how this was accomplished. In the life of constant tragedy and frequent death we imagine for them, it is easy to picture a rush to multiply, an anxiety to keep up with continuous losses. This fantasy is given a veneer of verisimilitude by the assumption that modern medicine has greatly extended human life. This also is not true. The capacity for longevity in man is not an accident but an expression of the realities of life during his evolution.

It is true that the death rate of infants among preindustrial peoples is much higher than among our own, but figures on average length of life among hunters have been distorted because of infant deaths, giving a misleading typical life span of twenty-four to twenty-eight years. Actually the age-group composition of modern hunter-gatherers is much like our own. For those surviving the first three years, life expectation among hunters is about that of Americans today. Though death may have claimed 50 percent of the infants, this did not much affect the continuity of individual associations composing the hunter group of about twenty-five, nor did it threaten a people shortage.

Today among all peoples there is a prenatal mortality rate of perhaps 75 percent—that is, three-quarters of the embryos conceived die, most of them before the woman knows she is pregnant. This is a service to mankind, for incompatible gene combinations are thus removed. This important function of early mortality was, in the past, extended through the first years of postnatal life. The death of infants, though sorrowful, was far less so than the death of children or adults. Indeed, it is not easy in our present swarming numbers to realize the impact of an adult death on a group composed of about twelve adults. It has been observed by anthropologists that the tribal collapse of North and South American Indians was due less to the actual mortality caused by the white man's diseases than by the social disintegration following so large a loss.

A 50 percent mortality rate among the newborn is a gift of life and health to the survivors. The modern medical reduction of that rate is an enormous alteration in human biology that we, as a species, may not be able to afford.

The birth rate in hunting-gathering societies is kept down by a variety of means, including contraception and induced abortion. Children are nursed by their mothers into their third year, and there is evidence that prolonged lactation inhibits ovulation, preventing further pregnancy. Social customs surrounding marriage do not exploit the human biological potential. The average age of marriage ranges from two to ten years beyond that of peasants. The total number of young born during a lifetime is smaller for most hunter-gatherer women than for their farmer counterparts. Infanticide is also practiced. In general there seems to be no great egotistic or familial pride in large families.

Recent studies show that the menstrual cycles of women working together tend to become synchronized. Apparently this is brought about by aerial-borne hormones, or pheremones. Such substances are not consciously detected but affect the physiology and behavior of those within smelling distance. If this were true among a group of the six or seven adult women of a hunting band, its consequences might have been far-reaching for birth limitation. It has been widely observed by anthropologists that menstruation was taken into account in both social, ceremonial, and practical life. A corollary is that the female cycle harmonized with the general round of life. If all the women ovulated about the same time, appropriately scheduled hunting forays away from camp or taboos or other deflections from copulation would have greatly reduced pregnancies. If such arrangements existed they would probably have come into being pragmatically rather than deliberately.

Studies of family size in modern societies also suggest a diminishing return of human quality in larger families. Large families seem to have a higher percentage of mental defectives, such as mongoloids. The first-born usually has the highest IQ throughout his life. If the mother is older (say, thirty instead of twenty), the IQ differential of the first-born is even greater over the second. Whether the reasons are genetic or environmental are not important here. Also, there is a higher probability of male children among early births, of female during later. (In a society with very small families where the mothers reproduce at an early age this would produce a preponderance of males, which would tend to reduce the reproductive rate of the group as a whole.)

Through successive pregnancies a woman accumulates increasing responsiveness against foreign tissue—that is, antibodies that attack the foetus. The probability of embryonic reabsorption or spontaneous abortion is therefore raised with each birth. This functions as a built-in device for limiting births—or, one might say, as a sign that the norm for the species is being exceeded. Thus small families appear to be superior in terms of quality of offspring and likelihood of survival, and probably reflect the species-specific state of the basic human family in a hunting-gathering ecology.

For all primates and all humans the tender loving care of children is normal, though in man its precise expression varies from culture to culture. In a farming civilization, the political state brought new pressures, a new sense of competition, and different motivations for parenthood. Farmers went for quantity. They wanted field hands, heirs, living evidence of paternal virility and maternal fertility, recruits for armies, replacements for losses into slavery, candidates for sacrifices, new bodies for the villages, and scions to honor and care for them in their old age. Such were the peculiar needs of tillers of the soil. Their culture gave this drive for more offspring its status and symbolic content in the formulation of a mythology that greatly emphasized fecundity. Rural societies have traditionally encouraged the desire for children and more children. They blessed big families and praised people who had a way with children, especially women whose lives were given exclusively to reproduction. The centuries have added military motives and sentimentality to this religious zeal, which has cloyed the reality of motherhood, paternity, sexuality, and morality with an emotional single-mindedness scarcely short of fanaticism.

Since the increase in human numbers from Paleolithic low densities was not the result of an increased food supply, the connection between the first farming and the burst of population probably lies in the alteration of the birth rate. An interesting parallel to this is found among certain macaque monkeys in Japan, who ordinarily live at population numbers well below the carrying capacity of the available food and space to support them. When additional food is added by men, their numbers increase. Apparently their reproductive behavior is altered in subtle ways that result in more macaques. For man, an increased carrying capacity of the land due to tillage was not the causal factor if the population was not already pressing food resources. Instead a dramatic cultural change must have altered society's regulation of its own generation; or, to put it from the standpoint of the hunters, the ancient ways, with their customs and norms of behavior, were shattered. The human species moved closer to realizing its innate capacity to increase, its biological breeding potential prompted by an enlarged plant-eater's psyche.

To Be Few Is to Be Wealthy

No one thinks of a herd of bears, a drove of tigers, or a flock of eagles. Our image of these animals is as individuals, as part of a singular grandeur, whose uniqueness of powers and spirit would be degraded by their gathering in crowds.

This is not simply a romantic notion. Solitary and small-group species are different from group animals. In addition to freedom from death by starvation, very different spatial relationships, self-regulation of numbers, low mortality rates, and population stability, large predators are free from epidemic disease. Men living sparsely are also less vulnerable to wide-spread contagious diseases. Many disease organisms simply cannot exist where the hosts are in such low numbers that transmission is impeded for months or years. Unable to endure the long wait between victims, or in larval stage in an intermediate host, they bear no acute epidemic threat. Their spread and virulence depend on ready transfer by host-to-host contact and on their ability to produce many generations in a short time—a vast proliferation that gives rise to new genetic strains.

This does not mean that species with small numbers are entirely free from internal infection. All get parasites from their food. All are subject to some communicable diseases. But it does mean that hunters have fewer parasites that might weaken and kill them or limit their populations. Low levels of communicable diseases and parasitic worms are indicated from the study of human fossil feces and from studies of living hunters. It appears that many of the diseases of modern man may not have existed for preagricultural people, and the number of human diseases has increased with world population. Disease organisms are associated with high human density not only because of the increased ease of transmission and contagion, as in measles and smallpox, but also because habitats have consequently been altered, favoring certain types of pathogens (disease-producing organisms), such as the cholera microbe, which flourishes in sewage-polluted water, or the malaria germ, transmitted by the mosquito. Malaria, which has probably killed more people than any other single cause, and many other infectious diseases are the heritage of agriculture. The early hunters had natural countermeasures to disease already present in their environment, in their bodies, and among the many herbs and other medicinal organisms known to them. The two factors in this were low population and the complexity of the ecosystem. The two tend to occur together since men deviating from hunting-gathering homogenize their surroundings as well as increase their numbers.

In view of this, is it possible for modern drug-diseased man to get closer to the hunter's situation without sacrificing what is valuable in modern pharmacology? The answer is yes, by retaining more of the natural environment. The richer the natural environment in kinds of plants and animals, the greater its chemical and microbial diversity. It may seem at first more rather than less dangerous for people to live in habitats enriched in germs, and of course this luxuriance does increase the number of kinds of potential disease organisms. But this is more than offset by the controls that organisms impose on one another, with the result that the diversified natural community offers greater stability and health to all its populations.

If the evolution of the human mind took place in a world of human sparcity and small-group life, it follows that the human mind malfunctions in areas of high density. The point is controversial because of man's adaptability and his inability to recognize social pathology; he has little with which to compare the conditions of his life except other distorted communities. Superficial studies have been made by crowding people into a room and giving them tests, which show that they are not affected, but mental disease takes many months to appear.

As in much of human biology, the real tests take many generations, require a control group, and so endanger human life that they cannot be done experimentally. Studies on other animals reveal that where groups of rabbits or rats are squeezed together the individuals begin to develop behavioral symptoms related to tissue changes in their nervous and endoctrine systems. These include failure of maternal behavior, increased gender-role confusion, and widespread social withdrawal to the point at which individuals become pathologically isolated. In such a "behavioral sink" there is an odd tendency for exaggerated clumping, for animals that normally move about during the daily course to sit in one place.

Humans are not rabbits or rats, but the parallels to human behavior in areas of population concentration are too conspicuous to be overlooked. Scientists are increasingly able to identify individual neurosis and social breakdown in animal groups and their relationship to altered spatial distribution. The cat, for example, is an unusual mixture of a solitary carnivore-hunter with modified territorial boundaries during the daytime and an intensely rank-ordered social being during the night. When cats known to one another are artificially crowded, even when provided with all their other material needs, the system collapses into a snarling tangle of tyrants and doormats.

Since human physiology and behavior are much more like those of other primates than of other animals, the recent lessons learned from primate studies are instructive. More than twenty species of nonhuman primates, mostly monkeys and apes, have been studied in their natural habitat. Ten of the same species have also been studied in zoos or other confinement. In every case the wild forms are described as generally peaceful and affectionate, sensitive to friendly, cooperative relationships, each kind with its own way of avoiding harmful physical conflict. In no species is the top-ranking individual in a group dictatorial. In all cases, where the same species are studied under crowded conditions (with plenty of food and water), their social organization as well as their immunity to disease deteriorates. Maltreatment of young and violent attacks on doormats by tyrants increase as much as ten or twenty times over normal.

Insofar as he is a carnivore, man's sensitivity to density may be even greater, and there is evidence that social breakdown, followed by violence and murder, is related to this. Recent studies by sociologists in Chicago were set up, with the variables of social class and ethnic group controlled, to ascertain the effects of the single variable of density on the birth rate, death rate, juvenile delinquency, and mental disease. There were shown to be positive correlations, not simply in numbers of people per acre but in terms of the way in which space was subdivided. The number of persons per room was found to be more important than rooms per housing unit or housing units per acre.

There is nothing romantic or even figurative about space requirements. They are real, and overcrowding may menace human health long before its other effects are evident. They are innate and have little to do with cultural expectations or the kind of interpersonal distances that individuals establish between each other during conversation or other social interaction. The mental health problems related to space should not be interpreted simply as an argument against cities but as a criticism of the way in which urban and non-urban space is organized.

As the industrial states send medical missions to preagricultural people, the latter are perceived through the window of recorded history: threat of plagues and pestilence, the memory of horrible epidemics, a recent past full of suffering, sickness, and violent death. Part of the problem is surely the failure to distinguish between primitive prepeasants, like the Papuan inhabitants of New Guinea, who suffer much of the debility of the agricultural revolution, and true hunting-gatherers—Pygmies, Bushmen, and certain other African tribes, Fuegians, particular groups of the upper Amazon and eastern Brazil, a few American Indians, Eskimos, the Borneo Punan, small groups in Siberia, India, and southeastern Asia, and Australian aborigines. These groups, except for those at the mind-breaking fringes of the human habitat in equatorial wet forests (without adequate large mammals to hunt), are among the world's most isolated people, and yet they are humane, generous, and hospitable. They suffer little from mutual aggression or from unredirected aggressive instincts resulting in "manager diseases" like renal atrophy, high blood pressure, and gastric ulcer.

On Species Rarity and Individuality

It has generally been claimed that modern Western religion or political democracy discovered the importance of the individual. More exactly, this was the pseudo-discovery by consciousness, for evolution defined this long ago. The primate order, to which man belongs, has carved out a way of life based on the intense interaction of individuals. The large carnivorous mammals the world over also live in such a personal cosmos, having the capacity to function in isolation and as group members. Human ecology emerged with the addition of the knife edge of carnivore cunning to the elegant foundation of primate sociality.

To belong to a species whose members are few and unique is a relative, not an absolute, good. Personal individuality is useful only until synchronized activities are necessary—cooperation, mutual defense, reproduction. Beyond that, eccentricity isolates and nonbreeds itself into a genetic dead end. Most animals have small margin for individuality. In the courtship of ducks, for example, the sequence of signals and responses is very precise. Deviations breaking the chain upset the whole procedure. Idiosyncratic ducks would simply disengage themselves from the flow of generations, wasting the energy the species invested in them. Species with large populations endure in spite of iconoclasts; a sparce species composed of prima donnas would die of eccentricitis.

The larger carnivores and primates, and man in particular, have circumvented this limitation on individuality by their capacity for learning. Among them, learned behavior is an adaptation for imitation and conventionalizing. The capacity to learn and remember similar patterns of behavior evolved with increased genetic diversity, which otherwise would have been destructive. Strong cultural standards were necessary to guide what was learned, in order to protect the species from the disrupting effects of individual variation.

The relative amount and effect of individual variation depend on the size of the population. As man's ancestors evolved from a tropical brush ape toward a steppe carnivore, their numbers per unit area probably diminished and were broken into smaller and more isolated subunits. Such a pattern was ideal for rapid evolution of larger brains, making increased learning possible, which in turn allowed for the retention of high genetic diversity, or polymorphism. The evolution of the capacity for culture was not, therefore, a biological means toward the idiosyncrasy of belief and behavior but toward overall difference. Human individuality and rarity were achieved because essential social activities could be coordinated in small groups of very different persons through a common system of beliefs and values.

Humanistic philosophers of human evolution contend that the peculiar human approach constituted a major breakthrough in the history of life, and they see man as heralding new modes of existence as revolutionary as the first invasion of land by aquatic amphibians. Caution is needed, since man is not the end of all evolutionary change, but only the terminus of one small branch, contemporary with and not descended from all other living species. Since complex behavior, nervous systems, and learning are widespread zoologically, one might ask, in the light of the alleged importance of man's advance: what are the ducks, zebras, pandas, and so on waiting for? Are we to assume that they are rushing toward expanded individuality and consciousness as fast as the evolutionary machinery allows?

More humility is needed in our perspective. The combination of species rarity and individuality based on a highly specialized life cycle and exceedingly complex brain is new and dangerous, and may not succeed; indeed its extinction is already threatening. Most kinds of animals are probably already as intelligent as it is possible to be in their particular niches; further refinement would simply diminish their survival rates. It is both erroneous and wrong philosophically, I think, to assume that all creatures want to be men or that human consciousness is the cosmic pass toward and through which all life must make its way.

The idea that learned behavior is an adaptation that makes us seem more alike while our genes become more different is the reverse of the usual view, which is that our biological natures are like great identical stones all cut from the same quarry, and that the seemingly enormous range of human and cultural differences is the result of flexibility or plasticity. In part this error was due to the poverty of primate studies and in part to our ignorance of learned behavior as a means of unifying behavior.

When human population dynamics broke down with the subversion of hunting and gathering, the latent genetic diversity previously hidden or controlled by tight social conformity was released. Just as the "goofies" poured out when the domestication of animals broke the balanced genetic systems of their wild progenitors, a thousand "goofy" ideologies have been exploding since agriculture shattered the life ways of the hunting clan.

Written history of the last two centuries has put its emphasis on personality, on those heroic leaders of the state who champion the departure from tradition by coupling political power to idiosyncrasy, and on creative genius as sources of culture. Yet the traditional (learned) behavior of higher animals and the study of prefarming cultures indicate that most change is destructive. The fundamental characteristic of a culture, which is a biological adaptation, is the conservation of persistent styles and themes, which its members accept and support, however brilliant they may be individually.

Perhaps, as the philosophy of history becomes more deeply affected by anthropology, modern history will itself be the best evidence against the idealizing of social change. The world population is now more than five hundred times what it was during the late Paleolithic. In this perspective it is evident that the political form of the state is less important in human freedom than the inexorable effects of population size.

On Population Density

Large human populations tend to degrade the environment, both as a source of food and as a medium of biological richness. Complex brains are an adaptation to biological richness and therefore require interesting surroundings. Over-high densities affect men directly and through the environment. Apes in zoos and men in dungeons develop symptoms of mental and social deterioration: seething dominance hierarchies, withdrawal, sexual perversion, hostility, intolerance, and group psychopathology in the tormenting and ostracism of selected scapegoats. Below a certain point of crowding the cause of this breakdown is not density as such. So many people per square mile is an abstraction, since people have never been randomly dispersed. Men always live close, in intimate groups, whose size is deeply ingrained as a species characteristic.

In our species there appear to be two basic levels of clustering: the single group or band, and a geographic network of such bands, the tribe. Studies of living hunters throughout the world and of paleoanthropological evidence from the Pleistocene show a consistent, universal size average for the living unit of about twenty-five. Tribes range from a few hundred to fifteen hundred but many are around five hundred. These two cluster sizes are so widespread that they probably represent basic human biology, group equilibrium systems that are psychologically satisfactory, settled upon during thousands of years of adaptation to the hunting-gathering life.

Among such people as the remote Venezuelan and Brazilian Indians, this band-tribe pattern of life was, and still is, the basis of a highly adaptive genetic system, preserving heritable variation within the species and fostering microevolutionary differentiation—that is, differences between local groups that are passed on by genetic inheritance. Its biological wisdom is expressed in the way in which it helps to limit population and stem communicable disease.

For such groups the rate of evolutionary change and adaptation can be a hundred times greater than that of a larger population. Obviously the present expansion and amalgamation of world populations deprive our species of this small-group evolutionary advantage, an advantage that may be important to future survival if any kind of worldwide catastrophe lies ahead, man-made or otherwise.

Another advantage of the band-tribe arrangement is the individual's personal acquaintance with all other members. This trait—widespread among all mammal groupings—is especially important in the lives of all higher primates.

How and why did such group sizes begin, and how were they related to hunting? Perhaps twenty-five was the largest number of people who could be regularly fed from a single bison, horse, or reindeer. A life unit of this size may have provided just enough adult males (about six) to stalk and kill a woolly mammoth and keep the carcass from hyenas or other fierce scavengers, while some individuals rested or butchered or assisted in transporting the kill. It may also have been the minimal number to fill the major social roles.

It has been called the "twelve-adult group," and it has been recognized not only by anthropologists but by mammalogists as typical of large primates and some other large mammals. Perhaps a larger group would tend to fragment or to develop conflicting cliques, while a smaller group would be less efficient in the storage and use of important traditional information. This size may also have been adapted to the patterns of camp establishment, sanitation, and mobility—that is, an appropriate number of people for the size of the region to be hunted and gathered over from a base camp. Such an area might have been expected to support two dozen people for a certain number of days or weeks—the residence period, which was important for the social-cultural activities or for the proper development of the young. More simply, the band may have been the optimum number of people able to occupy comfortably a cave or ledge shelter.

The size of the tribe also remained stable because it fit the needs of the bands. The tribe was sufficiently large to prevent deleterious inbreeding, as long as it had peaceful connections with other tribes, and yet it was sufficiently isolated to foster its own uniqueness and adaptation. By exogamous marriage among themselves the bands within the tribe maintained family and kin connections. The tribe stabilized occasional band disasters by providing a haven or replacements; in addition, the larger related cluster of bands yielded a regular increment of individuals with special talent and leadership qualities or occasionally produced an unusually wise old person whose genius would benefit the whole tribe.

In view of the highly dispersed small-group geography of hunter-gatherers, the whole tribe might occupy between five thousand and fifteen thousand square miles, an area defined by such terrain features as the basin of a watershed, a uniform geological or vegetational region, or combinations of parts of such major features. This contains band home ranges, and in this area the particular details are landmarks which, through systems of ceremony and myth, become part of the identity of the people.

If the human group size best for mental and physical health is about twenty-five, how do people survive in cities? The answer, in part, is that one function of this group size in shaping human behavior is in terms of familiarity. In spite of the actual number of people, each person strives to participate in a small group, and his circle of relatives and friends forms an abstract band totaling about the magic number. In the city perceptual screening devices enable the person to limit his contacts. This may account for the mechanical behavior of those in public jobs or the attitude of inhumanity or non-involvement by people on the street with those in distress.

Among hunters and gatherers the band is a mix of ages, sexes, familial relationships, and personalities. In effect the group is given, not chosen, and each member must make adjustments to the wide range of difference in human personality and potential.

ANCESTORS OF THE HUNTING HEART

Most of the basic traits of our species are not "originals" but have come into existence at different times in the history of the primate order. Thus we share visual traits with all who have descended from ancient monkeys, and a shoulder girdle with those descended from now-extinct apes. The characteristics of the family Hominidae have been traced from the late Miocene or early Pliocene periods, about fifteen million years ago.

The physical characteristics and ways of life of the genera and species of human ancestors have become increasingly known from accumulating fossil evidence. Each went through a period of evolutionary transformation, at the start of which it resembled its immediate ancestral species and at the end of which it graded into its descendant species. Each added to and subtracted from a pool of genes that has continued through time.

In the course of these transformations our line has increased in body size; improved its bipedality and running; graduated through seed gathering, scavenging, small-animal killing, to the pursuit of large mammals; increased the brain size; elaborated tools, including the use of fire; developed language, shelters, clothing, and made other changes in human ecology. In retrospect it is easy to look back on this sequence as though it were inevitable and, by projecting it forward in time, to see a future for man already written in the stars. Perhaps the paleontological perspective is especially seductive, for it has certainly led such eminent savants as the French philosopher Teilhard de Chardin to see life as a stage on which man plays the lead, in a drama moving inexorably toward angelhood. Perhaps we misperceive our branch of the tree of life as the main trunk. Even the extinct hominids—other genera and species of dryopithecines besides *Ramapithecus brevirostris,* other australopithecines besides *Australopithecus africanus*—were far from inconsequential failures; they existed for a long time, contributed in unknown ways to the enrichment of the planet and the evolution of life, and proceeded to the inevitable end of all species.

The significance of being shaped during this almost inconceivable length of biological time is that it implies a degree of inherent biological control over our lives which we are accustomed by our culture to reject. The idea of "biological determinism" has been so persistently denied that we have nearly crippled our appreciation of the organic factor in our lives. By identifying culture as the opposite of instinct we are in danger of putting the idea of culture at the center of a fantasy world.

Our origins would have been merely of academic interest if it were not that all behavior patterns—running, throwing, the two-dozen grouping—are more than dim reflections of outmoded customs from the ice ages, trivial souvenirs from the youth of our species. They are expressions of our physiological and psychological structures, continuous with muscles, glands, and the brain, imperatives for normal health.

Many of these do not have to be exercised in order for us to survive. Boys may be prohibited from throwing; people can live in solitary cells. Nonetheless, optimal human health demands the use of these muscles and glands in functional equivalents of the environments in which our primate forebears and the human organism evolved. Failure to find or provide the environment does not end human life but introduces stresses that injure individuals. A good example of this is vascular failure. Hypertension, thrombosis, and arteriosclerosis are symptoms of the malfunction of a system that is not properly used.

Statistics show that modern, sedentary men suffer twice as many heart attacks as active men, with four times as deadly an effect. Men who are 15 percent overweight are twice as likely to be victims, and men are five times more vulnerable than women. The human cardiovascular system evolved as part of the physiology of hunters, who regularly ran for their lives. The title of Laurens van der Post's book on Kalahari Bushmen, *Heart of the Hunter,* is not simply metaphorical. Men ran after and ate horses more or less consistently for some four hundred thousand years. The outcome of this is more than a love of horseflesh; it is a runner's body.

This does not mean constant activity. The hunter is less compulsive than the peasant about work. A typical Bushman hunter "works" two or three times a week, during which his total running time is not more than a few hours. The incidence of thrombosis among this group is extremely low. The implication is clear: an hour or so a week of jogging plus occasional sprints is the normal exercise for every male individual.

Almost all weight-control programs for normal people attempt to counteract the effect of lack of appropriate exercise on the assumption that diet alone will mitigate the disabling effects of a life without rigor. Associated with such a degenerate daily regimen are vascular and heart disease, joint and skeletal problems, neurophysiological, psychological, skin, and other organ-system deterioration. Good nutrition is useless without adequate activity.

For our species, evolution suggests three important activity sequences to offset premature aging and the pathological effects of our overanxious and underactive culture. The three sequences utilize sets of muscles associated with the origin of human physique. The first is swimming, the second hanging and swinging, the third running. A typical daily regimen for modern man would be as follows: swim steadily for five minutes, rest; hang head down and swing from ropes or bars by the hands for five minutes, rest; run for ten minutes. Women should modify this plan by reducing the running to five minutes, preceded by five minutes of stretching or dance. This program stresses vertebral segmentation and muscle complexes whose origins are associated with fish, primate, and hunter-gatherer.

In a commercial society everything that people do and need is exploited for profit. In the late 1960s jogging became fashionable in the United States. But it will survive fashion and fad simply because those who run will be healthier and live longer.

Whether our primate and carnivore habits threaten or help us depends on how we use them. There is increasing evidence that, short of malnutrition, underfeeding, which would be recognized by occasional hunger or even brief periods of intense hunger, is far more healthy for man than overfeeding.

Man is a fat-making, fair-weather carnivore who can eat more than three pounds of meat at a sitting. He is also a primate snacker, a connoisseur of ripe and unripe berries, of frogs, crabs, and insects. He has the best of two worlds—until he begins to confuse them. Then he not only fails to draw down the stored fat but begins to switch his snacking to fatty foods. Without heavy exercise some of the fatty substances are eventually deposited inside major arteries, more or less irreversibly. Tropical primate fruit-eaters pick and choose, then discard half-eaten morsels. But men "wolf" their food, gorging not once a week but, after their vegetarian instinct, several times a day, becoming gluttonous snackers.

The nonrunning gluttonous snacker undergoes deterioration of muscles, joints, bones, lungs, body metabolites, coordination, disease resistance, and psychological function. Cause and effect are often connected through intricate, sometimes obscure psychosomatic chains.

There is still another complicating factor in human food habits. Before men became eaters of flesh on a large scale, but after their ancestors had moved out of the heavy woodlands and the savannas intermediate between trees and dry grasslands, their attention turned to nuts, grasses, and tubers—plant-storage organs high in fats. Their use may have been a stage between chimplike fruit-nibbling or gorillalike stem-and-leaf-munching and eventual meat-eating. Man and his ancestors have long used these high-energy foods. Potatoes, cashews, and corn are good for the runner but dangerous for a non-hunting (non-running) individual who likes to eat between meals.

Patterns for women set in the evolutionary past are different from those set for men. Women, who probably less often ran after large game, have fat-storage systems that do not overload their vascular organs and contribute to heart failure. The rhythm and physiology of their lives are so different from those of men that it is almost as though they were another species.

Evolution of Sexual Dimorphism

The gender differences, or sexual dimorphism, of humans, as among all organisms, are a compromise between opposing selective forces. In general, among animals where social roles are strongly differentiated, so are musculature and appearance. Roles are related to habitat. Among the monkeys both sexes of most tree-living forms are very similar, while terrestrial monkeys and apes are sexually much more dissimilar. Male gorillas and chimpanzees are more than 100 percent heavier than the females. Within a single species of baboon, which is found from forest-edge habitats to barren country, there is more dimorphism among those living farthest from the trees and more pronounced dominance of the males over the females. Strong dimorphism is associated with intense male hierarchies and extended pairing. The more intensive the rank-order system, the more open the terrain, the more aggressive the males and submissive the females, the greater is the physical difference between the sexes.

If the differences between human sexes are compared to those seen in the range of primates, some educated guesses can be made about the habitat, social organization, and role differentiation during the long period of Pleistocene hunting-gathering. As man-the-hunter emerged from his forefathers, he retained face and chest hair patterns, which emphasized sexual difference. Beards, like manes in lions, intensify dissimilarity and trigger spontaneous feelings of awe, submission, and intimidation. Modern races of men who have lost the beard-growing ability, such as Polynesians or American Indians, commonly substitute tattooing, ornaments, or cosmetics.

The differences in role that are signified by external appearances are mainly those connected with food-getting. In the early dawn of our genus, or of its australopithecine precursors, there may have been no home base to which groups returned at night, and the prey was small- to medium-sized animals eaten on the spot. If so, the group moved and stopped as a whole, and the foraging for tubers and nuts as well as the killing of porcupines and antelope calves was participated in by all. But among *Homo erectus* and *Homo sapiens* the men departed from a base camp or a field camp, hunted large, dangerous mammals, sometimes for many days, and returned with meat. The very young and old probably remained behind. Women and children foraged during the men's absence.

Not only did this affect the kind of natural selection for physical traits, but new pair-bond mating patterns came into existence, stabilizing couples during their separation. Copulation intensified by orgasm and preceded by erotic play, emphasizing female postures and anatomy, became an intrinsic part of a pattern of life whose rhythms were dictated by the coming and going of the hunters.

The dramatic specialization of non-reproductive sexuality by the hunter-gatherers seemed to demand not only increased dimorphism and incitement signals, but culturally defined gender exaggeration. Our species developed the instinct for cryptandic cosmetics—that is, the universal penchant for self-decoration, for coiffures, body rouge and paint, jewelry, clothing, and other means of grooming—to enhance sexual traits. The advantage of these devices over extreme anatomical divergence is that they can be temporarily employed (for the return of the hunters) and, perhaps more important, local groups could develop unique cryptandic fashions or skills which lent themselves to the many fine social distinctions of totemic clan differentiation.

For a million years under conditions of the hunt women lived—and because of their biology still live—geographically more circumscribed lives than men. They have a poorer sense of large-scale spatial relationships and direction and are not good throwers or runners. They probably have superior social intelligence and inferior strategic cunning than men. These differences are genetically controlled and are part of the personality of all living women, taken as a group. Women are less subject to heart attack than men because of the way in which female hormones regulate fat deposit in the circulatory system and elsewhere. Their body fat deposits differ in location and somewhat in function. Even the psychological differences between men and women were shaped originally by the conditions of life in a hunting-gathering society.

It is perhaps not accidental that there is a large proportion of women among the students of wild apes. Examples are Jane Van Lawick-Goodall with chimpanzees, Dian Fossey with mountain gorillas, and the women whose part in husband-wife teams has been significant. Women in some measure share with the apes a prehunting perception and psychology, even a musculature, from which men are excluded: a world of frugivorousness and pensiveness, at once more intensely social and more tranquil than that to which man's symbolic carnivorousness led. Perhaps these similarities evoke an empathy that gives women an insight into and an advantage in studying, even joining, ape groups.

In a time of increasing confusion over gender differences, the evolutionary past provides a meaningful perspective. Admittedly the line between specialization of role and arbitrary social oppression as seen today is not easy to determine. But to distinguish between what is genetically given and what is cultural bias it is necessary to consider dimorphism in its psychological as well as social and biological aspects. The reality of innate temperamental as well as bodily differences does not justify just any social-status distinctions. Male chauvinism based on evolutionary determinism is reprehensible. But it is futile to pronounce, at the end of fifteen million years of hominid evolution, that men and women are alike. It is typical of the ideological approach to life to suppose that by political action we can make the human organism whatever we want it to be.

Among living hunters, men make the major decisions relating to their activity as hunters, explorers, and symbolizers, while women dominate in matters of children, diet, and social relations. An overall gender-based, dominance-subordination ranking does not exist among them. Hunters are not patriarchal authoritarians like cattle- and sheep-keepers. They perceive gender as the outcome of a cosmic philosophy of complementarity. Personified male gods of the sky and sun and female deities of the soil or sea, to whom omnipotent powers are attributed, are the fixations of planters and herders. Humanized gods among hunter-gatherers are seldom absolute rulers and are usually envisaged as benign, ancestral figures.

■

The past, having shaped our species, holds the clues to normal function. The cell, individual, and society all tend to create and adapt to and thereafter predict the kind of environment in which they work. Versatility of cultural form may seem to imply that for many the environment is relatively inconsequential, but in reality environmental requirements are greater and more exacting for humans than for most other species. Men need, in their nonhuman environment, open country with occasional cover, labyrinthine play areas, a rich variety of plants, animals, rocks, stars; structures and forms numbering into the thousands; initiation solitude, transitional and holy places, a wide variety of food organisms and diversity of stone and wood, nearby fresh water, large mammalian herds, cave and other habitation sites, and so on. Beyond the ecological and psychological constants needed for normal human health there must be an environmental margin of security to allow choice and to contribute to the individuality of experience and learned behavior.

Postindustrial men do exist without these things and in an enormous variety of social arrangements, but they live in constant crisis, stress, and poor mental health. Men are not free to create any form of society or any kind of environment they choose; they are free only within the bounds shaped by the past that is present in them.

A wide flexibility of behavior requires suitable environmental diversity. If an omnivore concentrates his attention on a single kind of food he will injure himself and his environment. If the runner does not run he will die of heartbreak (and so will the antelope). If sexually dimorphic forms subordinate the values and roles of one gender to the other or deny their dimorphism, they hamper individualizing (or individuating) processes and cripple the social and ecological life of the group.

It is sometimes said that higher complex creatures like humans do well in a changing world. In truth, such species, with flexible, learned behavior and diverse social forms, require a stable natural environment. Since modern forms were created by the past they depend on environments like those in which they were shaped. This is, of course, a highly heretical opinion in a society whose myths enshrine progress and change—a society puzzled by the decay of the quality of life and threatened by self-destruction. It is also said that "nature is change" and argued that such is the essence of evolution. But this observation is often used as a justification for arbitrary control of the environment and distorts the fundamental aspect of evolutionary change, which is its tempo. The dramatic alteration of planetary life over hundreds of thousands of years requires great stability of life cycles, individual experience, and social organization. Without such continuity and seeming changelessness over the shorter term, life and environment would be too chaotic for the delicate processes of human life to operate.

ON AGGRESSION AND THE TENDER CARNIVORE

Fighting between members of the same species is very different from the killing of prey by predator, and psychopathological fighting is very different from normal conflict. All animals are predatory (or parasitic) since they obtain and eat other organisms. Carnivores, which eat meat, must catch, kill, and dismember their prey. Man is in part a carnivore: the male of the species is genetically programmed to pursue, attack, and kill large mammals for food. To the extent that men do not do so they are not fully human.

Within their own species and societies, all animals are occasionally competitive, irritable, and antagonistic. Assault against their own kind, as when stags lock antlers over hinds or housecats thrash young adults as initiation into the brotherhood, is always subject to precise restraining signals that inhibit or deflect attack. The animal world is full of appeasement signs and diverted aggression, which allow the escape of beaten rivals. Among men the instinctive response to submissiveness is general enough so that the exact signals by which the defeated says "Enough!" may be modified by local custom.

For modern humans the question of whether or not man is by instinct a killer has been misleadingly centered on war and on the political ends to peace. War is the state's expression of social pathology. Ecologically, it is a breakdown in the distinction that a healthy species makes between inter-species and intra-species behaviors and in the use of organized predation. It occurs where men cannot regularly hunt and where population densities are too high. In a Frankensteinian fashion it fuses elements of the primate rank-order system as the basis for military organization, with the cooperative yet lethal talents of the human social carnivore. Every facet of soldierly conduct honored and reinforced by the military for the past fifty centuries is a perverted form of the desired qualities evoked in the ancient initiation rites of adolescents: fidelity, idealism, skill, and courage.

The main episodes of war—cooperative murder—can be seen in caged or stressed predators of any kind. But among neither free-living animals nor hunting-gathering men is war an inherent trait that was at some time in the past a regular part of daily life. Among all carnivores, individuals occasionally kill other individuals. Sometimes it is an accident of uncontrolled rage, but usually it is the outcome of a chronic disturbance that has led to instability in group composition. Among those primitive groups in which prestige is gained from the daring murder of a member of another tribe, there is usually evidence of abnormal stress. The socially sanctioned expression of violence is an attempt to cope with pressures deforming and threatening the human condition after more peaceful expiatory measures have failed.

The expression of normal, infantile "primary process" thought (desire for omnipotence, immediate gratification, unrestricted emotion, and acting out feelings) is submerged and restrained in myth and ritual. In mild degrees of stress, these are acted out in socially organized spectacles of violence, such as ritual mutilation, torture, and execution: desperate, shocking (and usually successful) measures to readjust the group neuroses by means of scapegoats. But—when a group is threatened by disintegrating forces such as sudden mass mortality, acute deprivation, alien invasion, unusual climatic events, widespread health or nutritional disorders, or the failure of important social and religious institutions, it normally reacts with genocide and war.

The incidence of mental disorder leading to mutual slaughter is perhaps the best evidence that the human cerebrum is near its tolerable limits in size. In the past it may have surpassed that equilibrium and have been reduced by natural selection, reversing the trend toward enlargement.

The crisis of mental overreaching does not end there. Hypercomplexity is determined by function as well as by volume. A changed environment may render the brain unfit. A brain of razor-sharp keenness useful in a world of human rarity may be too large in a world of billions of people. Today the symptom of the overdone head is no longer the scapegoat ceremony, however; it is the insanity by which mass society delivers itself into military hands.

An altered population density is not the only environment incompatible with a large brain size. In the interior of New Guinea there are people who have been much written about and filmed in recent years. The men engage in chronic inter-tribal war in the form of more-or-less organized spear-throwing and ambush. Their lives have been described as "an unending round of death and revenge." Their culture is dominated by ferocious sorcery cults whose grisly fantasies serve less as a safety valve than as perpetual machines of fear and hate. In spite of their celebrated primitiveness these people are not true hunters. Like the tropical forest peoples of the upper Amazon, they lack large mammals to hunt. Psychically, yam-harvesting is no more a suitable occupation for them than supermarket shopping is for a man in Detroit. As among industrial men, their deprivation has psychotic consequences. It is no surprise that the inhabitants of New Guinea, descendants of far-off hunters, now isolated in a land without large prey, mutilate themselves (although they have no automobiles for this purpose) and vainly display their lifelong frustration in a furious search for alternatives to the hunt.

Certainly no other animal exhibits anything like the degree of intra-specific killing and maiming that occurs within our own species. That wars have continued despite the variety of political forms that have been tried through the ages of written history suggests that something more fundamental is at fault than systems of ideas and programs. The New Guinea spear duels and the Big Powers missile race are equally biological malfunctions—instinctive but pathological. As in other forms of mental illness, the true causes are submerged in unconscious obscurity, shielded by conscious images and ideas that are opposite of the truth—such as the stereotype of the farmer as a man of peace. Modern war is attributed to failure of belief or will or leadership or failure to contain the animal and archaic savage beneath our skins. In fact, the swords of war are hammered from plowshares. To consider goat-breeding and soil-breaking virtuous is self-deception; war emerged with the shift in ecology, which produced the arrogant concept of land ownership and the struggles for resources, space, and power.

■

The seeming contradiction between the aggressive and peaceful attributes of the carnivore-hunter requires a somewhat closer look at carnivores in general. As has been noted, fighting is normally ritualized (becoming somewhat like a dance) among members of the same species. Between-species killing among large predators is rare —in spite of the staged displays of fights between lions and tigers, bears and lions, by circuses and irresponsible nature-film makers.

The large carnivores are few in kind, few in number, and highly intelligent. Their attention, unlike that of plant-eaters, is fixed on roving prey rather than on rooted plants or place, "thatness" instead of "thereness." Apes in captivity become visibly agitated when the food dish is moved, but coyotes and lions do not. The size of mammalian carnivores is inverse to their fecundity and is proportional to the relative amount of learning in their behavioral repertoire.

Carnivore-hunters are sound sleepers. Sleep, associated with complex nervous activity, is divided into specific phases in big-brained animals. One phase, dreaming, performs functions known to be necessary but not fully understood. The content and structure of dreams in man are related to both individual and species experiences, so that the analysis of dreams provides a unique insight into environments and activities "expected" by the organism and may help reconstruct the daily life and ecology native to our species.

The various kinds of hunting animals are not usually competitive. In a given area different-sized species live in hunting sets or clusters with a spread of hunting styles, habitat, food preferences, and daily rhythms. Wolves and lynxes occupy the same habitat but hunt very differently and kill different species of prey. Wolves track, surround, and attack from the rear, while cats stalk, ambush, and attack from the front. This picture of an integrated set of predators, each playing a part in the whole ecology, minimizing competition, with cautious and deliberate procedures, belies the image of the rampaging blood-thirsty killer or the fictional creature that "kills for the pleasure of it." The common analogy between a berserk murderer and a preda-tory animal simply is not true.

The ecology of all hunting involves a strategy that has been called "the prudent policy of predation." In the evolution of predation there are long-term considerations that outweigh sheer killing effi-ciency. It is to the predator's disadvantage as a species to maximize the kill if this is detrimental to the stability of the prey population, and therefore to future generations of predators. The prudent pred-ator is not an exterminator. It plays a role in a self-regulating system, taking a yield of the prey only up to a level of the replacement rate. Within this limit predation has the effect of increasing the birth rate of the prey by removing the old, the crippled, the non-reproducing, whose places are taken by vigorous individuals.

In a sense the carnivore is using the prey to manufacture food for itself from plants. The efficiency of this transformation never exceeds about 15 percent because the herbivorous prey has already used most of the energy from the plants it eats in its own metabolic activity. Its body tissues represent the remainder, but in order for the carni-vore to take this without harm to the prey species it must be har-vested in the right stage of the prey's life cycle.

The predator, of course, has not consciously figured out this com-plicated equation. Nor has the human hunter, in spite of his superior intelligence, for he usually lacks the information needed to adjust his hunting to top ecological efficiency. Like all hunters, men therefore take a pragmatic approach. Since to harvest too few or too many is detrimental to the system in which predator and prey are comple-mentary, the hunters adopt a mode of operation that achieves the same end that mathematical analysis would indicate: a certain predator population density (usually well below reproductive potential and the actual carrying capacity of the environment); a shifting harvest of different species of prey; and a choice of individual prey whose loss will least affect the continuity of the prey population, mainly those animals with the highest probability of dying soon from any cause, particularly the old and diseased. In most carnivores the ability to make such a choice is the outcome of instinct and experience; in many it is these plus the empirical taboos and rituals that restrict the hunt.

The strategy of the prey is to separate as clearly as possible those animals that will perpetuate the species and sustain group behaviors from those that are defective, senile, and degenerate. By providing some animals that transmit the energy of plants to carnivores, the prey can more effectively insure the survival of those who are the gene bearers of future generations. The prey is also engaged in the longer-term objective of sorting out bad genes and poor genetic combinations by shunting them out of the gene pool and thereby improving the quality of the species.

In considering man as a part-time carnivore, the essential fact is that he became a large-game hunter as he became human. The omnivorous, scavenging *Australopithecus* was intermediate in the transition. The later Ice Age hunters of the genus *Homo,* with their exquisite tools and cooperative tactics, stalked the largest living land animals. The last of the Paleolithic hunters raised the art of hunting to the center of a complex philosophy of life. Throughout, the basic principles of predator-prey equilibrium were never abandoned.

SIX

The Dance of Neoteny
and Ontogeny

IN THE IDEOLOGY of recent times—of progress and the self-making of the person and the society, of the ego's selection of choices of what-to-be, appended to a body—the child is a *sac physiologique* that is fostered and that grasps or obtains thought and intelligence. Epigenesis is a contrary concept of life cycle (or ontogeny). The person emerges in a genetic calendar by stages, with time-critical constraints and needs, so that instinct and experience act in concert. The mature adult is a late stage in this lifelong series of overlapping and interlocking events: not linear but spiral, resonating between disjunction and unity, but moving, so that each new cycle enlarges the previous one.

This complicated passage through separations and symbioses is human and primate. It evolved; it is based on an extended life—extended not only by time added at the end, but by an expanded youth. This retarded growth rate and its associated events are neoteny. It is most conspicuous in the slow growth of the body itself, the retention of babyish or even fetal bone-growth patterns, toe, finger, or head orientation, reduced body-hair covering, late tooth eruption and loss, and so on in dozens of modified organ and tissue development rates. Neoteny includes a prolonged psychogenesis. It extends, specializes, and orders experiences essential to the emergence of consciousness and the psyche.

Joseph Pearce, in his lovely book *Magical Child,* describes this emerging sense of self and separateness, the growth of a confident, centered being who reaches out to new experience, perceiving a universe in a plural reality. By symbiosis he means a connecting dependency, a kind of school for relatedness, a matrix or setting in which the structure of the world is forecast by previous experience, beginning with the body, and is discovered according to "expectations." The infant is programmed by his own nervous system to anticipate certain responses from the mother, which must be encountered in order to become the basis or matrix of the earth, a new counterplayer.

Learning in this sense does not mean preparation by logical operations with dialectical and ideological ends, by art appreciation or creativity, nor by overviews of history and cultures. It means a highly timed openness in which the attention of the child is predirected by an intrinsic schedule, a hunger to fill archetypal forms with specific meaning. Neoteny is the biological commitment to that learning program, building identity and meaning in the oscillation between autonomy and unity, separateness and relatedness. It takes about 30 percent of the whole human life span. It is a pulse, presenting the mind with wider wholes, from womb to mother and body, to earth, to cosmos. Each of these resolves tasks given in the growth of consciousness and intuition in infancy, childhood, and youth. Their goal is not to perpetuate the prenatal subjective merger state but, in a staircase of mergers and departures, to identify a self (or selves: a resolution of the inchoate "we," "they," and "it" as well as "I"), leading to a more mature sense of relatedness. In this way a good sense of being in the cosmos is the result of two decades of timed events that involve the person with others and with the nonhuman in an extraordinary interplay. Generally speaking, social bonds (infant-mother, juvenile-family, adolescent-community) accompany the successive matrices of being, as the ground from which novelty is explored and the self delineated, while ecological realities (flowers-bees, bears-salmon) become satisfying otherness in their own right and metaphorical sign images or messages about the inner world, the binding forces of human society, and the invisible spiritual realm.

The success of this sequence depends on good nurturing. Thus, the evolution of infantile stages is accompanied by the emergence of a parental and social capacity. To be the caretakers of such a highly specialized ontogeny is itself a complex task requiring successive appropriate responses and anticipation. Neoteny as such is only the plunge into immaturity. Delivery into maturity depends on certain unique characteristics in the human adult that have been called the capacity for culture. Much of the transmitted content and behaviors making up the characteristic features of a particular people are directed to the ontogeny of its members. The details of this material—the language, myths, tools, and ceremonies—vary from one people to the next, but the differences are on the surface; they fill forms that the species has long since evolved as firmly at its physical traits.

The complexity of human development is so great and the scope for error so broad that we might wonder how anyone gets through to full maturity. Some repair processes are built into its calendar. The most conspicuous is adolescent regression, an infantile aspect that may serve the individual in recuperative ways. Beyond that, psychotherapy (which occurs in some forms in all societies) is usually shaped around a reexperiencing that enables the patient to adjust to, if not mend, a psychodevelopmental flaw. The catalysts of mind, provided by the nurturers, are like the nutritional and hormonal factors of the neotenic body, except that they are required experiences. Like the timed events in a play (either dramatic dialogue or the execution of movements in a game), they may be poorly presented, muffed, or missed.[1] The play goes on, more or less imperfectly. The person, so deprived, bears the consequences as unregenerate elements of immaturity, glossed by repression and compensation, distorted by unconscious yearnings for overdue fulfillment and resentments against the nurturers. If, for example, there was no adequate earth matrix in the child's life between its fourth and tenth year, it can never achieve a fully satisfying philosophical rapprochement to the stellar universe or to any of the fundamental questions to which religion is always directed. The cosmic counterplayers are likely to be perceived in some disguised form of infantile symbiosis, imperfectly integrated with the vast middle ground of the earth terrain and its living forms.

In *Nature and Madness* I have attempted to show how civilization was served by deforming the ontogeny of its members. These effects have been cumulative, but the first epoch—agriculture—was the most decisive. Unlike the society of prototypical human beings, who lived by hunting and gathering, agriculture favored larger groups of people, who, in terms of individual personality, accepted decision making by aristocracies or priesthoods rather than by councils of the whole, the rewards of success by power rather than prestige, the authoritarian leadership seized rather than granted. Politically, agriculture required a society composed of members with the acumen of children. Empirically, it set about amputating and replacing certain signals and experiences central to early epigenesis. Agriculture not only infantilized animals by domestication, but exploited the infantile human traits of the normal individual neoteny.[2] The obedience demanded by the organization necessary for anything larger than the earliest village life, associated with the rise of a military caste, is essentially juvenile and submissive, reflecting proud but unreflecting loyalty, blood-brother same-sex bonding, group adventurist attitudes, tight conformism, and willingness to suffer and endure based on pride.[3] The abandonment of the totemic use of wild plants and animals and the congeniality of the ecosystem as a model for social speculating threw the mythopoetic leap to philosophy in adolescence back upon familial models, including domesticated-animal subordinates. Agriculture removed the means by which men could contemplate themselves through any terms other than themselves (or machines). It projected back upon nature an image of human conflict and competition and then read analogies from that to people (or, as Lévi-Strauss puts it, "naturalized a true culture falsely").

The result of this is that human groups foreign to one's own are read as other species, and on the historical misconstruction of nature as violent, the displacement, enslavement, and killing of the others are logical. One enacts rather than thinks the role of predator or prey. The poetic energies of puberty are deflected from their confrontation with the cosmic and nonhuman toward which that ontogeny had been directed for a million years, turning it back in myths that disguised the maternal symbiosis in celestial dress. In short, the unfulfilled maternal symbiosis of infant and mother leaves a vacuum that can be exploited to draw the new birth of adolescence backward, framing the world in terms of the myths of the Great Mother. While there is no doubt that the maternal symbiosis of infancy is fundamental to all further at-homeness, it is its coherence that is paradigmatic, not its enfolding, shielding, comforting surrender of responsibility. As William Thompson has pointed out, the social consequence of the prevailing myth of the Great Mother is the takeover by an even greater father.[4]

The correction of our modern abuse of the feminine and the recovery of rootedness in the earth is not an adult adoption of the subjectivity of early development. Simply magnified, the latter carries with it all that passive, mindless lack of understanding and questing for which the ancient Mesopotamian agrotheocracies were scorned by the Hebrews and the Greeks. It is not the recovery of mother fixation, with its ambivalence of hating and adoring, fearing separation and yet resenting maternal power, that we now need, for the ideologizing of that ambiguity leads to splitting everything, a kind of final divisiveness.

A broader sensitivity to the feminine rather than fixation on mother is the normal characteristic of the child's maternal symbiosis. The intense bonding of mother and infant involves not only body contact and feeding on demand, but time together in quiet repose and leisure, during which the tentative explorations of the child away from the mother are successful to the extent that she is available and attentive, though not fussy and directing. With the beginning of village life, the number of children born to a woman in her lifetime increased from four or five to as many as sixteen (with about 50 percent survival in both). The mother could give less attention and less milk to each individual baby. Not going so far afield as her foraging counterpart, she did not carry the infant as much and was more likely to seek surrogate caretakers. The resulting failure of symbiotic bonding is unity pathology: the fearful, tentative, slow-thinking, psychologically crippled child whose personality will always be marked by a stressful mother attachment, unrelieved by a new centering in the plural earth matrix. Moreover, it does not end with the schizoid deformities of the adult, but in adults who are sick mothers, whose infants, says Harold F. Searles, "strive to remain fragmented as therapy for her and, failing, achieve inadequate separation from her and eventually from the nonhuman."[5] Failure of separation makes self and parts of the world subjectively interchangeable or, at the other extreme, dichotomized and opposing. In both there is a failure of relational factors in a literal, fragmented world without metaphorical dimension.

The fantasies, anxieties, and hostilities of unresolved immaturity are acted on or repressed and redirected in many ways. In this dark shadow of adult youthfulness is an enduring grief, a tentative feeling about the universe as though it were an incompetent parent, and a thin love of nature over deep fears. What agriculture discovered was not only that plants and animals could be subordinated, but that large numbers of men could be centrally controlled by manipulating these stresses, perpetuating their timorous search for protection, their dependence, their impulses of omnipotence and helplessness, irrational surges of adulation and hate, submission to authority, and fear of the strange.[6]

This useful warping and impedance of epigenesis in the service of village life has continued to provide mankind with a solipsistic psychology appropriate to a man-made world and its defense against neighbors. Still, its deformities are hurtful. Civilized men have pursued redress and maturity while at the same time bending ontogeny in new ways to suit new ideologies. The desert fathers, reacting against the momism of the Bronze-Age Near East, formulated patriarchy. Wrathfully demythologizing, deritualizing, and desacralizing the earth, fostering mobility and the iconography of the Word, the Hebrew prophets, Christian purists, and Hellenic Greeks sought to wrench the human personality into a more grown-up style. Taking a cue from the ontogenetic principle of the masculine guide or spirit as mediator in the transition from one symbiotic plateau to another, they misconstrued it as maleness and amputated the passage. The sense of individual responsibility fostered by these Western progenitors, resembling the juvenile's superego, and their precepts of alienation from the earth caught up the idealizing adolescent, shorn of his karma of ceremonial initiation, his dreams and emotions directed into visions of power and escape.

Repudiating myth in content and ritual act, Western man broke bonds with the earth, soil, and nature to return power to the father and dissociated the human spirit from seasons and celestial rounds. To do so was to awaken fear of the body and world in their rhythms and inherent liveliness, to make man alien, to glorify separation anxiety. Perception and philosophy at the desert edge confirmed a split universe, sentencing the person to a lifetime of ambiguity and forcing personal identity at the terrible cost of unrelatedness. "As a prize for certified adulthood, the fathers all limit and forestall some frightening potentialities of development dangerous to 'the system'," says Erikson.[7]

In spite of their mockery of the heathen myths and ceremonies of initiation, these alienists created for their children an atmosphere of intense crises of belief and faith—matters traditionally supervised by men, even among the agricultural theocracies with their maternal symbolism. These desert patriarchs, scorning natural symbols, minimizing the plant, animal, seasonal, earthy, and feminine, exploited the adolescent capacity for abstraction—and made it terminal—by despising all such sources except the Bible and its exegesis.[8]

Both Mircea Eliade and J. L. Henderson have argued that adolescent initiation is the cultural response to an intrinsic need.[9] The desire to prove oneself, infantilisms, idealism, poeticising, and enlarged search for a new identity are age-grade traits. The tutorials, ceremonies, religious instruction, and vision inducing are administered by a cadre of adults who are themselves the product of the successful marriage of ontogeny and liturgical art. That marriage is at the heart of human cultural behavior. It is the response to the neotenic psychology of the young by mature adults. As part of the biology of human life, the ceremonies of initiation have an ecological function: they are the branch whose flowering completes a crucial phase of the life cycle by using the realm of nature as the language of religious thought. The natural world can become, in retrospect, an object of veneration if it is first an object of thought, as the prototype of coherence—and it is that because of the quality of early maternal care.

The West of the Protestant-mechanist era coupled that desert thought, with its attachment to an adolescent, ascetic, idealist escapism, to scientific mechanism and literary secular humanism in a further assault on the spirit of the autochthonous and feminine that forms the basis of place attachment in every individual.

The Protestant puritanical reformulation of the self-chosen and child-inflicted alienated consciousness of the Christian fathers and Hebrew prophets had its own twists and quirks—which can also be seen as an unconscious struggle to recover maturity. One was their ambivalence about the sordidness of the organic realm. Their contempt for the body and their revulsions against the pullulations of life and the horror of slime, decay, excretion, birth, and death are not rational disinclinations but the effects of a harshly built psychological distortion of childhood delivered up to adult consensus and rationalization. But like the child, the Protestants were fascinated by the body in their obsessive "play" with it and its products, which ontogeny offers as proof and elements of the livingness of the self, made whole by progressive inclusionist perception.[10] Lacking that perception and affirmation of plurality and diversity, it simply decays into duality.

In the pubertal youth this fixation on the body stirs with renewed force. In tribal peoples its "dirty" side is elevated to serve as a basis for pollution taboos, linking contamination to the inadequate observation of cultural practices and the adolescent drive for the purity of a shining idealism to social customs. Aversion serves a limited but positive function in group consciousness.

But if contamination is everywhere—as it is in the ideology of the puritanical version of the Fall—the metaphor becomes destructive.[11] Conditioned to despise and distrust his own intuitions regarding the body, the individual cannot incorporate a "wisdom of the body" in a philosophy of holism. The alternatives open to a society intervening in ontogeny in this way simply play out the unresolved opposition by extrapolating from either the perverse, infantile, erotic pleasure of self-attention or the prudish, horrified distaste for any natural gratifications: thus Protestant culture in North America produces the world's most devoted protectors of wildlife, its greatest leaders in conservation, its most romantic wilderness literature, the first national parks, and the angriest opponents of the soiling of air and water—and it produces an ecological holocaust, the raping of a whole continent of forests and rich soils by uncomprehending destroyers, wrapped in patriotism, humanism, progress, and other slogans in which they profoundly believe.

The adherents to both ends of this psychoideological spectrum act out their feelings, fulfilling the modern commonplace that "man makes his environment." The psychotic, says Edith Jacobson, tries to "change the world" to meet his needs, a fantasy of performing (as opposed to symbolizing) his impulses. International corporations exult in advertising that they are changing the world. Beneath that proud boast is a kind of protean mania, advising us that we must progress or fall backward. Such fear of regression, says Jacobson, is most acute in early adolescence, when the youth, on the verge of recapitulating infantile modes of renewal, is poised psychologically between "dedifferentiation" and the movement toward maturity.[12] The reformist environmentalist can be acting out, just as unconsciously and desperately, that changing of the world as the mode of changing the self, particularly in animal protectionism, wild-area (as opposed to the rest of the planet) preservation, escapist naturism, and beautification—all of which maintain two worlds, hating compromise and confusing the issues with good or evil in people.

The trouble with the eagerness to make a world is that, being already made, what is there must first be destroyed. Idealism, whether of the pastoral peaceable kingdom or the electronic paradise of technomania and space travel, is in the above sense a normal part of adolescent dreaming, like the juvenile fantasies of heroic glory. Norman Kiell observes that the "pubescent" is called on to reform while his precognitive self is at the world center, and hence acts to "save mankind from his own nonhuman status"—that is, from the temporary identity vacuum in the transition from the juvenile stage into adult life.[13] The difficulty for our time is that no cultus exists, with its benign cadre of elders, to guide and administer that transition.

■

And so we come to our own time. And the same questions are asked: To what extent does the technological/urban society work because its members are ontogenetically stuck? What are the means and the effects of this psychological amputation? We inherit the past and its machinations. White, European-American, Western peoples are separated by many generations from decisions by councils of the whole, small-group nomadic life with few possessions, highly developed initiation ceremonies, natural history as everyman's vocation, a total surround of non–man-made (or "wild") otherness with spiritual significance, and the "natural" way of mother and infant. All these are strange to us because we are no longer competent to live them—although that competence is potentially in each of us.

The question of our own disabilities of ontogeny cannot be answered simply as the cumulative invasions into it of the past. The culture of urban technicity works out its own deformities of ontogenesis. Some of these are legacies, while others are innovative shifts in the selective perpetuation of infantile and juvenile concerns. Many aspects of the urban hive are shaped by the industries of transportation, energy use, and state-of-the-art synthesis of materials and products. On the other hand, the city is shaped, designed consciously and unconsciously, by identity cripples, deprived in various social and ecological dimensions, yet also cripples in the sense of potential capacity, the possibilities of personal realization in the archaic and magnificent environments of the deep past.

Whether blindness is pathological to those living in a cave depends on whether you think of it in terms of personal adaptability or of the inherent potentialities of every member of our species. My view is the latter, but adaptability is the more vaunted trait—adaptability, that is, in the sense of flexibility, readiness to change jobs, addresses, beliefs, celebrated by the technocratic ideal of progress in convenience, comfort, safety, insulation, and the stimulus of novelty. This kind of adaptability is not of a citizenship that transcends place and time, but of not yet being adapted, of never finding one's place or time.

Cultural anthropology has often been used as evidence of this contemporary notion of heroic flexibility. A great many ethnographic studies do impress us with the various ways of being human, but few of them emphasize the inexorable direction in all human societies: what all cultures seek is to clarify and confirm the belongingness of their members, even at the expense of perpetuating infantile fears, of depriving the members of the object of their quest for adaptedness and making their only common ground their nonrootedness.

In this connection it is no surprise that the "adaptability society" celebrates childhood, admires youth and despises age, and equates childhood with innocence, wisdom, and spiritual power. Its members cling to childhood, for their own did not serve its purpose. To those for whom adult life is admixed with decrepit childhood, the unfulfilled promise cannot be abandoned. To wish to remain child-like, to foster the nostalgia for childhood, is to grieve for our own lost maturity, not because maturity is synonymous with childhood, but because then it was still possible to move, epigenetically, toward maturity.

Wide-eyed wonder, nonjudgmental response, and the immediate joy of being are beautiful to see; I hope some kernel of them remains in the heart of every adult. They are sometimes presented as appropriate models for adult attitudes toward nature. But the open ecstasy of the child has its special purposes: a kind of cataloging, preconscious order-finding, and cryptic anthropomorphizing that have to do with personality development—at least for the child with a good mother bond. The poorly bonded child goes through this nature-wonder period even though troubled, for it is a new "maternal" reality and perhaps is therapeutic. In any case, there is no figurative nature for the child; all is literal. Even in pretending, there is only one reality. The children playing delightedly on the green grass or in awe at an owl in the woods will grow up oblivious to the good in nature if they never go beyond that momentary fascination. When, as adults, they will weigh the literal value of the owl (already realized, for it taught them the name and owlness) against other literal values, such as replacing the forest with a hospital, a sewage system, or an oil well, their judgment is likely to be for progress. With poor initial mother symbiosis, with an inadequate or lackluster place and creature naturizing, or without the crucial adolescent religious initiation that uses the symbiotic, literal world as a prefigured cosmos, the adult cannot choose the forest and the owl. His self is still at the center of a juvenile reality. It may be true that the purpose of the childlike pleasure in the outdoors is an end in itself, but it is also necessary to the further work of the self going beyond the self.

I have oversimplified the choices in order to make a point. There is not a choice between the owl and the oil well at all. In our society those who would choose the owl are not more mature. Growing out of Erik Erikson's concept of trust versus nontrust as an early epigenetic concern and out of the Russells' observation that the child perceives poor nurturing as hostility—which is either denied and repressed (as among idealists) or transferred in its source so as to be seen as coming from the natural world instead of from the parents (as among cynics)—there arises an opposition that is itself an extension of infantile duality.[14] Fear and hatred of the organic on the one hand, the desire to merge with it on the other; the impulse to control and subordinate on the one hand, to worship the nonhuman on the other; overdifferentiation on the one hand, fears of separation on the other—all are two sides of a coin. In the shape given to a civilization by totemically inspired, technologically sophisticated, small-group, epigenetically fulfilled adults, the necessity to choose would never arise.

In effect, the historical episodes in such socially administered deprivation have become elements in the European-American personality: the eras of plant and animal domestication, of religious asceticism, of puritanism, and of mechanization. The American is not the profligate anti-European; he is, in respect to certain characteristics, the full embodiment of Western, Classical, Christian man, enabled by the colossal richness of an unexploited continent to play out the savaging of neoteny according to the agendas of domestication, desert-edge transcendence, Galilean-Calvinist dualities, and industrialization. Careless of waste, wallowing in refuse, exterminating the enemies, having everything now and new, despising age, denying human natural history, fabricating pseudotraditions, swamped in the repeated personal crises of the aging preadolescent: all are familiar images of American society. They are the signs of private nightmares of incoherence and disorder in broken climaxes where technologies in pursuit of mastery create ever-worsening problems— private nightmares expanded to a social level.

All Westerners are heir, not only to the self-justifications of recent technophilic Promethean impulses, but to the legacy of the whole. Men may now be the possessors of the world's flimsiest identity structure, the products of a prolonged tinkering with ontogenesis—by Paleolithic standards, childish adults. Because of this arrested development, modern society continues to work, for it requires dependence. But the private cost is massive therapy, escapism, intoxicants, narcotics, fits of destruction and rage, enormous grief, subordination to hierarchies that exhibit this callow ineptitude at every level, and perhaps worst of all, a readiness to strike back at a natural world that we dimly perceive as having failed us. From this erosion of human nurturing comes the failure of the passages of the life cycle and the exhaustion of our ecological accords.

In the city world of today, infinite wants are pursued as though the environment were an amnion and technology a placenta. Unlike the submissive cultures of obedience, those of willful, proud disengagement, or those obsessed with guilt and pollution, this made world is the home of omnipotence and immediate satisfaction. There is no mother of limited resources or disciplining father, only a self in a fluid system.

The high percentage of neuroses in Western society seems often to be interpreted as a sign of a highly stressful "lifestyle." If you add to it—or see it acted out as—the insanities of nationalism, war, and biome busting, a better case than simply that of lifestyle can be made in terms of an epidemic of the psychopathic mutilation of ontogeny. Characteristic of the schizoid features of this immature subjectivity is difficulty differentiating among fantasy, dream, and reality. The inability to know whether one's experiences originate in night dreaming, daydreaming, or viridical reality is one of the most familiar disabilities of seriously ill mental patients. Drug use and New Age psychedelic athletics in search of a different reality, even the semantics of using "fantasy" as synonymous with creative imagination and "to dream" as inspiration, suggest an underlying confusion. They are like travesties of the valid adolescent karma, the religious necessity of transcendence. The fears associated with this confusion in adults are genuinely frightening. The anguished yearning for something lost is inescapable for those not in psychiatric care or on weekend psychic sprees but living daily in time-serving labor, overdense groups, and polluted surroundings. Blurry aspirations are formulated in concealed infantilisms, mediated in spectator entertainment, addiction to worldwide news, and religious revivalism.

Much of this has been said before, but not so often in terms of the relationship of the human to the nonhuman. Even as socially intense as we are, much of the unconscious life of the individual is rooted in interaction with otherness that goes beyond our own kind, interacting with it very early in personal growth, not as an alternative to human socialization but as an adjunct to it. The fetus is suspended in water, tuned to the mother's chemistry and the biological rhythms that are keyed to the day and seasonal cycles. The respirational interface between the newborn and the air imprints a connection between consciousness (or wisdom) and breath. Gravity sets the tone of all muscle and becomes a major counterplayer in all movement. Identity forms from the subjective separation of self from not-self, living from nonliving, human from nonhuman, and proceeds in speech to employ plant and animal taxonomy as a means of conceptual thought and as a model of relatedness. Games and stories involving animals serve as projections for the discovery of the plurality of the self. The environment of play, the juvenile home range, is the gestalt and creative focus of the face or matrix of nature. Ordeals in wilderness solitude and the ecological patterns underlying the protophilosophical narration of myth are instruments in the maturing of the whole person.

Only in the success of this extraordinary calendar does the adult come to love the world as the ground of his being. As a child, immersed in the series of maternal/ecological matrices, there are inevitable normal anxieties, distorted perceptions, gaps in experience filled with fantasy, emotional storms full of topical matter, frightening dreams and illusions, groundless fears, and the scars of accident, occasional nurturing error, adult negligence, and cruelty. The risk of epigenesis is that the nurturers and caretakers do not move forward in their role in keeping with the child's emerging stages. If such deprivations are severe enough, the normal fears and fantasies can become enduring elements of the personality. The individual continues to act on some crucial moment in the immense concerns of immaturity: separation, otherness, and limitation. Wrestling with them in juvenile and primary modes, even the adult cannot possibly see them holistically. Some of these omissions and impairments enhance the individual's conformity to certain cultures, and the culture acts to reward them, to produce them by interceding in the nurturing process, and so to put a hold on development. In this way, juvenile fantasies and primary thought are articulated not only in the monosyllables of the land scalper, but in philosophical argument and pontifical doctrine. Irrational feelings may be escalated into high-sounding reason when thrown up against a seemingly hostile and unfulfilling natural world. The West is a vast testimony to childhood botched to serve its own purposes, where history, masquerading as myth, authorizes men of action and men of thought to alter the world to match their regressive moods of omnipotence and insecurity.

The modern West selectively perpetuates these psychopathic elements. In the captivity and enslavement of plants and animals and the humanization of the landscape itself is the diminishment of the Other, against which men must define themselves, a diminishment of schizoid confusion in self-identity. From the epoch of Judeo-Christian emergence is an abiding hostility to the natural world, characteristically fearful and paranoid. The sixteenth-century fixation on the impurity of the body and the comparative tidiness of the machine are strongly obsessive-compulsive. These all persist and interact in a tapestry of chronic madness in the industrial present, countered by dreams of absolute control and infinite possession.

There are two ways of seeing this overall sequence. One is a serial amputation of the maturing process, in which the domesticated world and dichotomous desert deflected adolescent initiation and rigidified the personality into clinging to the collective loyalties, feats of bravery, and verbal idealism of pubertal youth. The era of puritans and machines fixated on childhood anxiety about the body and its productions. The urban/industrial age keyed on infantile identity diffusions, separation fears, and the fantasies of magic power. These truncations of epigenesis are progressive amputations, first at adolescence and finally at infancy. The other possible sequence begins in infancy with such wounds as damage to the fetus and neonate in hospital birth, through the anxieties of the distraught mother, asphyxiation, anesthetics, premedication, the overwhelming sensory shock of bright lights, noisy surroundings, and rough handling, impairment of delivery by the mother's physical condition and delivery posture, and separation of the infant from the mother—all corroding the psychogenic roots of a satisfactory life in a meaningful world.[15]

Civilized culture has, in the last ten thousand years, successively eroded the processes by which immaturity was healed. And yet, healing is not the right term for that retardation of development, the immaturing of adults by delayed development we call neoteny. It was the most important biological specialization leading to the evolution of our species. It would be fair to say that neoteny, more than any other single trait, makes us human. But it could only work if those social processes made possible by neoteny—the initiations, inculcations, learning, and maturing perspective and consciousness—functioned to make us grow up. *Biologically speaking, the function of culture is to mitigate neoteny.* Therefore I have characterized neoteny and culture as engaged in a kind of dance. To remain a child is not an appropriate individual destiny, nor is it a norm for our species. But cultures have a way of conspiring to subvert their own maturing activities if it serves an ideology or the psychological foundations of power. In addition, environments have different maturity demands: rich, diverse, stable environments are complex and tend to elicit distinctive cosmologies among different (small-group) societies; in barren environments human culture is also simplified and lends itself to regimes of subordination and uniformity.

What can one say of the prospect of the future in a world where increasing injury to the planet is a symptom of human psychopathology? Is not the situation far worse than one of rational choices in an economic system or the equilibration of competing vested interests?

In some ways the situation is far more hopeful. An ecologically harmonious sense of self and world is not the outcome of rational choices. It is the inherent possession of everyone; it is latent in the organism, in the interaction of the genome and early experience. The phases of such early experiences, or epigenesis, are the legacy of an evolutionary past in which human and nonhuman achieved a healthy rapport. Recent societies have contorted that sequence, have elicited and perpetuated immature and inappropriate responses. The societies are themselves the product of such amputations, and so are their uses and abuses of the earth.

Perhaps we do not need new religious, economic, technological, ideological, esthetic, or philosophical revolutions. We may not need to start at the top and uproot political systems, turn lifeways on their heads, emulate hunters and gatherers or naturalists, or try to live lives of austere privation or tribal organization. The civilized ways inconsistent with human maturity will themselves wither in a world where children move normally through their ontogeny.

I have attempted to identify crucial factors in such a normal growth by showing what might have been lost from different periods in the past. Some of these, such as life in a small human group in a spacious world, will be difficult to recover—though not impossible for the critical period in the individual passage. Adults, weaned to the wrong music, cut short from their own potential, are not the best of mentors. The problem may be more difficult to understand than to solve. Beneath the veneer of civilization, to paraphrase the trite phrase of humanism, lies not the barbarian and animal, but the human in us who knows the rightness of birth in gentle surroundings, the necessity of a rich nonhuman environment, play at being animals, the discipline of natural history, juvenile tasks with simple tools, the expressive arts of receiving food as a spiritual gift rather than as a product, the cultivation of metaphorical significance of natural phenomena of all kinds, clan membership and small-group life, and the profound claims and liberation of ritual initiation and subsequent stages of adult mentorship. There is a secret person undamaged in every individual, aware of the validity of these, sensitive to their right moments in our lives. All of them are assimilated in perverted forms in modern society: our profound love of animals twisted into pets, zoos, decorations, and entertainment; our search for poetic wholeness subverted by the model of the machine instead of the body; the moment of pubertal idealism shunted into nationalism or ethereal otherworldly religion instead of an ecosophical cosmology.

But this means that we have not lost, and cannot lose, the genuine impulse. It awaits only an authentic expression. The task is not to start by recapturing the theme of a reconciliation with the earth in all of its metaphysical subtlety, but with something much more direct and simple that will yield its own healing metaphysics.

SEVEN

The Domesticators

OF HALF THE TIME since the beginning of the momentous revolution by which agriculture and village life began to reshape the condition of human existence we know almost nothing of the *felt experience*. Of how the world was seen we have only surmises based on bits of material culture, dug up like fossil imprints of ideas. Archaeology tells us that the first crops preceded the making of cities by about five thousand years. The fifty centuries from here back to that point of earliest urbanity, to the wheel and the advent of writing, embracing the whole tumult of civilized man, were prepared for and made possible by the quiet fifty centuries before that.

Few prehistorians suppose that those earliest farmers and first domesticators east of the Mediterranean were conscious revolutionaries or even that changes were dramatic in a single lifetime.[1] In many ways, life was modified gradually from that of their hunter-gatherer ancestors, whose modest relics in turn stretch back three million years to the beginning of the Pleistocene. Yet, by the time civilization began in the great city-states of Egypt and Mesopotamia, the tradesmen, bureaucrats, and tillers of the soil exceeded their hunter forebears in possessions and altered their surroundings—and were the creators and victims of new attitudes, expectations, and mythology. How that transition toward urbanism took place we may guess only with educated uncertainty.

A different style of consciousness among the ancestors of Western tradition in the savannas, grasslands, and forest margins of what are now Egypt, Turkey, Iraq, Jordan, Iran, Syria, Lebanon, Israel, and Russia between the Black and Caspian seas characterizes the psychohistory of the emergence of sedentary village life from nomadic foraging. It was not simply a matter of being outdoors or indoors. The archaic hunters were indoors when they occupied rock shelters or built houses, while some of the earliest food collectors and goat keepers, on the other hand, lived in caves and, like the hunters, spent seasons in the open. Foraging and gathering graded into collecting, planting, cultivating, and trading. The farmer and herder never ceased to do some hunting. The steps from gathering wild fruits to gathering-planting the seeds of the ancestral barley and wheat, from hunting to driving-hunting the wild ancestors of the goat and sheep, from the scavenging wolf-dog ancestor to the dog/man collaboration cover a long period of transition and overlap. Even after village life was established on a year-round basis and the seven- or eight-score inhabitants were dependent on plant crops and domesticated animals, artifacts of stone continued to be made. Pottery, weaving—the paraphernalia we normally associate with agriculture and village life—came bit by bit, here and there, in some places disappeared and came again.

Changes in thought, in perceptions of the outer and inner world, and in premises and assumptions about reality probably occurred in a similarly capricious, spasmodic way, themes formulated and voiced and ritually assimilated only to be lost and then rearticulated. It was a long period of tenuous concepts, intimations, oblique views of older wisdom, shifts in perspective toward concepts of the world that, by the time of the Egyptian dynasties or Mesopotamian civilizations would be extremely different from those of the Paleolithic past. These shifts have to do with the *quality of attention* rather than ideas; with the *significance of place* rather than the identity of nations; with the theme of *duality;* with the subtle effects of food and *trophic patterns* on thought and expression; with the accumulation of made things and *possessions* that was part of village life; and finally, with some of the subtler influences of *domestication* on the ways people saw themselves and the land, as well as their plants and animals.

■

Quality of attention means cultural and habitual differences in the style of day-to-day hearing, seeing, smelling, tasting, and touching the surroundings. These differences are perhaps not as striking in times of crisis or formal expression as in the more casual way in which we pay heed. What people notice, what they expect to encounter, the mix of senses used, even the quality of their inattention and disregard all reveal something about the kind of world it is for them.

These early farming villagers were probably much like their hunter forebears in their vigilant sensitivity to sound. Walter J. Ong speaks of this sensitivity as an orientation to interiority.[2] All sound is a voice—dynamic, revealing, and communicating. Even today such an attitude of listening is apparent among peasants or shepherds for whom the farmstead or flock is a dynamic mosaic in their care, sometimes not all visible from minute to minute. The cacophony with which the still-larger town would eventually bullyrag and deaden the ear was yet to be, although perhaps its first signs could be noticed in the differences between that vast and articulate silence surrounding men in wild landscapes and the soft babble of the rural village that blocked off the voices of the distant savanna and forest— in the daytime at least. In the village few sounds were surprising, and most were fixed in place, like the familiar scratch of a broom on a known doorstep at a regular time.

Attention to visual cues even more clearly differentiates the hunter from the villager. "The hunter," says Ortega y Gasset, "does not look tranquilly in one determined direction, sure beforehand that the game will pass in front of him. The hunter knows that he does not know what is going to happen . . . thus he needs to prepare an attention which does not consist in riveting itself on the presumed but consists precisely in not presuming anything and in avoiding inattentiveness. It is a 'universal' attention, which does not inscribe itself on any point and tries to be on all points."[3] For the most part the animals—or roots, berries, and nuts—the hunter-gatherer seeks are unseen and hidden. In this sense his gathering, though directed to plants fixed in place, is unlike the farmer's harvest. Although wild plants and animals have their seasonal and habitat tendencies, any one kind of dozens might be encountered, and the signs that indicate their whereabouts are myriad. As the food collector became the planter, much of that awareness of a moving or hidden object was exchanged for a different kind of mystery—that of generation itself—which invited the focused imagination at the expense of keenness of looking and listening.

The plants used by these earliest farmers were increasingly annual grasses; most of the garden vegetables that would eventually join them were annuals too. As planters they were thereby attuned to the weather and calendar, an awareness that would become meterology and astronomy. Their hunting ancestors were sensitive to these things but were not faced with the same potential calamities of weather, for their more varied diet and the longer cycle of animal growth and perennial plant foods blunted bad years. The change to the cultivation of annuals was critical in the reshaping of attention, for the seasonal pattern of the birth, growth, death, and rebirth of the crops would burn itself into the minds of these grain farmers so profoundly that it might be said to be the first feature—the kernel even—of civilized thought. If these farmers ceased to listen to a million secret tongues in the wilderness it was, in retrospect, to develop techniques of domestication with which to alter the earth and to gain a symbolic foundation for a vision of a cyclic cosmology and eventually a concept of immortality.

I do not want to overstate the narrowing effect of season and climate on the farmer. The hunter's attitude of avoiding inattentiveness persisted in the farmer's style inasmuch as hunting and gathering persisted, especially in the earlier centuries of agriculture. And, of course, the march of the seasons, which to our eyes seems coarse, is to practiced observers subject to the most delicate nuances, such as the schedule of flowering of wild plants, the breeding cycle of birds, and the emergence and behavior of insects. This phenology of emergence and metamorphosis has a daily and hourly character throughout the year, to which I suspect the early domesticators were, like good naturalists, as sensitive as their foraging cousins.[4] Perhaps the first subtle warpings of this consciousness were matters of emphasis, shaped as much by the diminished variety of wild things at hand in the village vicinity as by the needs of their domestic plantings.

■

A village alters the relative abundance of wild and tame creatures that are in concentric zones around it. Each such human community of domestication had its own history, its own relationship to terrain, water supplies, fuel, building materials, and so on that modified the general pattern of clustered dwellings and gradated intensities of use away from the center. The village and its landscape became a place physically as well as psychologically unlike the camps and transient shelters that men had made in earlier times.

The *significance of place* to such peoples as Australian aborigines can be very different from its significance to sedentary peoples—certainly far more profound than simple location. Individual and tribal identity are built up in connection with widely separate places and the paths connecting them. Different places are successively assimilated or internalized. They become distinct, though unconscious, elements of the self, enhanced by mythology and ceremony, generating a network of deep emotional attachments that cements the personality. Throughout life, those places have a role in the evocation of self and group consciousness. They are mnemonic: integrated components of a sacred history and the remembered and unconsciously felt past. The whole of the known region or home range becomes a hierophantic map, a repository of the first creation that parallels and overlies individual history. Something like this is known to be typical of many nonliterate peoples and was probably true of prehistoric peoples as well.[5] Juvenile imprinting on terrain (that is, indelible fixation on specific sites, giving them lifetime supersignificance) continues among modern urban people as well, so it is not unlikely that some form of dynamic integration of the identity formation of the individual with features of the terrain is part of human biology, a genetic heritage; but the mode by which sedentary peoples would employ the landscape psychodynamically, as a tool of self-recognition, is quite different from that of the hunter.

The hunter was mobile, like his prey, the big-game animals. The topographic features and creatures were diffused throughout a vast region. They were not all visible at once and human products were always mixed with the nonhuman. The villager did not rove through these physical extensions of the self; he occupied them. The hunter seemed to inhabit the land body like a blood corpuscle, while the farmer was centered in it and could scan it as a whole.

As villages grew and their populations increased, they became more territorial—embedded, so to speak, in a defended location. Hunter-foragers before them (as today among the relict tribes of Australia) had often a jealous sense of occupancy and strict mores respecting trespass, but the matter was settled in formalities and protocol. It became far more feasible for five hundred men to exclude outsiders from fifteen square miles than it had been for ten to bar interlopers from fifteen hundred square miles. Perhaps what is known today as "body-boundary phenomena"—the totality of feelings that constitute the private sense of one's own shape and surface—became more rigid and shell-like where the metaphors of self, tribe, and place became more tightly structured, the various levels of boundary reinforcing each other.[6]

Among villagers, the limits of territorial lands were marked by stones identified with protective spirits.[7] These boundaries often ran along watershed divides and were therefore in the highest places. The fertile lowland, circumscribed at the horizon and protected there by sacred pillars, may be seen as analogous to a gigantic body. Its contours, springs, caves, vegetation, and landforms are the surface of a giant, like a sheltering and nourishing mother. The concept of the Great Mother Earth is, in this way, a natural metaphor for sedentary peoples. So it became, for agricultural peoples, the dominant mythological figure.

The maternal image had not been celebrated so single-mindedly among their hunter predecessors. Although carvings that may represent pregnant women are known from the Pleistocene hunting cultures of Europe, there is no evidence as to how they were used or whether they indeed referred to motherhood rather than matehood; and there is little else from the Stone Age to suggest the concept of the Great Mother.[8]

But this concept was highly developed, in one form or another, in all the great agricultural civilizations of the preclassical Western world, a psychological reference point as well as a religious symbol. It shows a shift in the iconography of farmers, a focusing on the nourishing and protective aspects of the world, evoking the experience of being mothered. The gods were becoming more humanlike, the plants and animals subordinated to a kind of family drama. The world of the imagination, as well as the tangible surroundings, was in this way saturated with human bodies and faces, emphasizing personality and gender. The animals did not simply give way to humans in these symbolic roles but were subordinated in cosmology to manlike gods in a new and more presumptuous way.[9]

To the hunter, much of what he had seemed given; to the farmer,

earned by continuing labor. For the farmer the contrast between the
ease of childhood and the burdens of maturity had increased. For him
there was a lost, more perfect world, the images of which were enhanced by his awareness of this contrast.[10] Mircea Eliade tells us that
the myth of that loss is as wide as humanity, but the question must
remain—for it has not been addressed directly by him—as to the
difference in its meaning to farmers and their nonfarming ancestors.[11]
Surely the biblical Garden of Eden story must have seemed perverse
to those hunting peoples on whom missionaries inflicted it (but
whose courtesy and good humor compelled them to stifle their laugh-
ter). That myth has the fully developed features of a consummate
agricultural dream: no work, bad weather, or wild beasts; no depen-
dents, competitors, risk, curiosity, old age, or alienation from God,
no death, or women's troubles—not that some of these ideals would
not have occurred to hunters. What its collective form was among
the earliest planters we cannot know, but we can suspect this much:
the crops must now and again have failed, plunging the individual
into torments of anxiety reminiscent of those earlier "failings" of
their own mothers. Over the centuries, soils and productivity declined, were eroded away, or salted in, requiring more work for
a meager subsistence. Alternative foods in the wild lands were ex-
tirpated. Drought and parasites found the worn community more
vulnerable. The inevitable decline from original productivity and
stability was known by tradition and carried with it a sense of
grievous loss and punishment. In the decline of its former radiance,
the earth seemed to be sullied, and the fault or guilt to lie with
man himself.[12]

While the farmer would eventually come to see himself at odds
with the wandering hunters and pastoralists and would resent their
freedom as shiftlessness and the relative ease of their lives as sloth,
these earliest farmers were still part-time hunters. "Eden was no garden," writes Nigel Calder, "but it was a gathering paradise.[13]

In any case, the Earth Mother herself would come in for some suspicion in the same spirit in which Eve would be blamed. The bad Mother Earth—as well as the good—was implicit in the attribution of gender to the soil, for there is a time in infancy when the mother is indeed two persons, one of whom is fearfully and infuriatingly withholding.[14] I suppose that men who till the earth everywhere have in some fashion experienced and codified the environment as parental, although their particular social and kinship systems both evoke and represent the parental cosmos in unique local ways. How out of blood and marriage ties the different kinship patterns arose, the anthropologists have not yet fully explained, though it is a fair guess that there are consistent differences between hunters and farmers and between grain farmers and root farmers.[15] If so, attitudes toward the feminine earth may be influenced by the role of women in a particular society and the land used accordingly—land use and mother use mutually interacting. Also, the mother is very different to the small infant than to the child and different again to the pubertal youth, so that a whole series of different "mothers" is accumulated during the growth of each individual. A culture may foster certain of these in its symbolic life and neglect others. External nature may become part of the language as well as the object of such portraits.

Crippling as the image may be of the land as a fecund goddess— even as the basis of a supposed matriarchate in Crete and Anatolia— we should perhaps reserve judgment as to its ecological efficacy. The metaphor of the great goddess enables emotions and bonds of kinship, compassion, and responsibility to be felt not only within the human group but to be directed to the earth, helping the group to survive in health the experience of the ecological double bind: the fertile earth that sometimes fails to produce.

The negative effects are obscured by the forces of repression. What are the results of a lifelong subordination to mother? Among them are resentment and masked retaliations, displaced acts of violence, and the consequent guilt—all of which can be exploited to intensify the maternal dependence. Here I wish only to raise the question whether lifelong subordination to a vast Earth Mother might not affect humans in similar ways.

■

In many ways the sensory impact of village life fostered an impression of opposition, or *duality:* things were in or of the community and village or they were not, they favored the crops or hindered them, were wild or tame, weeds or crops, useful or worthless. The same thunderstorm that could have multiple and diverse effects on the hunter's life because of the variety of his interests and foods was plainly destructive or quenching to the village whose garden and drinking water would suffer drought or flood of increasing severity as the natural vegetation and soil diminished.

In the simplified ecosystem of agriculture it would be possible to adopt, as it were, the posture of jural duality that enables the juvenile, newly caught up in the spirit of his burgeoning sense of ethics, to make judgments with overweening certainty.[16]

The simplified world of the ancient dry-land farmer was, in spite of its clarity, not necessarily a more coherent one than that of his ancestors. Its ambivalence was not in its multiplicity, but in the inherent conflicts of things in opposition. Instead of a peacefully integrating dusk, the night swept away the light of day like a cavalry charge. Dryness and wetness struggled for the land. The hunters, says Eliade, tended to face up to these ambiguities and to reconcile them in their mythology, while the farmers, among whom they were perhaps more tragically crucial, repressed them.[17]

The resolution of such seeming contradictions is a mark of mature thought and personality. For the small child, a kind of bimodality of cognition is normal, a part of the beginnings of classifying and making categories, an essential step in the adult capacity to make abstractions. The world at first is an either/or place. The human mind makes a hazardous trip, beginning in an undivided unity—the I-am-everything paradise of the fetus—proceeding through a world of contraries, and arriving at maturity able to work in multiplicity and plurality. Getting stuck in the binary view strands the adult in a universe torn by a myriad of oppositions and conflicts.

But this kind of splitting remained to be fully realized in the patriarchal societies. For the planters the reconciliation was symbolized by the figure of the earth as a woman and her marriage to a son who must die, the virgin mother-wife and murdered son-king. Such a mother is the unconscious ideal of preadolescent boys, whose spontaneous affection for their mothers is never completely lost, nor in some important ways surpassed by love of wife. The "death" of their childhood does not catapult them into a totally masculinist world as it does among patriarchal peoples, but only foreshadows a new birth in a "uterine" relationship with a larger mother.

The psychology of this celestial round—life cycle and crop cycle—is one of regression rather than growth. This mother worship on a cosmic scale is achieved by exaggeration of that preadolescent state, formalized in the endless round by the ritual supplication and courtship of the Great Mother Earth. It centers on a fantasy that perpetuates a defense against oedipal tension and blocks its resolution and the mature possibilities that follow.

Hunters were certainly aware of the cycle of annual renewal, but the early farmers had reason to be more intent on the metaphors of seed germination and the estrus of cattle. Much of the ancient art now in museums reveals an obsession with the great round of the year, perhaps because of the increasing uncertainty of yield and because the farmer had fewer alternatives than his foraging ancestors. With agriculture it was likely to be boom or bust, and in the bad years nature seemed to withhold that to which the farmer, after all his labor, felt he had a right.

There can arise, says Harold Searles, "a transference to all of outer reality as personifying, in unconscious experience, a dominating, withholding mother."[18] In effect, the child of a mother who *seems* to be malevolently deficient—or, for that matter, absent—can begin to see the whole world through the same lenses of projection and re-crimination.

■

The figure of the great mother goddess is central to the food or *trophic pattern* that governs domestic life. After nearly ten thousand years of living with that apprehension about food and the binding force of its psychic disablement, it is not surprising that civilized people find it difficult to understand the absence of such worries among hunting-gathering peoples, making them seem careless and imprudent.[19] The repressed distrust of the mother and the maternal earth can then be redirected onto those blithe savages, picturing them as unfeeling for the well-being of their families and coarsely inured to hunger and the other imagined afflictions of a brutish life. This scornful fantasy is easily enough projected upon the rest of brute creation, making it easier to believe that all animals are insentient.

It is not only an abstract Mother Earth who is the victim of this psychic deformity, but all wild things. Characteristically, farmers and townsmen do not study and speculate on wild animals or "think" them in their poetic mystery and complex behaviors. With civilization, typically fewer than twenty kinds of plants and animals in one village were tended, herded, sheltered, planted, cultivated, fertilized, harvested, cured, stored, and distributed. Sacrifice and other ceremonial activities were restricted accordingly. Even the gradual broadening of agriculture to embrace many more kinds of organisms left it far short of the rich cosmos of the hunter. Civilization increased the separation between the individual and the natural world as it did that of the child from the mother, amplifying an attachment that could be channeled into aggression.

The farmer and his village brethren assumed an executive task of food production, storage, and distribution that would weigh heavily on them for the same reason that all executives wear out their nerves and glands: responsibility in a situation of certain failure—if not this year, then next, or the year after that. Being held responsible for things beyond their control is especially crushing for children, for whom the world may become hopelessly chaotic.[20] They, in their chores of goat tending or other work tasks, like the adults who managed the domesticated community, were vulnerable to weather, marauders, pests, and the demons of earth and air. Blights and witherings were inevitable, bringing not only food shortage but emotional onslaughts. The judgment is guilt, for which the penalty is scarcity.

In such a world the full belly is never enough. Like the dour Yankee farmer who sees in the clear blue sky of a Vermont spring day "a damned weather-breeder," abundance would only set the mark by which shortage would be measured.

But quantity was not the only variable. As the diversity of foods diminished—the wild alternatives becoming scarcer and more distant from villages—the danger of malnutrition increased. It is widely observed that domesticated varieties of fruits and vegetables differ from their wild ancestors in carbohydrate/protein/fat ratios as well as vitamin and mineral content. Where selection is for appearance, size, storability, or even taste, some food value may be lost. Virtually all the processes that aid storage or preservation have a similar price in decline of quality. The point is that the lack of food is not the only spur to a kind of trophic obsession, but the hungers of those who are superficially well fed might also add to this general picture of chronic preoccupation with food.

The argument can be made that anything that fixates the individual's attention on food can be associated with ontogenetic regression. I mean not only the infantile impatience to eat and the whole alimentary oral-anal romance to which he is so responsive, but the typical conservatism of older children and adolescents—the first, perhaps because of a sensitivity to strong or strange new flavors; the second, because of a psychic state in which the groping for a new selfhood is partly one of recognition of codes that identify a group. Teenagers are the weakest gourmets because they have not yet achieved a confident-enough identity to free themselves to develop personal preferences. The young are wary about what they eat, probably for adaptive as well as culturally functional reasons.

The young of hunter societies are probably cautious too, and certainly such cultures had a highly developed sense of food taboos. Nonetheless, the small foraging band ate dozens of kinds of flesh (including invertebrates) and scores of kinds of roots, nuts, vegetables, and leaves. The idea that this range was born of desperation is not supported by the evidence. There were certainly seasonal opportunities and choices, but apparently to be human is to be omnivorous, to show an open, experimental attitude toward what is edible, guided by an educated taste and a wide range of options. As among all peoples, what is eaten or not eaten had cultural limits among hunter-foragers, but these did not prevent somebody in a group from eating at least some parts of almost anything.[21]

The food-producing societies that succeeded the hunter-gatherers attempted to make virtue of defect by intensifying the cultural proscriptions on what was to be eaten in a world where, for most people, there were fewer choices than their archaic ancestors enjoyed. And how was this tightening of the belt and expanded contempt achieved? It was built into the older child and adolescent. It could be frozen at that level as part of a more general developmental check. It may have been inevitable in the shift from totemic to caste thought about animals, corresponding to the change from hunting to farming, in which wild animals ceased to be used as metaphors central to personal identity, to be less involved with analogies of assimilation and incorporation. The growth of self-identity requires coming to terms with the wild and uncontrollable within. Normally the child identifies frightening feelings and ideas with specific external objects. The sensed limitations of such objects aid his attempts to control his fears. As the natural containers for these projected feelings receded with the wilderness, a lack of substitutes may have left the child less able to cope and thus more dependent, his development impaired.

■

Perhaps there was no more dramatic change in the transition from hunting-gathering to farming than in the kind and number of *possessions*. Among archaic people who use no beasts of burden, true possessions are few and small. What objects are owned are divided between those privately held and those in which there is a joint interest. Among the latter, such as religious objects or the carcass of a game animal, the individual shares obligations as well as benefits, but in neither case does he accumulate or seem to feel impoverished. The wariness of gifts and the lack of accumulation found in these people are not due to nomadism, for the desire would still be evident.[22] Nor can these characteristics be explained away as a culturally conditioned materialism, as that would beg the question.

This absence of wanting belongings seems more likely to be part of a psychological dimension of human life and its modification in civilization. "Belongings" is an interesting word, referring to membership and therefore to parts of a whole. If that whole is Me, then perhaps the acquisition of mostly man-made objects can contribute in some way to my identity—a way that may compensate for some earlier means lost when people became sedentary and their world mostly man-made landscapes. Or, if objects fail to fully suffice, we want more and more, as we crave more of a pain-killing drug. In short, what is it about the domesticated civilized world that alters the concept of self so that it is enhanced by property?

My self is to some extent made by me, at least insofar as I seem to gain control over it. A wilderness environment is, on the contrary, mostly given. For the hunter-forager, this Me in a non-Me world is the most penetrating and powerful realization in life. The mature person in such a culture is not concerned with blunting that dreadful reality but with establishing lines of connectedness or relationship. Formal culture is shaped by the elaboration of covenants and nego-tiations with the Other. The separation makes impossible a fuzzy confusion; there is no vague "identity with nature," but rather a life-long task of formulating—and internalizing—treaties of affiliation. The forms and terms of that relationship become part of a secondary level of my identity, the background or gestalt. This refining of what-I-am-not is a developmental matter, and the human life cycle conforms to stages in its progress.

Now consider the process in a world in which that Other has mostly disappeared. Food, tools, animals, structures, whole land-scapes are man-made; even to me personally they seem more made than given and serve as extensions of that part of the self which I determine. My infantile ego glories in this great consuming I-am. Everything in sight belongs to me in the same sense as my members: legs, arms, hands, and so on. The buildings, streets, and cultivated fields are all continuous with my voluntary nervous system, my tamed, controlled self.

In the ideology of farming, wild things are enemies of the tame; the wild Other is not the context but the opponent of "my" domain. Impulses, fears, and dreams—the realm of the unconscious—no longer are represented by the community of wild things with which I can work out a meaningful relationship. The unconscious is driven deeper and away with the wilderness. New definitions of the self by trade and political subordination in part replace the metaphoric reciprocity between natural and cultural in the totemic life of the hunter-foragers. But the new system defines by exclusion. What had been a complementary entity embracing friendly and dangerous parts in a unified cosmos now takes on the colors of hostility and fragmentation. Even where the great earth religions of high agriculture tend to mend this rupture in the mythology of the symbolic mother, its stunting of the identity process remains.

Although he formulated the cognitive distinctions between totemic culture, with its analogy of a system of differences in nonhuman nature as a paradigm for the organization of culture, and caste or agriculture, which find models for human relationships in the types of things made, Lévi-Strauss avoided the psychological developmental implications with admirable caution. But it is clear from the developmental scheme of Erikson that fine mastery of the neuromuscular system, self-discipline of the body, the emergence of skills, and awakening to tools are late-juvenile and early adolescent concerns. In farming, the land itself becomes a tool, an instrument of production, a possession that is at once the object and implement of vocation as well as a definer of the self.

As farming shifts from subsistence to monoculture, village specialists who do not themselves cultivate the soil appear. Their roles are psychologically and mythically reintegrated into society as a whole. Smith, potter, clerk, and priest become constituents of the new reality. That reality is for them all like the pot to the potter: (1) The wild world has reduced significance in his own conscious identity and may therefore be perceived (along with some part of himself) as chaotic; (2) he himself, like his pot, is a static *made* object, and by inference so is the rest of society and the world; (3) there is a central core of nonlivingness in himself; (4) the ultimate refinements in his unique self are to be achieved by acts of will or creativity; (5) daily labor—routine, repetitive motions for long hours at a time—is at the heart of his being; (6) his relationship to others is based on an exchange of possessions, and the accumulation of them is a measure of his personal achievement; and (7) the nonhuman world is primarily a source of substance to be shaped or made by man, as it was mythically by God.

These are but fragments of the world of the artisan. Gradations exist between that world and totemic cultures. The transition took many centuries before man's concept of the wilderness was indeed defined by the first synonym in Roget's *Thesaurus:* "disorder." In the earliest farming societies perhaps there were only nuances of the psychology of domestication. The individual would not see himself as a possession or conceive of being possessed by others until tribal villages coalesced into chiefdoms and he was conscripted or enslaved or his labor sold as a commodity, events that may have been as much an outcome as a cause of the new consciousness. That was many generations in the future as the first harvesters of wild wheat began to save some grains to plant. Yet we see them headed, however tentatively, toward the view of the planet as a thing rather than a thou, a product instead of an organism, to be possessed rather than encountered as a presence.

This attitude connects with the psychological position of early infancy, when differentiation between the living and the nonliving is still unclear. The badly nurtured infant may become imprinted with the hardness of its cradle or bottle so irreversibly that it cannot, even as an adult, form fully caring human relationships. But that is the extreme case. The earliest farmers were inclined to represent the landscape as a living being, even, at first, to conceive life in made things. But as those things became commodities and infancy was reshaped accordingly, the cosmos would become increasingly ambiguous. Attempts to resolve this conflict between the "itness" and the numen of things—both in the landscape and its reciprocal, the inner self—are a major goal of the religious and cultural activity of civilization.[23]

■

The *domestication* of animals had effects on human perception that went far beyond its economic implications. Men had been observing animals closely as a major intellectual activity for several million years. They have not been deterred, even by so momentous a change in the condition of man/animal relationship as domestication, but the message has been altered. Changes in the animals themselves, brought about by captivity and breeding programs, are widely recognized. These changes include plumper and more rounded features, greater docility and submissiveness, reduced mobility, simplification of complex behaviors (such as courtship), the broadening or generalizing of signals to which social responses are given (such as following behavior), reduced hardiness, and less specialized environmental and nutritional requirements. The sum effect of these is infantilization.[24] The new message is an emotional appeal, sense of mastery, and relative simplicity of animal life. The style conveyed as a metaphor by the wild animal is altered to literal model and metonymic subordinate: life is inevitable physical deformity and limitation, mindless frolic and alarms, bluntness, following and being herded, being fertile when called upon, representing nature at a new, cruder level.

One or another of the domesticated forms was widely used as a substitute in human relations: as slave, sexual partner, companion, caretaker, family member. Animal and human discriminations that sustained barriers between species were breached, suggesting nothing so much in human experience as the very small child's inability to see the difference between dogs and cows. Pet keeping, virtually a civilized institution, is an abyss of covert and unconscious uses of animals in the service of psychological needs, glossed over as play and companionship.[25] The more extremely perverted private abuse of animals grades off into the sadistic slaughter of animals in public spectacles, of which the modern bullfight is an extravagant example.

Before civilization, animals were seen as belonging to their own nation and to be the bearers of messages and gifts of meat from a sacred domain. In the village they became possessions. Yet as ancient avatars, they remained fascinating in human eyes. A select and altered little group of animals, filtered through the bottleneck of domestication, came in human experience to represent the whole of animals of value to people. The ancient human approach to consciousness by seeing—or discovering—the self through other eyes and the need to encounter the otherness of the cosmos in its kindred aspect were two of the burdens thrust upon these deformed creatures. To educate his powers of discrimination and wonder, the child, born to expect subtle and infinite possibilities, was presented with fat hulks, vicious manics, and hypertrophied drudges. The psychological introjection of these as part of the self put the child on a detour in the developmental process that would culminate in a dead end, posted "You can't get there from here."

■

These six aspects of civilized thought originating in agriculture—quality of attention, significance of place, duality, trophic anxiety, attitude toward possessions, and domestication—are not so much characteristics as trends. After all, some wild things survived even in dooryards, and human foraging continues. But the combined effect of all the changes in plant-animal abundance, including replacement of a multitude of wild forms in the village surround by a small number of domestic forms, was the creation of a new kind of landscape, itself made more immature. Ecologically, husbandry destroys the mature ecosystem or climax community. In its place there appear assemblages of plants and animals typical of earlier stages. Ecologist Eugene Odum speaks of the whole series as a developmental sequence, analogous to that of human growth. Generally, the earlier phases are simpler, less efficient, and less stable than the later, but if left to themselves, go through a predictable species replacement until, after many years, that replacement tends to diminish and the community has regained its climax, its primeval or virgin condition.[26]

The husbandman, however, does not want his meadows to get brushy or his gardens to get weedy. By keeping stock in the meadow, he stabilizes its altered, youthful state; its continued stabilization results in a plateau of unaltered immaturity, a disclimax. The disclimaxes that appeared with the first farming in the foothills of the Near East, like all subsequent disclimaxes, seem thematically harmonious with the ambience of immaturity of human thought and the human community proper. In an essay in 1942, Ortega y Gasset speaks of the mature climax ecosystem as "authentic countryside." He writes, "Only the hunting ground is true countryside . . . neither farmland, nor battleground, nor tourist country." Only there, in the "first countryside, the only 'natural' one, can we succeed in emigrating from our human world to an authentic 'outside,' from which history represents the retreat or anabasis."[27] Mindful of the achievements of history, it is nonetheless this chance to get outside oneself that concerns us here, for it is needed repeatedly, in different stages of individual development, and in different forms. Ortega y Gasset's countryside and Odum's climax community are common ground. They are for the older child and adolescent a penultimate encounter at the end of a sequence of experiences of otherness that began with the awareness of mother as a separate being.

■

In the foregoing pages I have suggested a number of ways in which crop tending and village life made problems for the farmer that were psychologically similar to and in tandem with typical difficulties of the early growth of the individual. Each of them in some way seemed to increase the physical and perceptual distance between the person and those forms of the nonhuman world most remote from him. By aggravating the tensions of separation from the mother and at the same time spatially isolating the individual from the nonhumanized world, agriculture made it difficult for the developing person to approach the issues around which the crucial passages into fully mature adult life had been structured in the course of human existence.

New beginnings are always in some sense regressive. The farmer, caught in the net of the seasons, is a victim of his own earth metaphors. His ceremonial life, expressively formulated in homologies of the self and the cosmos, invades the whole of his annual round with avatars of germination, fruition, and early death. His horizons become more limited in space as well as time, suggestive of the prepubertal fears of wandering too far. His restricted geography is like a hobble on his distancing from the womb, contrasted with those tests and trials by which his forefathers measured the maturity of the individual by sending him alone into wild countryside and solitude.

Everything worked to bind the new farmer aggressively to locality, to encourage the vision of the land as part of himself and to dream of a better world, of a lost unity—with its silent evocation of his unconscious memory of the natal state. Even when the mother figure was extended to the land, it reflected a symbiosis more akin to the infant's love/hate for her than to the interrelated but independent species in an ecosystem. Matriarchy as a political system may never have existed, but the exercise of male power was, in the end, to master those processes that would produce and reproduce for him, even while the final maternal secrets were out of his reach. Male sway would gain him possessions, too, which the ancient hunters had known would ensure neither a true self nor, in the last analysis, respect; to give away what they had was the lesson they had learned. It was not that the villager *would not* learn that lesson, but that he *could not*. His identity was spread around among things, insufficiently internalized and consolidated. Foremost among them were the products of his labor. The classes of made objects seem, almost as though by some mysterious dynamic, to have superseded totemic membership as the touchstone of those episodes of initiation by which the adult learns who he is. With the made thing at the center of his being, the villager felt that he himself was made, and he would, thereafter, see the world that way too.

He came to live more and more with his own fabrications as the environment. Being of his own making, the things around him were indistinct from himself, and he was less differentiated than he wanted to be. At such a level of psychological individuation, what remained outside his jurisdiction—the otherness of wildness (internal and external), death, and the mysteries of growth and decay—would be repressed by his anxious fears, and this, too, would push him back toward those ready-made defenses that protect the infant from his own helplessness: unconscious fantasies and projections. These would disguise the wild beasts with his own ferocity and mask the tame with his yearning and vulnerability.

As the infant normally grows away from being ruled by his stomach, the new farmers and their artisan neighbors were increasingly ruled by the collective stomach. To become so absorbed with the auguries and techniques of food production gives a final ironic twist to their departure from the totemic culture that faded as farming increased. The totemic thinker mused on the classification of plants and the behaviors of animals, on food relations and food chains, and translated his impressions through the idiom of mythopoetic thought to marriage and kin relationships. Thus it was that the endless patterns of nature as food were scrutinized with infinite care as signs and markers, as the language of human relatedness. The farmer's literal preoccupation with food is like a parody of the taxonomic collections of the child, who wants endlessly to know the names of things, who is, so to speak, storing away elements of concrete reality from which to create a world. For the child and the farmer, those things seem to be an end in themselves, whereas in true maturity they are only the beginnings of thought. The farmer spends more time engrossed with the future, imagining tomorrow and its possible prodigality or paucity. It is as though the human capacity for absorbing mythic stories as personal psychodrama had played the mean trick of stranding the dreamer in endless accountability for tomorrows, some of which would inevitably be disastrous.[28]

An individual unsure of the distinctions between himself and his nonhuman surroundings accepts such an awesome duty, thrust upon him by his own blending of his identity with the landscape, positing it in priesthoods and churches. For him, to be in control of the fertility of the soil is desperately bound to his person in an autistic envelope. Such was the farmer's and villager's monolithic view of a dependent symbiosis with a Mother Earth. Such a dyadic concept might alleviate the heaped-up, duty-bound, guilt-laden burden, saturating the relationship with ecstatic adoration and contentment. But in her cruel moments of dearth that mother would be worse than any dangerous beast, and the memory of that painful episode would leave its schizoid print on everyone in society, scars that the bountiful harvest could not erase.

The care of crops, stock, and children fixed the daily routine and increased the amount of work. Like casual gathering or preambles to the chase, the work was probably light in the earliest centuries of planting, but in time it would take everything. The world of drudgery would eventually seem normal, the savage would be scorned for his indolence and lack of expectant suspense, and the only escape from tillage or bureaucratic time-serving would be death. These anxieties would elicit a certain satisfaction in repetitive and exhausting routines reminiscent of the swayings of the autistic child or the rhythmic to-and-fro of the captive bear or elephant in the zoo. Early farming represents a "state of surrender," says anthropologist Daphne Prior, and the farmer was a defeated captive.[29]

Like a prisoner of war, he would survive if he could psychologically adapt. As for relishing monotony, where is one to find the developmental precursors to the workaday world? We have already touched on the food conservatism of the adolescent, which, in fact, is only one detail of a much broader mind-set. The strictures apply as well to clothing, daily routines, catchwords, and circle of friends—a powerful pubertal resurgence of childish clinging, the two-year-old's clutching familiar places like a limpet, hating trips and strangers and new tastes. He wants his accustomed stories and toys: woe to the liberal parent who, supposing that "creativity" is primed only by novelty, takes an insecure child on a long vacation, for the parent will be punished and chagrined by the clamor for familiar things, home, and the same old books read exactly in the same way.

Probably these rejections of strangeness play a healthy role in the normal stages of the life cycle: among nomadic hunter-foragers, they may keep small children from wandering too far; in the young child, the reluctance to adventure may be part of consolidating gains already made in a strange new world; among adolescents, conformity solidifies loyalties as the subadults approach the limbo of nonbelonging between childhood and grownup status. But clinging conformity is an appropriate model for maturity only if the problems of the child or adolescent remain unresolved, as they do in the children of parents who themselves are psychologically troubled and inept.[30] For the child in such a family, the unremitting infantile behaviors and psychopathic modes to which they lead are adaptive: they are the means for surviving defective home environments and, ultimately, for surviving distorted worldviews. But they do not lead toward psychological maturity, a view broad and forgiving, recognizing the limits of membership and the importance of selfhood within the group—like that of Chiefs Seattle and Smallahala, who saw the invading whites as wrong and yet as human. Such an attitude, it seems to me, involves a sense of the larger gift of life, a realistic perception of the self and the Other, and a sense of the talents of generosity and circumspection, all of which were at odds with the needs of the early village craftsman, on whom the domesticated world imposed the framework of rewards, competition, and exclusiveness, hoarding of seed strains, rejection of cross-tribal marriage, and abandonment of the metaphysical potency of all creatures for the utility of a few. Loyalty and conformity were absolutely central, enkindled in the callow human fears of foreign ways and nonbelonging.

Of course, this generalized description of the farmer/villager is used as a mode; there are exceptions. The loving acceptance of the strangeness of life, the wit to become fully oneself and yet not estranged from the infinite diversity of the Other, the leisured, free openness to self-unfolding instead of clinging to a made world may indeed be achieved by the individual farmer who knows birdsong as well as the cackling hen, who gathers and fishes as well as plants and cultivates. On the subsistence farm of nineteenth-century Illinois, in sixteenth-century Flanders, at the homesteads of ancient Jericho, such leisure may have been possible—as it may be anywhere on rich uncrowded soils in favorable climates. The final phases of maturity, in which the seasoned individual becomes capable of mentorship and spiritual guidance, are in some degree within reach of all in such places.

The Near Eastern human habitats at the end of the Ice Age were also rich and fruitful, and the earliest planters may have been as much the beneficiaries of the full cycle of individual psychogenesis as their ancestors and their farmer heirs on the fruitful soils of the north. But the land changed. Subarid desert fringes are especially vulnerable to both abuse and climate. Men were forced to find in their own psychological makeup the resources to meet the demands of the domestic community in an ecologically deteriorating world. Slowly and without planned intent, the subjective experience changed in its equilibrium with the external world. In Freudian terms, the id or instinctive impulses as the expression of instinctual wildness became synonymous with the desert; the ego came to attend more and more to human products; and the social matrix of the superego grew in focus and complexity.

But no Freudian terms are needed to see that village life put demands on the minds of adults that resembled distorted versions of the growing pains of typical children of *Homo sapiens* everywhere. Perhaps the greater complexity of life in village society did not actually counterbalance the simplification of the nonhuman environment. Thus, the difference between the psychological world of the adult and the child in the villages was not as great as that between adults and children among the ancestral hunters. This is not what one expects from the traditional view of history. But history itself, an idea accounting for a made world, was invented by villagers as a result of five thousand years of strife and struggle to hold environment and self together. As a simplistic, linear, literal account of events and powers as unpredictable as parental anger, history is a juvenile idea.

EIGHT

Ten Thousand Years
of Crisis

THE DAWN OF CIVILIZATION, associated with the first agriculture, is generally seen as a great sunrise before which men lived in a mental and social twilight, waiting, straining to become fully human. We see those vague predecessors as incomplete, with a few crude tools, living days of fear and monotony, nights of terror and discomfort, with a short, brutish existence as the only reward for the struggle to survive.

Today's myth of progress and gospel of radical change, orientation to tomorrow and frantic exchange of old things for new are modern only in terms of the whole human span that preceded them. Though we may picture ourselves as very unlike old-world peasants, it is in the agrarian mind that modern life begins.

Nobody knows for certain how or why agriculture began. How man began the earliest tending of plants and animals may remain a secret forever, but the epidemic of acquisitive proprietorship and territorial aggrandizement that resulted from this development is apparent. It was neither a worldwide event nor a single event, but a shifting mixture of hunting, fishing, and planting, at first in a rather limited geographical area from Turkey to the Caspian basin and south to the Red Sea and Palestine and later expansions from centers in equatorial Asia and America.

Despite many specific domestications and forms of early agriculture in other parts of the world, particularly Southeast Asia and Central America, the set of techniques and of mind seems first to have taken form at the eastern end of the Mediterranean Sea and to have spread from there by cultural contact. In time, Asia and America became "centers of domestication" as agriculture spread around the globe.

The climate, species of plants and animals, types of available food, and the man-made combinations of tools and ideas had been changing for a million years. Men had expanded their range, shifted with the slow tides of glacial ice, learned the ways of other living creatures, and achieved a rich humanity long before metals, pots, wheels, kings, and theocracies appeared.

Because of the limited archaeological evidence, it was still thought until recently that domestication appeared abruptly, as an inexplicable breakthrough that transformed human life about ten thousand years ago. Now it is clear that its sudden appearance in archaeological diggings was a local accident. Between outright gathering and full food production there were stages of food collecting and incipient domestication, lifeways mixing hunting and gathering in different proportions, and finally the culling or artificial hunting of animals and collecting from an extended garden plants that were more or less constantly protected and probably genetically altered by men.

The story of some caveman genius bringing home a baby wild sheep to raise or capturing a cub-wolf from its den, or realizing in some bold flash of intuition how to grow tomatoes, thus inventing in one mighty stroke a new way of life that was thereafter imitated by the genius's friends and descendants, is nonsense; it is part of the same civilized myth that would have us believe that in some miraculous way the farmer discovered agriculture and thus raised himself above his predecessors.

A sequence of events east of the Mediterranean some twenty thousand years ago may have led by uncertain steps toward agriculture. Whether these stresses and deformations of human society were the consequence of the climate and the glaciers of the last ice age has been argued inconclusively for half a century. The great wetness of the time has suggested to some that men who had previously chased big game were impeded by the waterways and swamps, that hunting faltered as large mammals became locally extinct, that fishing may have seduced men into a sedentary life, which made for a different kind of attention to the plants and earth around them. It has been suggested that after the wet came the dry; that the principal wild herd animals remaining were aurochs (the wild cattle) and the ancestors of domestic goats and sheep; and that grasses flourished on the slopes so abundantly that their seeds became an increasingly available food for people. If the use of cereals was the crux of man's prehistory, then it was inseparable from the use of fire for cooking, making them edible in large amounts.

During this stage of deteriorating cynegetics (that is, hunting and its culture) local tribes apparently tried a great variety of foods that earlier had been rejected by the reindeer hunters who preceded them. Archaeological records have shown signs of crisis during the four thousand years preceding the first farming communities. It was a time of intense food experimentation in which acorns, nuts, seeds, snails, clams, fish, and other aquatic animals were gathered. The mastery of stone tool-making faded, but there were new utensils of wood, leather, and bone, evidence of swimming and the use of boats, flint sickles, the pestle and mortar, and the bow and arrow. These innovations by seed-gleaners, shore-scavengers, and sheep-followers in the Tigris-Euphrates watershed and on the slopes of the Zagros and Palestinian mountains preceded the earliest concrete signs of domestication—the bones of livestock and seed types found only in association with man.

This was a time of trial and difficulty for the societies and cultures that had created an art and a religion that had endured for twenty thousand years over much of Europe and Asia, yet it favored experiment and goaded men into versatility. By the time the climate warmed around the Mediterranean, some twelve thousand years ago, sedentary, seed-conscious people were munching local mutton in villages. For them the bison, the woolly mammoth and the rhino, the wild horse, cave bear, and reindeer had all but passed from memory.

The lands they occupied may have looked very different from the more northerly tundras and steppes or the more southerly savannas where hunters still flourished. The rolling, open, upland terrain was flecked with patches of woodland and streams separated by grassy swards. Roaming herds of sheep and goats gradually became habituated to people, tolerating human presence even within the "flight-distance" at which wild animals normally flee. They were an increasingly easy kill for men whose durability, strength, and cunning had been honed through generations by their hunting forebears. But compared to their ancestors' grand chases and spearing of wild horses, plugging goats with arrows must have been a profound though perhaps unconscious disappointment.

The virtual collapse of hunting and gathering, the central activity of the ancient culture, would surely have affected the very heart of human existence. The great mystery of domestication is therefore not so much how men achieved control of plants and animals, but how human consciousness was reorganized when the cynegetic life was shattered—that is, the mental, social, and ecological complex based on hunting. All major human characteristics—size, metabolism, sexual and reproductive behavior, intuition, intelligence—had come into existence and were oriented to the hunting life. How, for example, did the male prerogative shift from the chase to the harvest of plants? Even though men at all times have continued to hunt with great élan and pride, just as women have continued to gather and to be the center of the household, it is astonishing that such a shift in vocation took place.

In the course of a few thousand years men assumed control over the harvest, however much it was ritualized in female symbols. Throughout history agriculture has been represented in feminine

terms and images. Even so, men generally dominate the political order in such societies—as among biblical peoples. Perhaps this is because, from the earliest times of farming, a major purpose of man's
pastures and fields was the production of meat from grazing animals,
and the harvest of meat was the ancient domain of the male as a
hunter. Or did control of surplus grain in some way acquire the prestige and potential power traditionally associated with the hunt and
the hunter's honor in distributing the parts of the kill?

Driving the bezoar goat and urial sheep, however it may have been
compensated in social status, must have seemed, as the animals became more and more tame, less worthy of a man's life. Cut off from
hunting reindeer, horse, and elephant, men lost both the models and
the means by which personal prestige was achieved and measured
within the group by peaceful means. They found a substitute in
the biggest and most dangerous potential prey remaining—men
themselves.

The collapse of an ecology that kept men scarce and attuned to the
mystery and diversity of all life led as though by some devilish Fall
to the hunting and herding of man by man. To defend his fields a
farmer needed many kinsmen: sons, and codefenders, and cofighters,
and ultimately brother ideologists.

What must surely have preceded farming was a shift in style and
in man's sense of his place in the world; a shift whereby man would
presume to own the world and wild organisms would be screened for
those having a certain infantile, trusting placidity that could be nurtured and increased in captivity. Long before some degenerate auroch
or wild cow was hitched to a set of stone wheels in Egypt, the density
of the planet was altered. A group of deprived hunters, caught in a
geographic and biological crisis, took up crayfish stomping and seed
gleaning—activities that had not occupied the full attention of their
ancestors for millions of years, since the earliest genus of man, *Ra-*

mapithecus, ambled about pond and prairie edges and the father of modern men, *Australopithecus,* scavenged, sought small game, and snatched crustaceans in the shallows of ancient African lakes.

HUSBANDRY, A FAILURE OF BIOLOGICAL STYLE

It is hard to speak of domestic animals as failures because we are so fond of them. To us they are fellow beings, whereas we regard wild creatures as curiosities or shadows whose wills oppose our own. To denounce farming and rural life, so relatively serene at a time of urban crisis, seems to flout the last landscape of solace and respite. But in my view the urban crisis is a direct consequence of the food-producing revolution. In a sense, although farmers domesticated particular varieties of plants and animals, the farm domesticated the habitat. For whom was food mass-produced and food surpluses stored if not for the town?

"Domestication" means much more than the dictionary definition, "to become a member of the household." Individual wild creatures brought into the house, no matter how much they are loved or how long they are kept, do not become domesticated. If they live they may not thrive as well as in the wild; if they thrive they still may not reproduce or generate a lineage; and if they breed, the offspring may still prefer to go free if they can escape. There is an inborn difference between domesticates and all other animals.

"To domesticate" means to change genetically, to alter a group of organisms so that their behavior and appearance are quite different from their wild relatives, and these changes are transmitted to their offspring. By selecting parents, culling undesirables, inbreeding and crossbreeding, man uses the same processes that operate in nature.

Each gene in an individual organism acts in the context of many other genes. Hence the genetic changes resulting from domestication may affect the whole creature, its appearance, behavior, and physiology. The temperament and personality of domestic animals are not only more placid than their wild counterparts, but also more flaccid—that is, there is somehow less definition. Of course there is nothing placid about an angry bull or a mean watchdog, but their mothers were tractable, and once an organism has been stripped of its wildness it can be freaked in any direction the breeder wishes. It may be made fierce without being truly wild. The latter implies an ecological niche from which the domesticated animal has been removed. Niches are hard taskmasters. Escape from them is not freedom but loss of direction. Man substitutes controlled breeding for natural selection; animals are selected for special traits like milk production or passivity, at the expense of overall fitness and naturewide relationships.

All populations are composed of individuals who differ from one another. Among wild animals, the diversity is constantly pared at its fringes. Reproductive success and survival are best for individuals of a certain type. In this way, natural selection is a stabilizing pressure, shaping populations into distinctly different and recognizable species. This pressure does not exclude genetic variation. Indeed, the appearance and behavior of a wild species holds true to type in spite of genetic variation. Apparent uniformity masks genetic difference. When natural selection is removed, much of that hidden variation emerges and the population is flooded with external diversity.

Our subjective experience of this is in terms of individuality, and the concept of individuality in our society carries such a strong emotional force as well as political overtones that individualizing as a by-product of domestication may not easily be seen as undesirable. Though domestication broadens the diversity of forms—that is, it increases visible polymorphism—it undermines the crisp demarcations that separate wild species and it cripples our recognition of the species as a group. Knowing only domestic animals dulls our understanding of the way in which unity and discontinuity occur as patterns in nature and substitutes an attention to individuals and breeds. The wide variety of size, color, form, and use of domestic horses, for example, blurs the distinctions among different species of *Equus* that once were constant and meaningful.

It is important to know, when any two organisms are compared, how they are related. However trivial that distinction may seem at first, its triviality simply signifies the poverty of biology in modern philosophy. With domestication, arbitrary reestablishment of inconsequential groupings and relationships damaged the perceptual powers of mankind. If evolutionary human ecology had only one lesson it would be that the development of human intelligence is linked to man's conscious exploration of the species system in nature. But this lost-sensibility aspect carries us away from the biological consequences of domestication.

The glandular and anatomical alterations of animal domestication are fairly well known. Consider the white rat, whose history has been comparatively well documented since it was created from the wild brown rat in the middle of the nineteenth century. In breeding for ease of keeping and uniformity, a variety of related and inadvertent changes have occurred. The tamer, more tractable, less aggressive, more fecund white rat, with its early gonadal development, less active thyroid, and smaller adrenals, is cursed with greater susceptibility to stress, fatigue, disease, and has less intelligence than its wild relative. Many of the deleterious changes have been unavoidable side effects, because of the interplay of gene action or because genes favored by the breeder are closely linked to undesirable genes on the chromosomes.

The strong, firm style of the wild animal is due to a mix of genes that work well together—in other words, it has a stable epigenetic system. The similarity of individuals is shielded by this system against disruption by mutation. In addition, certain chromosomal aberrations may serve to keep blocks of genes together in the wild form; that is, they tend to reduce mixing or recombination in later generations. In domestication the breeder breaks up these blocks, allowing new combinations to appear in the offspring, which would render most of them unfit in nature. Some of these will be especially desirable to him, others simply monsters. Once a cluster is broken up by man-controlled breeding, producing genetic "goofies" that are protected from the rigors of the wild, new sets of captivity types can then be winnowed from them on the farm or in the laboratory. Even in zoos, where the majority of wild animals soon die, the captives that survive are those that, because of their genetic difference, are least exacting about territory, least subtle about social signals and cues, least precise in behavioral discrimination, the loss of mates and companions, and fear about human ubiquity. All domestic animals are highly social, but their social relations are degraded and generalized, just as their physiology is radically altered. They have been bred for readiness to accept human control. "Releasers"—those signals from others of their kind that trigger complex behavior sequences—are lost, along with genetically regulated responses. For them the world grows simpler.

Ritual behavior becomes abbreviated. Symbolic fighting to settle conflicts peacefully is less frequent among domestics than among wild species. Mating patterns lose their elaborate timing as segments are lost. Hormonal changes, such as a decrease in adrenocortical steroids, lead to submissiveness. The reproductive systems of the kept animals lose their fine tuning to the season and to display postures, which in nature are a tightly woven sequence of steps from courtship through parental behavior. Differences between male and female— the secondary sexual characteristics—are diluted. The animals become crude pawns in the farmer's breeding game, shorn of finesse and the exquisite detail so characteristic of wild forms. The animal ceases to be an adequate representation of a natural life form. Its debased behavior and appearance mislead us and miseducate us in fundamental perceptions of the rhythms of continuity and discontinuity and of the specific patterns of the multiplicity of nature.

Interpretations of this debauched ecology were formulated for civilization by its "educated" members. Effete dabblers from the city looked over the barnyard fence at the broken creatures wallowing and copulating in their own dung, and the concept of the bestial brute with untrammeled appetites was born. This was the model for "the animal" in philosophy, "the natural" from which men, understandably, yearned for transcendent release.

Among animals, suitable candidates for domestication are social, herd-oriented, leader- or dominance-recognizing forms. Their response to their own species (possible sex partners) and their own habitat is more a matter of learning and less of fixed responses to fixed signals. Husbandry seeks out and exploits three characteristics of these animals: the tendency of the young to follow whoever is caring for it by imprinting—the process of irreversible attachment; the gradualness of the transition from nursing to eating; and the way in which different social relations may be mediated by different senses. For example, mother-daughter nurture relationships may be based on an imprinted taste. A Scottish milkmaid lets the cow lick her bloodied hands (as well as the calf) at birth, and thereafter the cow will "let down"—give milk—for the milkmaid and the calf, but only for them.

Inborn metabolic errors condemn wild animals to swift destruction. In captivity such cripples are sometimes not only protected but prized. These flaws ("hypertrophies") in growth result in the production of extra meat, wool, silk, eggs, and milk. All such freaks carry a burden of genetic weakness. The nurture of these weaklings is a large part of modern animal science, which may be defined as the systematic creation of animal deformities, anomalies, and monsters, and the practice of keeping them alive.

Another mutant trait common to domestics is excessively delayed maturity and sexual precocity combined with rapid growth. In culling out the irascible and stubborn individuals, the hard, mature, lean line is sacrificed for animals with submissive and infantile responses. Individuals maturing at slower rates are favored. Cows and horses have long-enduring mother-child relationships just as primates do. By exploiting this relationship, new social interdependencies can be created. Infantile animals are less attached to their own kind and readily join other barnyard animals or the human household. Children are eager to adopt them as "people," and adult humans are attracted by their helpless appeal and immature faces—for juvenile qualities are as apparent in face and body as in behavior. The effect of all this is that domestic breeds are creatures who never grow up in spite of their sexual precocity.

The protected environment of domestic animals cushions them from the sculpturing forces of nature and cuts them off from many physical resources. Only when their place-preferences are removed by breeding is this loss tolerable for them. Instead of being more flexible than his wild ancestor, the domestic is specialized to accept human judgment concerning habitation and food. The capacity for living with deficiency is not a true liberation of behavior but the weakening of the choice-making faculty. Wild cattle range widely over diverse types of soils and vegetation in search of plants for which they have a special need at certain times or for trace elements and other minerals that they lick directly from the earth. They seek mud or sand, shade or bright sun, humidities and winds—the conditions that are right for them. Their deliberate instinctive exposure to rain and snow is precisely regulated to their requirements. Many have special relationships with birds, who feed near or on them, and with other animal and plant parasites, internal and external, beneficial to their health. Each step in their life cycle is carried out in the right surroundings, which may be different for feeding, giving birth, courting, resting, hiding, playing, or socializing. In zoos, mental and physical breakdowns are common because the animals lack the extensive range of choices necessary to a healthy physical or social existence. Some species simply cannot be kept alive, necessitating a constant flow of "living material" to replace the dead or dying.

Domestic animals, who also live in restricted environments, are not stir-crazy and malnourished because they are the survivors of hundreds of generations of captives. They are the well-padded drudges, insulated by blunted minds and coarsened bodies against the uniformity of the barnyard, having achieved independence from the demands of style by having no style, coming to terms with the gray world of captivity by arriving at the lowest common denominator of survival.

If this seems to slander some favorite dog or horse or pig, remember that artificial selection of juvenile qualities also favors immaturity, flexibility, and adaptability. The qualities that are admired—responsiveness to men in dogs and trainability in horses—are achieved through breeding at the expense of the traits of maturity. No one can judge the pathos of the domestic animal who has not watched its wild cousin in its natural habitat over a period of months. As long as civilized mythology ranks wild animals as poor relations to barnyard forms it will be almost impossible for most people to make unbiased comparisons.

Occasionally man himself is included in lists of domestic animals. But man is civilized, not domesticated. Domestication is the process by which the genetic make-up of organisms is modified by man to make breed lines and by which civilized man regulates the genetic inheritance of organisms that constitute part of his own habitat. These lines are disengaged from the niche of the wild stock, stripped of biological integrity, simplified in behavior and requirements.

Among domestic animals social relationships are reduced to the crudest essentials. Pre-reproductive parts of the life cycle are minimized, courtship is reduced, and the animal's capacity to recognize its own species is impaired. Since these changes have not taken place in man, man is not properly a domestic animal, although civilization has disrupted his epigenetic stability and loosed a horde of "goofies."

THE INVENTION OF DRUDGERY AND CATASTROPHE

The first cultivation was south and west of the Caspian Sea on uplands covered at that time with sparse woods and grass, much of it steppe and oak-pistachio savanna. The climate was warm, though glacial ice still occupied high mountain valleys. The soil on these open-forest flanks of the Zagros, Lebanese, and Palestinian mountains was light and could be worked easily. The routine was no worse than the gathering of wild grain and the digging of wild roots.

The eminent American geographer Carl Sauer has suggested that casual planting in the form of seed-waste disposal may have preceded cultivation. However, there is no evidence of early vegetable growing, and grain-producing grasses require at least a modicum of soil-breaking. By 9000 B.C. there were at least two groups of early Near East farmers, the Natufian and the Karim Shahirian. These people lived in caves and small clusters of mud huts and had domestic sheep, goats, and two grains. In archaeological digs a preponderance of immature animal bones have been found, along with flint sickle blades, grinding stones, and celts (stone axes). Living in the same region were other men subsisting entirely by hunting and gathering, some in the open, others in caves or huts. "Pure hunters" continued to persist for another two thousand years in the Near East, though as the climate grew steadily warmer, game animals like the red deer diminished. As cool habitats migrated up the mountain slopes, human population increased. When hunters finally gave way entirely to farmers in that area about 7000 B.C., the towns of Jericho in the Jordan Valley and Jarmo in the Zagros Mountains each contained as many as a hundred and twenty-five people living in houses. Subsistence farming was under way.

During this time the early techniques of agriculture were spreading from the Near East, evoking other domestications in Asia and America, which then returned new varieties of crop plants and breeds of farm animals to the Near East.

Production of storable cereals that could feed large numbers of nonfarmers marked the transition from subsistence farming to institutional agriculture. By 5000 B.C. there were farmers in alluvial valleys of the Tigris and Euphrates who were using slaves to cope with the weeds and heavy soils and to cultivate vast fields planted to a single crop of hybrid grain. Agricultural surpluses and new distribution and storage systems made craft and class specializations possible and necessary.

Pigs, pottery, and weaving were developed, and the first temples signified the rise of cosmologies based on a model of the universe as a barnyard, of hierarchical theocracies, political states, tyranny, war, and work. The coincidence of the first domestic cattle with the temples and signs of sacred bulls indicates that cows were first kept for religious rather than economic reasons.

A thousand years later there were towns of ten thousand people; farmers had occupied the floodplains of the Nile and Danube; and nomads with herds of cattle were munching their way across the Sahara, Persia, Arabia, Morocco, Ethiopia—expanding the traditions, arrogance, and destructiveness of pastoral nomadism. In Europe, in time, the use of tree-cutting axes combined with the teeth and hooves of livestock to destroy the great forests that had closed in on ground vacated by glacial ice. Mankind stood at the gate of the modern world.

There are many kinds of farmers and herders in the world, but they differ mainly in the mixture of certain common qualities, and the qualities derive from the basic nature of tilling and tending. The early agriculturists varied widely among different peoples in the mix of hunting, gathering, and planting. The qualities derived from planting are most clearly seen in the later peasant farmers of the civilized or historical agricultural state. They adhere to the native soil, revere their ancestors, are sober-minded, and have strong codes of conduct. They are simple, industrious, tenacious, and predictable. But simplicity can mean dull wits, and industry can be a kind word for toil, the price and token of security, respect, and piety. The other virtues are euphemisms for the simplified, repetitive life of people whose bulldog grip on their humanity is misinterpreted as contentment and wise serenity.

The peasant has wedded domesticity to agriculture. His household is like field work: banal and monotonous. Like the mating of ram and ewe, the partnership of marriage is usually arranged—at most a choice of convenience. Procreation is the household extension of production, the means of ensuring children as field hands. Prudence and practicality rule family relationships. An economy of normal abundance, combined with the fear of scarcity and famine years, creates the authoritarian family based on dogged partnerships, dominance, and submission. Children grow up holding a grudge against their elders. Where the father is a tyrant, meals are eaten in silence. The desperate, unhuman plight of the serf in an agricultural society forces him to repress his family frustrations in order to survive, to convert them into a bitter conformity, and to redirect hatred outward—toward competitors, aliens, and wild nature. Fierce unity and loyalty become the core of class struggle and ideological exploitation, expressing the fellowship of slaves.

Peasants face the outside world with coarse sullenness, emotions concealed or deadened except for scorn for the soft-hearted. Decorum and sobriety substitute for manners and gaiety. Resentment and suspicion run deep. A stoic numbness and lack of imagination are inseparable from religious faith. Ask the peasant what he enjoys and you get no answer. Depth interviews reveal an intense dislike of his situation and a strong desire to leave the bleak rural environment. It

is likely that many of us see some of these traits in our urban con-
temporaries and in ourselves, far from the pigsty and plow. The peasant is in us all and his warp and values are part of modern culture.

With his anthropomorphic view of the world, as expressed in the
invention of humanist gods—matriarchy and patriarchy forever contending—the peasant and villager see all misfortune as caused by
someone, to be countered by magic or vengeance.

Men obtain images of themselves from the natural world. Planters
and tillers see themselves as domestic animals in a cosmic garden.
Reserving part of the harvest for the gods is part of the custom of
renewal ceremonies. Hence sacrifice came into existence; the murder
of the first-born is a logical myth of men as numerous as weeds.
Herders see themselves as sheep who follow "a great shepherd." Living amidst collapsing ecosystems, agrarians accept a religion of arbitrary gods, catastrophic punishments by flood, pestilence, famine,
and drought in an apocalyptic theology.

It is common in sociological studies to distinguish between the
planters or tribal herdsmen of the earliest agriculture and later peasants and farmers. The first do not live in such a highly structured and
complex society of rulers and workers as do, say, the traditional peasants of Central Europe. However useful these distinctions are for social comparisons, they are ecologically inconsequential. All agrarian
societies share hatred of predatory wild animals, show blunted body
or blunted sensitivity, lack of interest in noneconomic plants and animals, and the willingness to drudge, with its deep, latent resentments, crude mixtures of rectitude and heaviness, and absence of
humor.

■

In official history 3000 B.C. marks the beginning of civilization,
corresponding to the rise of equatorial valley irrigation monocultures, the urban-rural complex of specialized, single-crop farms and

ruling bureaucracies of the great river valleys. In the archaeological residue of the Mesopotamian states there is evidence of ox-drawn carts, trade, writing, slaves, wars, and theocratic kingships. During this same period there was debilitation of the total natural complex, pillaged ecosystems that never recovered. The signs of this were the local extinction of large wild mammals, deserts replacing forests, the degradation of grasslands and disappearance of soil, the instability of streams and drying up of springs, and the depletion of land fertility—all of which affected water supply, climate, and economy. The creeping dereliction was largely invisible then, as it seems extraneous now. Individuals were born into harsh, stony surroundings where floods and drought seemed to be eternal, a world given to rather than made by man.

The connection between the rise and fall of great alluvial valley civilizations was clearly traced by Dr. W. C. Lowdermilk, an American soils expert.[1] First Lowdermilk noticed that the bottomlands along the great rivers are still fertile, though they now support only one-fifth as many people as they did three thousand years ago. The debacle that overtook Babylon, Kish, Ezion Geber, Timgad, Petra, Carthage, and other cities of the Near East and North Africa was not simply exhaustion of the land. Two kinds of clues helped Lowdermilk to puzzle out the role of ancient hydraulic agriculture in the ruin of these now-buried cities. One was the silted-in waterways, buried irrigation channels, and hydraulic works. Even the cities themselves were buried, as any spade-wielding archaeologist will testify. Jerash, once a city of 250,000, now lies under thirteen feet of earth, on which exists a village of 3000.

The other was the barren rocky slopes beyond the city walls, so characteristic of the Mediterranean world from Portugal to Palestine, of most of the Near East and North Africa, and much of India, China, and Mexico. The evidence is incontrovertible that the land was once covered with soil, grasses, and woody plants. In the Judean hills and on the slopes of Shansi province, Lowdermilk found ancient upland temples whose walls kept out livestock and whose sacredness repulsed the woodcutter. Within the walls forest groves survived on good soils, oases in thousands of square miles of man-made desert. On Cyprus, where lowland temple walls held off mudflows, the plain is now eight feet above the churchyard. The church has a new floor laid over a silt flow thirteen feet deep. Twenty-three feet of silt had therefore come down from the slopes since the church was built, the result of clearing, burning, and grazing.

The barren slopes and buried cities were only part of the story. Intensive land use was not primarily the cause of urban collapse. Lowdermilk reasoned that a great burst of population had followed the mastery of irrigation agriculture, which incorporated the use of the plow and the strategy of crop rotation. Faster than famine and wars could cut them down, the human hordes increased. Density in the city and floodplain sent surplus people farther upstream, up the tributaries, and up the slopes of the watershed itself. Clearing and cultivating the lower slopes drove the shepherds and their four-legged locusts higher. Timber for ship and other construction was logged from the highlands—which were occupied in turn by charcoal-makers, subsistence farmers, and stockkeepers. The silt that began to crawl down the slopes became a perpetual revenge, so that the vast terrace systems and valley flumes required constant maintenance, not only by farmers but by armies of laborers—mostly slaves. The city that preceded the present Beirut was an example of this sequence: expansion of the population of Phoenician Semites through hydraulic monocultures; increased manufacture and trade; the export of migrants; the clearing and cultivation of an upstream watershed once covered for two thousand square miles by the cedar of Lebanon tree; followed by an unremitting struggle to secure the waterworks against siltation. When some social upheaval interfered with the routines of control, the state fell.

As increasing populations and demands on the land led to further subdivision and fragmentation, either the farmer relapsed into a bare subsistence economy or agriculture was reorganized on a feudal basis. In the latter case some formerly "free" men became serfs and slaves. In time a growing landless, underemployed proletariat came to be a menace to the ruling classes and was placated by the state with bread and circuses.

Rome is a later example of a process that began when the ancient theocratic state reached the limits of production and, in the desert, of water. The growing population could do one of three things: starve, emigrate to the hinterland and farm the slopes, or enter urban roles of begging, brigandage, or military service. This last required increased taxation and regimentation, to implement as well as to resist it, which generated revolt or evoked invasion from without, eventually followed by bureaucratic collapse—and the flumes, ditches, pipelines, conduits, terraces, reservoirs, and dikes disappeared under an avalanche of mud. War, invasion, insurrection, epidemic, and famine could each break the temporary balance maintained by infinite drudgery against the consequences of the agrarian revolution.

The destructive combination of hydraulic agriculture and theocratic state has been the major force in the creation of our apocalyptic culture.

Historians have blamed the Moroccan demise on Arab nomads who hated trees, just as the Mongols were blamed for the collapse of the Mesopotamian irrigation systems. Ideology has been used to explain ecological situations. It is as though there were some mental block against recognizing the fatal mishandling of the natural environment by the agricultural society and its urban overlords.

In China men struggled to control the Yellow River for four thousand years, while at the same time other men ravaged the upper watershed, creating gullies six hundred feet deep. The mud that came down settled in the river bed, gradually lifting it high above the surrounding floodplain, and the river was contained entirely by manmade dikes. Flooding runoff from the denuded slopes occasionally overtopped the dikes. The great flood of 1852 shifted the mouth of the river four hundred miles and drowned hundreds of thousands of people. The biblical Flood of the Old Testament about fifty-five hundred years ago, which was probably the Euphrates River, had the same basic cause. There is evidence that the early Sumerian civilizations did not know floods of the Euphrates, and that flooding began with upper watershed destruction. The soils that were ripped off the earth by hooves and teeth and sent down the Tigris and Euphrates, forming a delta that advanced 180 miles into the Persian Gulf, as though the skin had been peeled from the earth and heaped into the sea, making 35,000 square miles of salt marsh from topsoil.

Such destruction was not necessarily the result of poor agricultural practices. It was rather the nature of husbandry itself. The record of agriculture everywhere on the planet is that of a blind force extending sand dunes and other wind damage by excavation and burial, lowering water tables, increasing flooding, altering the composition of plant and animal communities, and diminishing the nutritive quality and stability of ecosystems. The loss of certain substances from the soil—especially phosphates, nitrates, and calcium—decreases crop food value. Changes in floral composition affect a complex, stable species by replacing it with a simpler, shifting association. A forest may remain a forest or grassland remain grassland, yet be drastically altered in richness, productivity, resistance, and soil-building ability. Changes in composition are brought about directly by overgrazing and indirectly by the cultivation of surrounding lands; they are invisible to most people, even cattlemen and other pastorialists.

No other organisms are more intricately associated with civilization than the cereals—wheat, barley, rye, corn, rice: all modified annual grasses on whom the masses of mankind depend. Ecologically, the cereals are takers, not makers of soil. By contrast, perennial wild grasses work as pumps; their deep roots bring fresh nutrient minerals to the surface and structure the soil. They live in conjunction with a wide variety of flowering legumes and composites, two groups of plants essential for good soil formation, which are dependent on insect pollinators for their continued existence and in turn support a rich animal life.

As men undertook the cultivation of vast fields of cereals, they turned away from an ancient relationship with the wild nectar- and pollen-seeking bees, flies, butterflies, and beetles. Such insects had made possible the arboreal life of early primates in flowering and fruit-making tropical forests. Then they were instrumental in the evolution of prairies and savannas, which supported the first pre-human ground apes. Finally, pollinating insects supervised the evolution of the steppe and tundra flora, where the great herds of Pleistocene mammals fostered the final hunting phases of mankind.

The earliest subsistence agriculture did not abandon its dependence on flowering plants and their pollinators, but when men moved into the great river valleys and planted vast fields of grain they repudiated ancient connections with a host of tiny animals who compose the richest and most diverse fauna on our planet. The cereals are wind-pollinated annuals, shallow-rooted, ephemeral, without soil-forming virtues, and their association with flowering forms or pollinator insects is minimal. By supporting large, minimally nourished human populations and by their destructive effects in the environment when grown in cultivated uniformity, the cereals are truly the symbol and agent of agriculture's war against the planet.

It may seem quaint to write fervently of "land-use practices" at a time when pollution is the fashionable topic of environmental concern and the space and solitude of the sheep-herding life seem idyllic. With such a small fraction of society in the industrial state "living by the soil," erosion, forest destruction, and desert making hardly seem urgent, but the soil was the source of complex life long before men or agriculture first appeared. It is as fundamental to our well-being now as ever, though most of us never put our hands into it.

The ancient catastrophes no longer seem so ghastly as they did when Lowdermilk made his report. Those immense tides of people and cities seem, in the light of our atomic era, to have fallen in a peaceful ebb. In view of their modest technology it seems almost academic to recall them now. Yet we share with them a worldview generated by monocultures. Current technology has become more efficient and complicated without changing the direction established by ancient irrigation states. However noble the spirit and grand the human aspirations since the earliest Egyptian dynasties may be, the written record and the fortunes of the state have usurped the human record. Its vision of a man-centered universe and its impoverished ecology, bedecked as destiny, is a heritage too uncritically accepted. In view of the enormous scope of human time and experience, perhaps mankind has unwittingly embraced a diseased era as the model of human life.

The crippling of the natural realm by hooved animals and the replacement of the rich and varied flora of evolution with domestic varieties set precedents for the machine age. Scalping with the bull-dozer succeeds gleaning with the goat; disinfecting the forest with pesticides is an extension of cleaning kitchen pots and pans with soap; polluting the air with fumes is not much different from the Sumerians polluting the water with silt. But the most damaging blows of all are the extinctions of the "useless" forms of life, those wild things that seem outside our economy and inimical to agriculture. The success of that practical philosophy is measured in human numbers. The great increase in human population began in earnest ten thousand years ago; by 1980 there were five billion and there will be about eight billion by the year 2010. We have loosed a population epidemic since men ceased to hunt and gather that is the most terrifying phenomenon of the million years of human experience.

NINE

The Desert Fathers

IF IDEAS HAVE HABITATS in which they originate and prosper, then the desert edge might be called the home of Western thought. Historically this is common knowledge, for the peoples of the dry landscapes of Egypt, Sumer, Assyria, Palestine, and the eastern European and Eurasian borders of the Mediterranean Sea fashioned many of the concepts that define Occidental civilization.

To understand this aridity of culture we must stand apart from the conventions of history even while using the record of the past, for the idea of history is itself a Western invention whose central theme is the rejection of habitat, the formulation of experience as outside of nature and the reduction of place to location. To it, the plains and passes of the desert fringe are only a stage upon which the human drama is enacted. History conceives the past mainly in terms of biography and nations. It seeks causality in the conscious, spiritual, ambitious character of men and memorializes them in writing.[1]

The desert is a powerful, unique sensorium. Silence and emptiness are the ambiguous descriptions of sounds and landforms. The desert is at once a place of sensory deprivation and awesome overload—too little life, too much heat, too little water, too much sky. Its cool shadows offer "thermal delight," and yet the desert evokes the terrors of the inferno.[2] Its distance and scale, the sweep between horizons and the loftiness of stars, its winds and mirages, its hidden life and conspicuous shapes seem at once to dwarf and to emphasize the human figure. Its sensory impact is profoundly stimulating and disturbing, a massive shock to the human limbic system—the neural basis of emotional response—that seems to demand some logic or interpretation.

Between the senses and the logic is perception—that is, the bio-psychological screening devices, filters, combined forces of inherent tendency and individual experience that direct attention and focus possibilities. Thus, what the desert means is preceded by precon-scious selection of what is seen and how it is seen. Myriad qualities of the desert beg for interpretation: the firmness of outline; the lin-earity of horizon and movement; the separateness of things and their static, fixed quality as though made by some absent artisan; the way light and dark, sky and earth, life and death insist on contrast and duality; the ephemerality of creatures and transience of man; the flickering vitality of things distant, such as the planets; things un-seen but heard, opposed to the frozen immobility of stone. These are some of the preconscious pointers toward interpretation.

Although it seems inimical to human life, the desert—the great dry belts that straddle the tropics of Cancer and Capricorn—is the home of the world's civilizations. At the waterholes and along the rivers of the arid subtropics of Asia, Africa, and Europe where the three continents join, history began—not in the sandy desert proper, but at its edges. These margins are not desert habitats proper, but ecological *ecotones*. They include the spare shrub communities at the fringe of sandy plains or stony plateaus, the patches of grassland on slightly moister slopes, traces of savanna, the evergreen dry forest of the mountain islands, the verdant park and wetlands of the oases and river margins proper, and the derelict phases of all such vegetative communities degenerating toward barren rock as a result of climatic change and human abuse.

It was never the occupation of desert that mattered, but its iso-lating effects. It began with dramatic suddenness at the edges of val-leys where cultivation and settlement leave off, always reminding farmers and their urban cousins of the separation of fertility and bar-renness. The desert of the Near East was once the home of wild an-imals, barbarian nomads, and mounted invaders from the east and north, with whom settled peoples also engaged in commerce.

Village, town, and city life in the great valleys, as understood from the archaeological record, was a stew of seventy centuries of turmoil and havoc as well as building and growth. Recurring disasters are evident in their litter, often including the downfall of the great theo-cratic cities. Their ruins, numbering more than a hundred, are among the great spectacles of the earth. City after city was built upon the decimated foundations of its predecessors. Today, scores of tiny villages squat on the shattered wreckage of centers that once con-tained many thousands of inhabitants. The pattern of expansion and collapse emerging from the excavations of these ruins is one of rising power and prosperity followed by environmental deterioration and social catastrophe, the fateful tides of powerful theocracies made vul-nerable by their own success.

The cycle typically began with the concentration of authority and organization expressed in warlike expansion, territoriality, and the engineering of water supplies and irrigation. The amount of pro-ductive soil was increased by the carefully managed distribution of water. Gradually irrigation became extended complex hydraulic sys-tems. As the population exceeded its available resources, emigrants went upstream on the heels of timber cutters and charcoal makers, many settling as stockkeepers in the watersheds of the tributaries of mainstreams like the Tigris and Euphrates. Over the years, their live-stock increased and denuded and trampled the slopes, destroying their vegetative cover and soil. The land lost its water-retaining ca-pacity, increasing the runoff after rains and reducing the ground-water supplies in springs and wells. The seasonal variation in water supply was exaggerated by this flooding and scarcity. Silt threatened to clog the impoundments and the miles of intricate water-feeder systems upon which the agriculture depended.[3]

Cultivation, once it reached the limits of tillable land, was intensified. Crop specialization, control of weeds and pests, and increased intensity of demand on the soil set the stage for periodic outbreaks of crop diseases and invasions of pests and parasites whose wild foods were gone. Nutrient-element deficiencies and soil salination also helped set the stage for debacle.

As chiefdoms were swallowed by kingdoms and kingdoms confronted other kingdoms, defense put heavy demands on manpower, straining the bureaucratic management of the land. The semi-isolation of the great city-states converted the whole region into a giant experiment in communicable human diseases, so that, in spite of his resistance to contaminated food and water, to local strains of bacteria, viruses, nematodes, and flatworms, the citizen of such a state became vulnerable to new forms of diseases brought by traders and invaders.

Thus emerged the Four Horsemen of the Apocalypse: conscription, enslavement, famine, and disease.[4] Cataclysms of whatever kind were followed by hydraulic failure and mud deposits so suffocating that neither conquerors nor stragglers could easily renew the buried waterworks that had taken decades or even centuries to build. Eventually a new city would emerge, a cult and power center of the district. Its inhabitants, like their predecessors, would seek the ritual protection of their gods, whose connection with the earth and its seasons entailed a mythology of the soil and its autochthonous forces, of the springs and streams, the weather, and the secrets of germination. They would try harder to harmonize their society with the powers of nature. But they too would fail.[5]

Since the tempo of this cycle of catastrophe and renewal was in terms of many lifetimes, it was probably more or less invisible to those who lived it. A record-keeping observer, an interested hovering alien, however, might see the futility and illusory security even though he might not recognize its ecological aspects. Most desert tribesmen were disengaged, but they were not so analytic or so interested. Another watcher from the desert was the self-styled outcast. By self-definition the Hebrews were the "outsiders." Although they adopted a nomadic style, the Hebrews were never true outsiders and contemptuous of the city in the manner of Arab nomads. Hangers-on at the fringe, mixing scorn and yearning, the little tribes of place-less people perceived with keen and biting insight the folly of the great pagan theocracies that worshiped the wrong gods.

On the most ambitious scale in the history of the world, the ancestors of the Old Testament made virtue of their homelessness. They struck a gold vein of moral analysis by assimilating certain themes of transience from genuine nomads while rejecting their fatalism. In a Semitic storm god they found a traveling deity who was everyplace and therefore not bound by location. Owning nothing, they created a theology of contingent divinity, and heroic escape.

The Hebrews discovered and occupied a force field of human relations that has been one of the most distinctive features of the Near and Middle East from the time of the earliest agriculture: the gap between pastoralist and farmer. The farmer was economically and politically allied with the city. The domestication of plants and animals led to a Neolithic dialectic, a split in husbandry between pastorality and tillage. This Cain and Abel motif is deep in the blood of Western origins. It is fundamental to the ideological psychology of "us" against "them" that the desert seemed always to echo in its physical contrasts.

Although basically economic, the dialectic resonated with other dualities. What to their ancestral hunter-gatherers had been a polar equilibrium whereby men hunted and women gathered was sundered into masculinist and patriarchal societies of animal breeders on the one hand and Great Mother–worshiping, plant-tending cultivators of the soil on the other.

City and country were not then the symbols of opposition, but allies against the wandering peoples of the desert. The mythology of the ancient city-states was profoundly imbued with feminine principles and dominated by pantheons of powerful goddesses. Central to religion were the cosmic cycle of life, the sacredness of soil and water, the spirituality of particular places, and reverence for seasonal rhythms and harmonies of growth and decay, birth and death. These values were shared by the craftsmen, tradesmen, bureaucrats, and others of the city, centered there in a temple priesthood.

Pastoralists have traditionally shown distaste for a life of manure shoveling, mucky sluice reaming, and the drudgery and passivity of tending and waiting. To this adopted attitude the critical and analytic Hebrew added a revulsion for the heterodoxy of the city's foreign traffic, with its bastardizing, accommodating, and polluting of religion and invidious pursuit of vanity and money. It seemed apparent to the Hebrew prophets that false gods, wantonness, and materialism destined all such centers to destruction. True pastoralists might have agreed, turned their backs and gone their way, but the Hebrews watched and learned from the crack in the dialectical world. Outside the city gates, self-exiled, deriding those inside, sharpening powerful new weapons of objective analysis, they formulated a *via negativa*. The inevitable catastrophes that had left ruins in every direction since the beginnings of civilization testified to an inevitable providential nemesis. God was just, as well as distant from all this ritual elaboration and collaboration between men and the soil. It was not any particular Mesopotamian myth that was wrong; it was myth itself.

So the Hebrews did not choose pastoral myths, although they incorporated pastoral style: patriarchal authoritarianism, the principles of mobility, durability, frugality, a penchant for abstraction and distancing, a conscious disengagement. The giver and maker and destroyer would topple all walls and priests and kings at times and by means of his own choosing, not as the manifestation of the outraged divinity incarnate in things, but as an unknowable master outside creation. The occasion of all his acts would escape prediction and cyclic formats; his means would be his own: flood, famine, plague, invasion. The spectacular pattern of ruins around them told nothing of the when and how of calamity. Nothing about ordinary experience could inform one about such a god.

The Hebraic ideal was an extraordinary ambition: self-styled exiles, fugitives, wanderers, a community of alienated souls who disavowed both the substance and form of the bonding ties by which men had acknowledged kinship with earth and tribe from the dawn of consciousness and which they had given form in the exemplary and metaphorical model of myth. The ancient notion of the multiplicity of truth, of hidden spirit in all things; the mystic simultaneity of past, present, and future; the credence in spoken, sung, carved, drawn, or danced affirmation of the cohesion of all things; the reading of nature as the divine language: all were seen as illusory in the eyes of the chosen prophets and chosen people.

The Hebrews understood that, however comprehensible natural events might be in their own right, they were meaningless in any cosmic sense. While the world was still to be revered as belonging to Him, it was to be understood that He did not regularly speak through the mysteries of birth, growth, death, the beauty and variety of life, the mutual ties among natural and social forms, or by means of incarnate, numinous hierophantic objects.

The Hebrews invented a special myth that denied the message of regularity and causal interconnectedness that had been the stuff of pagan myth. The human psyche was still to be nurtured with stories—not accounts of analogical beginnings uniting present and past, but of origins actually distant in time; not familiar oral recitations or rhetorical episodes of an epic, but quotations from the written word; not affirming a methectic, but rather a cathartic world where estrangement was the condition of all men. Just as the ancient Hebrew lived in the crevice of the Neolithic split, Occidental men would come to see themselves as neither wholly spiritual nor wholly natural, as fragmented rather than plural in nature.

The new antimythological myth was history. Psychologically it served as all myths do: as a story of the past that explains origins, establishes exemplary models of behavior, and provides the conventions of a particular group. Yet it was psychologically dysfunctional in order to sustain the ideal of estrangement. Its most revolutionary aspect was its repudiation of the cyclic pattern of events, its insistence on the truly linear flow of time, and its pursuit of its own abstract, self-confirming truth as opposed to indicators and signs in the concrete world.

Because historical events were unique, they were not analogous to the body, family, or natural processes. They were interpreted by envoys, through words written rather than spoken, proclamations tinged with strangeness, a kerygmatic, or preaching and prophetic, form. The evangelical assertion of the new Word was not intended to make man fit into the world, but to verify his isolation and emphasize the unpredictability and disjunction of experience.[6] Where traditional myths had been part of a great man-culture-nature-divine cybernetics, the new myth extolled the mystery of God's purpose and the discontinuity of events.

Even its linear pattern gave minimal form. Unlike the cosmological matrices of Neolithic culture, historical progression was at best a broken point-to-point sequence, full of random turns, like literary fiction. In contrast to the satisfactions of a universal harmony, it had only a lean and bare claim that things happened, but expressed little of their "whatness." It was conductive to a skepticism previously unknown. It favored a new attitude of self-scrutiny and uprooted the temptation to close with the visible world or to accept it as an expression of divinity. Life was a sensuous snare, alluring with intimations of a centered reality on earth, full of spurious signs of purpose. The doubting, sometimes mocking, rummaging, questioning attitude toward the world was extended also to a new inward scrutiny. It would reveal the artificiality of all culture and the selfishness of human motives, not only the self-delusion in all explanation, but the frailty of criticism itself.

To observe that this renovation of consciousness took place at the edge of the desert is not to say that it was caused by the desert. Perhaps it is not possible to separate causes and evidence at the level of preconscious perception. Yet, such a consciousness might include attention habitually directed to the sky, the relative insignificance of all things organic, the sense of hidden, invisible, unknowable power that seems more akin to the wind than to concrete things. Waiting, silence, emptiness, and nothingness seem to imprint themselves on the concept of truth, the self, ultimate states. In general, none of the great world religions is life-affirming. They all seem to dislocate and abstract *as though* taking some sign from the insignificance of life in the overwhelming geometry of mineral and astronomical forces around them. "The desert," says Herbert Schneidau in his *Sacred Discontent,* was "the concrete image of transcendence" appropriate to an unknowable God, though not his home—something "wholly other," a place of contrasting, negating oppositions.[7]

Its emptiness, as Aldous Huxley observed, is conducive to concentration, hallucination, sensory deprivation, spiritual exaltation, madness, and death.[8] Its desolation is the vestment of those who want no home on earth and find a solacing humility in their own nothingness and liberation from the body. For some, the desert quest is to resolve discontinuity and seek an ultimate unity. For the Egyptians, along the predictable Nile, stability, symmetry, and coherence ruled the cosmos. For the Hebrew fathers, however, there was no afterlife, no access to God beyond prayer, and no intrinsic order on earth.

History is a collective memory of the past that denies the telluric dimension of place. History was the only way to keep myth while holding that the desert was no more than a stage.[9] Eventually its authoritarian, masculinist, ascetic ideology would spread into the cities themselves, defeating the feminine mysteries associated with riverine and oasis agriculture, a victory for transcendence over the natural and indigenous.

Though important to the roots of Western spiritual life, the desert for the Hebrews was not valued as a place. It was a vacuum, idealized as a state of disengagement and alienation, a symbol of the condition of the human spirit. Its physiological potency for visionary ecstasy is evident in the lives of holy men, from the prebiblical patriarchs to Moses, Jesus, Mohammed, and thousands of pilgrims, hermits, monks, and their followers.[10]

This purist or puritan heritage ranges throughout Western religious inspiration, an idealism constantly threatened by the telluric powers of heathen cults, is irrepressible as weeds. However much seasonal festival and mythic intuition the Jew and Christian clung to in their daily lives, the dominant thrust of the West was, at bottom, estrangement and abstraction.[11]

Perhaps something of the same can be said for monotheism itself. As theory, it persists with the capacity to outlive and undercut liturgical practices. Like the demythologized world, a one-god cosmos may be beyond the sustained capacity of the normal individual. "The creed of Sinai tore up the human psyche by its most ancient roots," writes George Steiner. God became as "blank as the desert air," and "the Judaic summons to perfection" was so impossible as to be a "blackmail of transcendence."[12] Steiner attempts to account for the persecution of the Jew and the Holocaust as examples of the periodic outbursts of revenge against the originators of monotheism.

	MYTH		TWO VIEWS OF LIFE:
	The Nature of Life	Eternal and recurring patterns, to which fertility and fatality are crucial, hence death is positive and recyclic. Time is synchronous: the past and future are enfolded in the present. Metamorphosis is central but oriented to stability rather than change.	Nothing is fortuitous. The principles of totality, predictability, and regularity are important. Nature and culture are in sacred symbiosis; alien cultural systems are merely different expressions of that same embeddedness. Man is at home in the world.
	The Earth and the Cosmos	God takes multiple forms and the sacred appears in all areas of life. Nature has many clues to divinity, and there also exists a culture-divinity continuum. God embodies institutions, and in them shrines, forms, images, and art are central. Life	reanimates a larger cosmographic scheme. Man participates in this according to an epigenetic level of responsibility. Terrain forms, graves, and other sacred places reflect telluric and autochthonous forces.
	The Basis of Knowing	All men possess an oral preunderstanding, an intuition extending from their own bodies. Mnemonic thought is applied to an analyzable world in an avidity for parallels, ritually enacted and celebrated. Science is concrete, enlarging meaning; nature offers clues to logos. Binary speculation and systems of difference are	fundamental. Metaphor is the mode of divine access; forms are metaphors of powers. Myth is inseparable from ideology and morality. The record is mythopoetic, oral, and musical. Estrangement of the individual is only an interval in an integrative rite.

MYTH AND HISTORY

		HISTORY
Emphasis is on diachronicity and linear change in time. The world is more provisional, contingent, and even random in its patterns. The purpose of life is not evident in nature, so that nature and culture are either oppposed or categorized as science and history. Strangeness, estrangement, and fragmenta-	tion are characteristic. Doctrines and cults rise and fall; other cultures are mocked as erroneous. Masculine and feminine seem to be opposing. Society sees itself as nomadic, pastoral, and patriarchal. The causes and purposes of things are not inherent in them.	*The Nature of Life*
God is apart from the world and institutions, including art and culture. God is arbitrarily unlocalized and his actions are intrusive, unexpected interruptions. Events are linked in disparate	strata of time. God is not in nature, nor is truth multiple. Guilt and a sense of deserved disaster are part of the "thouness" of history. Myth is seen as a shield from the truth.	*The Earth and the Cosmos*
Understanding is dialectical, Platonic, or ideological. God gives messages to chosen spokesmen, and they are not repeated. Kinship is less important than chosenness. Meaning comes from prophecy or dramatic, broken, probing, or literary inter-	pretation. Metaphor and ritual and art are peripheral. All meaning is precarious and unique. "The beginning" has literal rather than homological significance. Personal affects are skepticism, alienation, and self-analysis.	*The Basis of Knowing*

NOTE: Based on Herbert Schneidau, *Sacred Discontent* (Berkeley and Los Angeles: University of California Press, 1977).

What is it about human psychology that finds monotheism intolerable? David Miller believes that polytheistic religious experience means being gripped by a story in which the diversity of the many characters is "the symbolic expression of a lively process." The gods and goddesses "teach us an acceptance of the variousness of ourselves and others." The monotheistic search for a single sense of identity makes us feel guilty for not getting it all together, which is impossible in a plural universe. Thinking is polytheistic, "a reality in which truth and falsity, life and death, beauty and ugliness, good and evil are forever and inextricably mixed together." The powers and forces are dramatically revealed in an acceptable way. The story form keeps what James Hillman calls "the feeling function" alive, harmonizing the "in here" with the "out there."

If he cannot find evidence for a single center in a diverse world, the monotheist feels lost, experiences a disconnectedness, and senses the "death of God," which is to say, the deadness of abstraction. Belief divorced from tangible support is tiring, dull, out of touch. Theology becomes "irrelevant to faith and philosophy irrelevant to everything." Miller concludes that monotheism socially becomes fascism, imperialism, or capitalism; philosophically it is unmetaphorical, unambiguous, and dichotomous; and psychologically it is rigid, fixed, and linear.[13]

Miller's polytheism in the service of a lively narrative contains not simply a heterogeneous collection of gods, but a sequence of "worlds of being and meaning in which my personal life participates." These are not merely reflected aspects of the psyche, but the means by which thought is divinized and the earth sacralized, modeling not a one-and-many but a multivalenced world. History, however plural, is not concerned with multiple bases of an ongoing creativity or the spiritual significance of concrete diversity, but with an account of events subordinated to a single divinity. It is, says Miller, inadequate as an explanation for the way our experience actually feels; it does not link up coherently. Out of our desperation we grasp at any center that gives pattern and meaning. Ideology is born: dialectic belief, religious or secular, that fills a vacuum in the absence of religious enculturation based on lifelong immersion, with its preunderstanding continuously confirmed by sensory experience and the logic of natural relationships.

Ideology, according to Louis J. Halle, is ultimately defined as the "us against them" mentality.[14] It is the expression, often social, of an implacable and irrational dualism. It is especially powerful in desert lands because the desert seems to confirm a law of opposition to the senses, despite ideology's own scorn for such natural reference. The "cradle of civilization" is also the cradle of fanatic ideology—witness the interminable wars, large and small, that boil across its deserts. The ideologist pursues not only an idea to live by but to die and kill for, horribly distorting juvenile loyalty to kin and adolescent conformity and idealism. Perhaps this is the meaning of Kenneth Rexroth's snort that "the entire Judeo-Christian-Muslim period in human history has been an episode of unparalleled perceived and social psychosis and international barbarity."[15]

The logic that blames the Hebrews who invented monotheism for all its effects is, of course, unreasonable. The Christians, the Persian cults, the Platonic-Aristotelian Greeks, and the Dark Ages of Europe worked the idea toward its bitter ends. At first, the payoff of the Hebrew prophetic tradition, like that of all minority extremists, had been security, in spite of the felt impotence. It required centuries of devoted effort to realize the either/or possibilities of monotheism and the desert fringes as its appropriate setting. Paradise before the Fall, Paul's rapture, and the celestial realm all became interchangeable, as opposed to the real world, the desert, which represented sin, according to Basil (d. 379) and Gregory (d. 390). Persian duality helped the Christians transform all ambiguity into opposition instead of metaphor. The efforts of religious energy to reanimate the cosmos merely had the effect thereafter of creating sides, populated with demons and devils on one hand and saints and angels on the other. Augustine saw the desert itself as a war. Animals represented evil. The anchorites, like their modern fundamentalist heirs, were eager to fight devils "in the freedom of the vast wilderness," according to John Cassian (d. 435), in order "to find that life which can be compared to the bliss of angels." The hermit-animal traditions, involving Jerome (d. 420) and John the Baptist, meant subduing that ferocity which was supposed to have resulted from the Fall.

As the Testaments went northwest into Europe, so did the desert. Internalized after a thousand years, it became a necessary adjunct to evangelical desacralizing of place and to the demythologizing of the pagan tribes of the north. The concept of the wilderness became for the West the umbrella beneath which the divine discontent of the desert and the gothic fears of the northern forest could be lumped.[16] Christian evangelism would invent such sweeping condemnations of nature as the Christians progressed from a rural minority toward urban power and urban thinking.

The relationship of the desert environment to the Western myth of history, to monotheism, and to ideology seems to invoke a debate about environmental determinism, but such a debate is no longer possible, for it was grounded in the defunct idea of the early twentieth century that genetical inheritance and the experience of the individual were opposing or competing forces, that the history of culture had something to do with escape from instinct and nature. The real difficulty with the discussion of the relationship of history to place is that the question is framed in an historical mode that has already decided the issue. History is inimical to compliance with nature, having arisen in a tragic perspective of man against nature, or nature as neutral. Using nature as a parable of politics, it sees all events in ideological texts.[17] Determinism is itself a linear, causal concept, an historical rather than cybernetic way of thinking. It is as though it were invented in order to overstate the role of natural control in human matters, which are then seen, in reaction, as matters of choice, chance, or supernatural intervention.

The Hebrew inventors of history did perceive accurately: the earth gods did not save the Sumerians from recurring disaster. Why now should we therefore find their transcendental vision any more at fault than that of the cybernetic, mythic peoples? Certainly not directly on ecological grounds. A score of Neolithic cultures decimated the ecosystems they occupied in spite of their attunement to the seasons, to the auguries of plants and animals, and to their rituals of soil and place. It is ontogeny rather than ecology of which we must speak.

What the desert fathers—in the form of history, Hebrews, patriarchs, and monotheists—did to the ontogeny of the person must be seen in the context of the swaths already cut by agriculture. Those were in the psychological debilitations of diminished maternal care in large families and in the loss of wildness and otherness from the juvenile's world. The desert fathers, like their Arabic, pastoral models, scourged adolescence. They could amputate and cauterize pubertal epigenesis because they would further transform the relationship of the infant to its mother.

Having taken the desert vacancy as its sensorium and the nomadic pastoralist Arabs as paradigmatic fathers, the Hebrews and their spiritual cousins could not have escaped the consequences. For example, the price of patriarchy is that it "denies to the woman and the child any weight, any autonomy, and any reality. The only serious world is that of the adult male. . . . It is the function of social customs and rites which surround birth, weaning, circumcision, excision— all forms of passage, in short—to prolong this fact, to accentuate it, to acknowledge it—or rather, on the contrary, to conjure it away, to liquidate it, and to make all traces of it disappear. . . . The world of mothers will be buried in the depths of an idealized past, and enveloped in fantasies. . . . This is what permits the unmasking of nature's mysteries and the decoding of her signs, as well as the annulment of the prohibitions which cover nature," says A. Bouhdiba on Arab-Muslim society.[18]

Landscapes, in such an abstract world, tend to become symbols of ideas. George Williams has traced out the transformation of "wilderness" and "paradise" into states of mind. The Puritans, especially the Protestants, made much of the idea of paradise. The word itself comes from the Persian for "garden" and is a forerunner of the idea of utopia. It has been interpreted as a Muslim expression of a land of "instinctual gratification" dominated by the pleasure principle.[19] For the Christians, its ambiguity works its way into the very center of the idea of the Fall, in which their scorn for sensual gratification, as experienced by Adam, marks their swing toward repression. But the ambiguity about paradise was there long before the first Christian.

The over-mothered infant in patriarchal society and, among boys, their severance from the world of women exploits the theorizing openness of the adolescent. In him the dream of paradise will be nourished by that loss and will feed his fantasies and his hopes for the future. Its emotional intensity will also heat the opposite of paradise, the wilderness. Yet the two, in their polarity, have analogous points in purity and remoteness, in their romantic perfection. The quality of this remote yet yearned-for purity is native to the state of adolescence itself, and bears to adolescence a functional psychological role.

Peter Blos, Norman Kiell, Anna Freud, Erik Erikson, and many others have described the characteristic subjectivity and behavior of adolescence.[20] Perhaps the most peculiar of these features is a regression to certain infantile traits: playfulness with sound making and word meanings; body sensibilities and self-consciousness; "acting out" of feelings and emotions; extreme variability and instability of moods; a reinvigorated fraternal and paternal attachment; and fantasies of power and heroics. In addition, the adolescent typically is preoccupied with larger questions: the meaning and purpose of life; concepts of infinity, space, time, and God; and the ideal human relationship and community. Piaget speaks of this as a formal or abstract level; others call it symbolic thought.

Much of this is familiar and common knowledge. Yet, in an historical-existentialist society the right questions may not be asked. Adolescent behavior can be made to seem a response to the circumstances in which a youth finds himself: the uncertainty and choices faced by the subadult, the somewhat irresponsible status granted him by adults, and the ambivalent experience of being between childhood and maturity, like a melon not quite ripe.

In the light of human evolution, however, the adolescent traits can be seen not only as symptoms of a growth spurt or as adjustments to social limbo, but as a highly specialized process of emergence. In small-group, tribal societies, adolescence is perceived as a gestation followed by the birth of the adult. The whole group is intimately involved in this process. Mircea Eliade, the eminent scholar of comparative religions, has described its basic format, even though its details vary among different societies: the ceremonial death of the child, the acquisition of new skills and knowledge, the new capacity to endure and suffer, rites of rebirth in initiation, and a vision quest. Central to these administrations is attention to his indigenous desire for cosmic understanding and profound devotion.[21] Because his comprehension of the religious significance and origins of life can only be grasped metaphorically, the language of these ultimate matters is mythopoetic, based on metaphors from concrete experience, especially, says Joseph Campbell, the "imprints of infancy."[22]

The adolescent becomes psychologically infantlike on his own in order to be reborn culturally as an adult. Each of the infantile behaviors lends itself in some appropriate way to this transition. The so-called primary thought and infantile self-centeredness of the first months of life serve as a state of mind from which wider relationships are developed, as they will be again in adolescence, on a new plane. It is not the infant's fantasy of omnipotence or its love/hate feelings toward its mother, but its movement beyond that duality that is crucial to the successful outcome of adolescence. Graduation from the mother matrix into the larger sphere of a maternal earth matrix in early childhood is the basis for good, concrete object relationships and is also part of the later adolescent graduation exercise into adult status. The wordplay and poetry-mindedness of the adolescent and his new sensitivity to symbolic thought moves him away from the classifications of concrete reality—of animals, plants, weather, rocks, planets, and water—that had been the central tasks of speech in childhood.

Like land birds instinctively setting out on transoceanic migration, given assurance, so to speak, from the experience of the species that there is land on the other side, the human adolescent organism reenters the dangerous ground of immature perception on the premise that society is prepared to meet his psychic demands for a new landing—that is, that society is organized to take these refractory youths through a powerful, tightly structured gestation; to test, teach, reveal; to offer, as Erikson says, things worthy of their skill; to tutor their suffering and dreaming; and to guide their feelings of fidelity. If the infancy to which they look for an exemplary protocol of growth has been blighted, or if the adult group is not prepared to administer the new and final birth, then the youths create autistic solutions to their own needs and, prolonging the quest of their adolescence, sink finally, cynically, back into their own incompetent immaturity, like exhausted birds going down at sea.

The scenario created by Western cultures was different, however. The kind of society sought by the Hebrew prophets repudiated the nature-lore parts of a developmental process by which maternal connections are subjectively transferred to the earth, subsequently locking their alienated youth into the intense idealism of adolescence without the intermediary experience of belonging to Mother Earth. The loss of mother thwarts a middle factor, plunging the individual forever into infantile dualism, without a connecting ground that melts the alternatives of either hating the protective, nourishing She who abandoned him or fixedly adoring the feminine in the guise of his own mother's face, to the detriment of his capacity to establish a mature relationship with the other sex or with any Other. This prolonged, crippling disease of attention and the fantasies of omnipotence as they ripen in adolescent idealism, perhaps more than any other traits, mark the desert-fringe civilizations.

This faulty developmental scenario separates society from the rhythms of natural life and substitutes a critical posture toward all schematizing. Events erupt into history. There is no preunderstanding in the Hebraic prophetic archetype of fiction, in Attic probing of tragedy, in Socratic isolation, or in Greek self-scrutiny. In time, art and science became data-making instead of tools in myth and ritual. Fictional literature, the art form most peculiar to the descendents of the desert mind, is, says Herbert Schneidau, a defamiliarizing, dissolving solvent that, unlike myth, has a unique plot development and end, as well as an individual author and point of view. It is, like history, a probe that deconstructs, serving ideology in its verification by conviction.

The one-sided domination of Western cultural style by masculine values is typical of mounted nomadic peoples and was adopted and reformulated by the Hebrew fathers. Their sexual chauvinism is more or less true of the Neolithic as a whole. Even though the sedentary societies of the ancient world (including that side of Hebrew life) were locked in wonder at the powerful mysteries of place and soil, they were politically dominated by males.

The alternatives of male- or female-centered philosophy may seem in our time to be ideological forces to be adjusted by education, but their respective ascendency waxes and wanes in the psychological development of the child. In traditional tribal peoples, the prepubertal youth is commonly separated from his mother in order to undergo a new birth designed by men, as the first was by women, with the goal of moving the candidate toward a more holistic and polar complementarity between the sexes. It is the theme of this book that the individual is inherently mentally and emotionally tuned to those shifts in focus. The adolescent is prompted by his own intrinsic mood changes to be away from his mother's control. Then everything depends on what the mentors do, for they may, on the historical side, prolong, exaggerate, and make conscious an adult model derived from the pubertal child's tendency to dichotomize the sexes; or they may, on the mythic side, elaborate the separatism temporarily in order to further the purposes of an ultimate integration.[23] The novice's initiatory exercises and other educational experiences may strongly influence whether he proceeds psychologically and philosophically to a mature integration. Perhaps society and the individual are more vulnerable to an arrested development fixated on masculinity, rather than on femininity, for two reasons: first, the preoccupation with male forms and fathering is the last of alternated male/female phases before maturity; and second, the physical domination of all societies by men can mislead the immature-minded into thinking that patriarchal values and ideals are synonymous with universal power.

The task of adolescence is to become whole at a new level of consciousness. The individual is deeply aware of this, though it is not clear to him what that means or how it is to be done. When teachers and counselors take him away from the household, they create the conditions in which the potential adult within him can be realized. But his new circumstances can mislead the individual into thinking that the changes that he feels to be urgent are to be made in the outer world. If in some way (such as the denial of the natural world as a language or the truncation of myth) the overall process is frustrated, the youth may remain stuck in the notion that his ideal can only be achieved by reforming the world.[24] Since any number of possible ways of doing that may be imagined, each supported by verbal logic, he is persuaded by his own limited judgment—first by one system of ideas, then another. His compulsion to succeed feeds mainly on his own sense of internal disharmony. Such an ideologist is a poor mentor, as he will perpetuate his own adolescent obsessions and thwarted rites of passage and guide his charges toward ideological choices.[25]

Because of his "fight with nature" the man of the desert must strike aggressively, says Watsuki Tetsuro.[26] After the model of the herdsman moving his flocks to wherever the grass is, the Westerner (like all men) enacts his own idea of the sacred in his life. A god, jealous and vengeful, who makes incursions into nature and human affairs is like the Arab herdsman or Assyrian horseman, sweeping things clear, testing his alliances. The fanatical idealist and his cynical alter ego see the world as a stage, fascinated by their self-image.[27]

To such pseudoequestrians the world is a designed set, says the writer Charles Lapham, speaking of this raiding aspect of our modern society in his essay "The Melancholy Herd." Democracy is a "pastoral wandering through a department store" where expectations of power and wealth by the Bedouin-like American are like grass greening. Most noteworthy is the short span of attention, a transient-mindedness so dominated by moving on that even the modern city is merely a camp, its inhabitants fixated on change and fear of permanence. The transient mind is dominated by an interior desert of alienation, disappointment, self-hopelessness, and insignificance, for which war, prophecy, and visions are palliative. To those for whom wealth has literally sprung from the earth like milk from a teat, there is at best a poor sense of the cost of things, the value of work or of soil. Politics are like gossip, leadership inseparable from celebrity. The melancholy effect of all this is a hopeless desire for more than the world offers.[28]

Lapham portrays our aristocratic desert-mindedness as a catalog of childishness, a sort of teenybopper frothiness and macho juvenile vapidity clearly not synonymous with the seriousness of the Hebrew desert fathers. They would have been scandalized at our scatter-brained yet patrician ignorance of history, our dabbling pursuit of entertainment and accumulation of things. Yet the similarity of Americans to mandarin Bedouins is neither accidental nor due to direct cultural heritage. It incorporates that body of adolescent traits and pastoral attitudes first assimilated into Western consciousness by Hebrew prophets and later reworked and secularized by Greek philosophers and modern Protestants. It is dominated by themes of alienation, disengagement, and unrelatedness—hence chaos.[29]

It is not my contention that the pubertal child (or, for that matter, the infant in whom the adolescent is immersed retroactively) is himself alienated; the ten-year-old with a moderately good nurturing is happily at home in the world. Pediatrician Arnold Gessell describes him in almost beatific terms. In the West, it is the failure of the adolescent's religious mentors in the succeeding four or five years to translate his confidence in people and the earth into a more conscious, more cosmic view, in which he broadens his buoyant faith to include the universe. The amputation of nature myths causes a grievous dislocation, for which he will seek, in true questing spirit, an explanation in terms of "ultimate" reality. He does not become an alienated person until he can give some logic to his flawed relationship to the world. The fiction granted him by the pseudopastoral desert philosophy of the West is that his painful incompleteness is the true mature experience and that the meaninglessness of the natural world is its meaning. In itself, this philosophy is merely inadequate, no worse than other intellectual dead ends. But, acted upon, it wounds us, and we wound the planet. The injury to normal individual development passed on to Western culture by Hebrew ascetics, their puritan emulators, and the Greek demythologizers persists at the root of our assumptions and attitudes about the world. The child's development is not aided by the intellectual masters of the West who control secondary education and are, in their turn, products and arbiters of a desolated adolescent quest.

The central dogma of the West insisted on a separation of spiritual matters from the phenomena of nature. Such a view is sustained not only by formal dogma, but by impairing the orchestrations of the growth of each generation. It is the philosophical expression of that phase of subadult life when the world seems abruptly altered and decentered, when the purposes of childhood have become irrelevant, and the bindings linking the adolescent as an adult to an awesome and complex new home are not yet perceived. Arrested at that point, denied the methectic workings and mythopoetic vision of man in nature, he will for the rest of his life struggle with existential problems that are normally the work of a few critical years in his second decade of life. I do not mean that the adolescent normally gains instant wisdom, but that the framework of nature as metaphoric foundation for cosmic at-homeness is as native to the human organism in its adolescent years as any nutritive element in the diet.

Lacking this framework, he will always lack true reverence for the earth. The remaining choices for a logic of creation are an otherworldly orientation, materialist exploitation, or existentialist absurdity. The first calls upon an abstraction that lacks the psychological resources in the concrete, natural, named, and structured world of the juvenile matrix, the foundation for later metaphors, and regresses to the infant's schizoid fears of the loss of the good and bad mother. The second is fixated on juvenile literalness. The last builds its view upon a fragmented, meaningless world like that seen by the blind who are suddenly healed by surgery, like the barren, phenomenal world of the newborn.

In the developmental spiral of epigenesis, the clues to the meaning of things and events in each new matrix are in terms of those of the old. The landscape, for example, is given coherence by the preceding experience of the body and the mother's face, just as face and body had made sense in harmony with the rhythms, tastes, sounds, and cuddled comfort that were predicted by the womb. Biologically, this sequence proceeds to the final commencement, adolescent entry into a world of invisible realities anticipated by and including the physical terrain, its coherence emerging from the collective meanings that preceded it. Thus the normal regression of the adolescent at the brink of a mature vision revivifies and transforms the three archetypes—womb, body-face, and natural world. Each will in some way be available as images and reenactments by which his particular culture portrays the universe.

In Western pseudopastoralism, however, the desert is noplace; nature is a limbo (to the later puritans an evil snare). This view devastates the child's organizing work in two directions: it tends to diminish the potential of his understanding of social relationships by excluding the tangible nuances of events in nature that, by analogy, enrich early familial experience; and it sheds no symbolic light on the larger cosmos. The beneficiaries of eye surgery are usually subject to intense anxiety; the longer they have been blind, the more likely they are to abandon the pursuit of visual meaning and lapse into knowing by sound and touch.[30] Crawling babies explore the natural world joyously and fruitfully only if their mothers are reassuring and encouraging. If their mothers are overcautious and anxious, the child becomes fixated on the mother's emotion, reflects her fear and uncertainty, and instead of organizing a new matrix in the land, mechanically adopts the mother's fearful attitudes.[31]

The broken sequence of mental growth fostered by the fathers of the West cannot be represented simply as a bad link in an otherwise healthy chain. Unreconstructed adolescents make bad mothers and bad fathers. The parent whose oversimplified view of things places the natural world on a lower plane or in opposition to the social world will express this anxious, schizoid attitude in many ways to his children and will fail to make occasions for their own healthy growth beyond it. Humans intuitively see analogies between the concrete world out there and their own inner world. If they conceive the former as a chaos of anarchic forces or as dead and frozen, then so will they perceive their own bodies and society; so will they think and act on that assumption and vindicate their own ideas by altering the world to fit them; and so will they rear their children.

TEN

The Virgin Dream

THE SPIRITUAL EFFECT of the wilderness runs deeper than any other encounter in nature. Great distances and vast empty spaces, impenetrable forests and mighty waves suggest the power and omniscience of the supernatural, a presence ultimate and final, somehow more real than small-scale places, closed yards with apple trees and sparrows. To those who sit by the lone sea breakers come the heartbreaking terror and the mantle of prophecy, the ecstasy of divine fear, and the sudden, awful awareness of self in space and time.

Our response to the sight of the Grand Canyon is deeply moving, a romantic experience. Yet in the Western world that experience has had little to do with formal philosophy in general. Religious thought has not seriously entertained the notion that man in the wilderness is any closer to God. Pantheism is generally regarded as obscuring the ancient Hebrew foundation of Christianity, that God is not of this world. This creation of two worlds where there had been one was begun by the leap of Mediterranean pagan gods onto Olympus and from there into the sky from the disenchanted terrestrial earth, and it was completed in the eighteenth century when Immanuel Kant launched the ship of existentialism, of indeterminism, setting men and their egos apart from nature. In those lands where the gods have not yet leaped, missionaries continue to cleanse primitive minds of demons and to separate spirituality from nature and earth from heaven, and everywhere technology demonstrates that nature is merely the stuff from which men create worlds.

But the human heart is fickle. No creed absolutely disavows guidance, divine or otherwise, in nature, however much it etherealizes human experience. Many of my naturalist friends are quick to assume that Christianity is a mortal enemy of the love and protection of nature, but much depends on which saint, which emphasis or doctrine is attended to. As Charles Raven, in his *Natural Religion and Christian Theology,* has pointed out, Christianity is full of ambivalence.[1] It has absorbed the mythopoetic wisdom of whole cultures and pagan ceremonies. The great moments of inspiration and decision in Christian history occur in certain landscapes. Although Christianity is the great enemy of the natural world, it also contains the most extreme love of nature. It is surprisingly flexible, as Robert Redfield discovered in the Yucatán, where Christianity is smoothly interwoven with indigenous pagan gods and the worship of limestone sinkholes. It has the hybrid vigor of multiple origins. The Augustine-Pauline ascetic fires pasteurized Christian theology, denigrating the body, depreciating the animal nature of man—in short, denying life. It was the greatest effort in history to reduce the aim of human existence to abstractions and shadows. Yet no religious ideal could exclude the vitality of organic existence for long. Pagan gods reentered Christianity ever more rapidly after the ninth century. Ancient calendars, holidays, names, the classical heroes disguised in biblical garb, art— all came slowly back. However thinly disguised and crudely readapted, they imparted new earthiness and vigor to a system of belief that had become too ascetic for large numbers of people, too unreal in the sense that most people will always mean reality. By virtue of their patience and the validity of their conception, pagan spirits regained their place in the form of astrology, control of the calendar, and thereby the daily and seasonal workings of the universe.

One extraordinary effect of this secular resurgence within Christianity has been the transfer of our feeling of awe from sky spirits to stars and planets and then to earth. Esthetics was derived from religious experience, adapting from it a mode of feeling that is now commonly assumed to be part of a normal response to great events, works of art, and grand scenery. The division of the universe into heaven and earth had separated God from this world as surely as the other planets were distinct from earth. At the beginning of the Middle Ages, "sublime" referred to God, his angels, to the heavenly bodies and their mythologies. With the renewed study of the heavens by Copernicus, Kepler, Galileo, and Newton, who did not separate science and religion, a step toward the reunion of heaven and earth was taken. Galileo firmly believed in the efficacy of prayer in his work and in that work as a form of revelation. That terrible embarrassment that the Church refused to face—that the universe was composed of suns and planets of which the earth was merely one—nonetheless implied that the earth was a typical planet and a clue to the splendid mystery of other planets and the sublime events of the sky. The earth was, then, itself a sublime heavenly body.

This perspective encouraged a vision of the earth as a whole and descriptions of the earth's surface as if seen from a great height. The landscapes by Patinir are views seen by a bird, god, or angel. Birds had long been considered among the most mercurial and esthetic of forms. An imaginary flight was an excellent vehicle for new geographic descriptions and new literature. Renaissance humanism and medicine affected the new geological-astronomical study, by descriptive analogy comparing physical entities to the human body (mountains were symbols of pride or "pregnant" with minerals). Psychology emerged as the study of sensation, of feelings, and as an attitude of speculation, adding a new kind of self-conscious or self-analytic esthetic to the tradition of visionary flights and voyages whose imagery was a flight through the sky or an ocean voyage.

The early panoramic landscape paintings have been called "Christian optimism," appreciations of the richness and diversity of the world created by God for man. That world was worth knowing for itself, as well as a source of knowledge about the universe. Naturalists such as Konrad von Gesner, travelers after Polo and Mandeville and the ecclesiastics to whom pictures no longer seemed heathenish, as the medieval church had regarded them, and historians and geographers all engaged in a delineation of the world's great places and events.

Then and now the desert provided the purest sublime experience, so acute that even tourism with its evasive maneuvers could not ameliorate its raw intensity. Aldous Huxley examined the metaphor of the desert as that purest gleam at the heart of religious insight. Boundlessness and emptiness are the two most expressive symbols of an attributeless Godhead, in whom we sink with Meister Eckhart "from nothingness to nothingness." These spatial metaphors are abundant in religious literature, silence and emptiness as symbolic of divine immanence. Judaism and Christianity originated in or near deserts. Their imagery lives on, strangely transformed in temperature climates, taught in Sunday school to children who have never seen a desert. One of the anomalies of modern concepts of nature is an imagery often inappropriate, obsolete or at best exotic. Yet, out of the wreck of that obsolescence rises the inspiration to fit new environments such as man-made wastes.

A grand view of earth is also had from a mountaintop. The shifting of attention in the late Middle Ages from the sky to the earth was signified by Petrarch's famous fourteenth-century ascent of Mt. Ventoux, the idea for which he may have taken from Dante. Modern tourism was far away and Petrarch's lively curiosity wilted abruptly as he sat on the mountain, the price of looking down instead of up. Petrarch took Augustine's *Confessions* along. While on the summit he read, "And men go forth, and admire lofty mountains and broad seas, and roaring torrents, and the ocean, and the course of the stars, and forget their own selves while doing so." That stung Petrarch for his worldliness and he scurried guiltily down.

Men had lived on mountains before, to find seclusion and send their thoughts flying upward, as at the Thessalian Meteora, the honeycombed cliffs in Spain, and the cliffs of Africa's Thebaid. After Petrarch there was secular climbing to escape the city's turmoil and to survey the countryside, to permit the exploring eye to rove like a wandering hawk, perhaps to relish the sensation of personal smallness and insignificance in the face of cosmic power and omniscience.

A disciple of Erasmus, the naturalist Konrad von Gesner, wrote in 1541:

> I have determined, as long as God gives me life, to ascend one or more mountains every year when the plants are at their best—partly to study them, partly for exercise of body and joy of mind. . . . I say then that he is no lover of nature who does not esteem high mountains very worthy of profound contemplation. It is no wonder that men have made them the homes of Gods, of Pan and the nymphs. . . . I have a passionate desire to visit them.

But it was to be another century and a half before Gesner's views were widely shared. Then it was not from the motive of the naturalist, which in turn was part of the joy and discovery of nature, but by way of travel esthetics. More typical of Gesner's time is the sentiment of Richard Lassells, who wrote almost nothing of mountain scenery in his widely read guidebook *The Voyage of Italy* except for a paltry paragraph on a climb to the crater of Vesuvius: "With much ado we got to the top of the hill; and peeping fearfully (remembering Pliny's accident) into the great hollow from the brink of it, found it to be like a vast kettle. . . . Having gazed a while at this chimney of Hell (for Tertullian calls Aetna and Vesuvius *Fumariola inferni*) we came down faster than we went up."

After his visit to the Alps in 1671, a cosmologist, Thomas Burnet, revived a twelfth-century theory that the earth was originally egg-like, its shell was broken by the weight of the deluge. A furious controversy surrounded Burnet's *Sacred Theory of the Earth*, with its account of the origin of mountains as tilted fragments of the earth's crust, fractured by the Flood. At this time the heights of mountains were enormously exaggerated. Speculation over the origin of fossils added to the contention. The subject was further complicated by the popular analogy of the earth to a human body, likening earth's interior to intestines and arteries, mountains to bones. All this contentious speculation helped make Europeans conscious of mountains.

Burnet wrote, "Places that are strange and solemn strike an awe into us and incline us to a kind of superstitious Timidity and Veneration." He was "rapt" and "ravished" by the vast panoramas. Marjorie Nicolson observes that his work, though intended to be scientific and theological, was even more important to esthetics.[2] He established a new way of seeing mountains. Since mountains were pieces of the earth's crust, the earth was nothing more than a "broken and confused heap of bodies, the rubbish of a great ruin. . . . What can have more the Figure and Mien of a Ruin than Craigs, and Rocks, and Cliffs? . . . all these Caves and blind Recesses . . . say but they are a Ruin and you have in one word explained them all . . . our cities are built upon ruins and our fields and countries stand upon broken arches and vaults." In the confusion of the rocks and disorder of caves, Burnet found a magnificence that haunted his imagination, though it was contrary to the esthetic axiom that proportion and symmetry were the ultimate measures of beauty.

Although others, such as Edward Norgate, anticipated the love of Alpine scenery early in the century, it was John Dennis, a literary critic crossing the Alps in 1688, who aptly phrased and organized Burnet's emotions as an esthetic:

> The ascent was the more easie, because it wound about the mountain. But as soon as we had conquer'd one half of it, the unusual heighth in which we found ourselves, the impending Rock that hung over us, the dreadful Depth of the Precipice, and the Torrent that roar'd at the bottom, gave us such a view as was altogether new and amazing. . . . In the mean time we

walk'd upon the very brink, in a litteral sense of Destruction; one Stumble, and both Life and Carcas had been at once des- troy'd. The sense of all this produc'd different motions in me, *vis.* a delightful Horrour, a terrible Joy, and at the same time that I was infinitely pleas'd I trembled. . . . I am delighted, 'tis true at the prospect of Hills and Valleys, of flowry Meads, and murmuring Streams, yet it is a delight that is consistent with Reason, a delight that creates or improves Meditation. But transporting Pleasures follow'd the sight of the *Alpes* . . . mingled with horrours and sometimes almost with despair.

Burnet was a link between the astronomers and the estheticians in apprehending the earth as a cosmic ruin, but it was Dennis who for- mulated this awareness in literary terms, who called the delightful horror of mountains "sublime" and who listed the sources of this elevated emotion: gods and angels, heavenly bodies, mountains, the four elements, wind, rivers, and the sea.

Dennis's superlatives and exuberant excitement make him sound like a voyager in fantasy. The "sublime" experience of the visionary refers to the more traditional meaning of the word, to the trans- ported feeling that usually takes the form of weightless aerial travel during a trance. "Transporting" unifies travel and rapture, the per- fect expression of the disembodied passage. Though shaped as an es- thetic, Dennis's sublime looked back to monastic martyrdom, exiled saints, and prophets in the wilderness. Isolation, abstinence, fasting, ritualistic chanting, sacred foods, flagellation, asphyxia, malnutri- tion are the stuff of which visions are made, or at least induced. Al- though landscape painting, like travel literature, depended upon the birth of an esthetic from a religious matrix, it has never separated itself completely from visionary (i.e., visual symbols of the uncon- scious) experience. Da Vinci's and Brueghel's and Patinir's mountains and whole landscapes by Giovanni di Paolo and Veneziano are vi- sionary in that sense.

The sublime has been called the esthetics of the infinite. As a result of the invention of the telescope and the secularization of Western culture, the sublime was adapted from God and the heavens to a cosmic vision of this world or to scenery of a certain kind. The two were combined in Milton's *Paradise Lost* in the view of the vastness and diversity of the world shown to Christ by Satan from a mountaintop. After his visit to the Alps in 1699 Joseph Addison devoted several issues of the *Spectator* to the vast, "confused," "rude" piles of rock he had seen. They were horrible, yet pleasurable. After him the poets frequently used astronomic or cosmic terms for terrestrial description. The cosmic voyage became the terrestrial excursion. Addison's introspection caused him to separate the sublime into intellectual and rhetorical. The intellectual was an actual confrontation of vast objects; the rhetorical, a vicarious, pleasurable horror from literary imagination or looking at pictures of wild places. His contemporary Lord Shaftesbury insisted that the sublime did not properly have to do with literary style but with a profoundly moving experience and a sense of God. Both, particularly Addison, prepared the way for Englishmen to appreciate scenery on the Grand Tour, the tour that had begun in the sixteenth century as an educational gesture to the superiority of Italian culture by scholars and scions of noble families. By Addison's time the Grand Tour had become commonplace among the new gentry, the princes of industry, and among both sexes as a voyage amid classical remains, for seasonal escape from the English winter, and for social prestige. Dilettantes, connoisseurs, enthusiasts, and artists on their way to see the works of antiquity were exposed to the sublimity of Alpine passes.

Pictures played an important part in this education of "sensibilities." Throughout the seventeenth century Dutch limners were busy in England, and English travelers brought pictures home from the Grand Tour. Many Flemish paintings had Italianate scenery, preconditioning British eyes to wonderful and impossible notions of classical and Alpine landscapes. In the beginning of the century the wilderness and mountains were only backgrounds to figures. The Flemish retained the landscapes as they copied these Italian themes, but replaced the saints with rustic figures such as bandits. Pieter van Laar was an early exponent of this substitution, as was Adrian Van Diest, whose *Mountain Landscape* is a pictorial analogue of John Dennis's prose. Throughout the century the proportion of landscape over portrait paintings on English walls increased. After mid-century the English tourists particularly favored and collected the work of a Swiss-born Italian painter, Salvator Rosa.

Few of Rosa's landscapes are panoramic. They show sky beyond dark, windy subpromontories among the large rocky debris at the base of the upper slopes, cliffs bounding streams near their juncture with the valley floor, sparse trees thrusting through rocky outcrops with the flush valley soils adjacent. Figures—gods, angels, bandits—are very small. As bandits were no longer actually dangerous, Rosa found the freedom of their lives exciting. Just as the French nobility of the fourteenth century escaped courtly life by playing shepherd, Rosa escaped the seventeenth-century rational life by joining bandits. Both of these escapes are indicators of changing values and images of nature, one at the peak of neopastoralism and the other at the emergence of the wilderness esthetic.

Rosa's figures move along limestone cliffs, bent trees, rushing streams, and crumbling walls of the Apennines. The implication of escape and individual freedom is another of those anticipations by painters of cultural trends, in this instance anticipating the attitudes of Rousseau and Byron.

Thomas Burnet had described mountains as ruins, the chaotic detritus of the Fall. Ruins were pregnant with meaning in a world newly dedicated to the discovery of the glory of ancient Greece and Rome. Georges Louis de Buffon, the French naturalist, upon reading Burnet's *Sacred Theory* and knowing something of fossils, suggested that the day of creation would have to be pushed back at least twenty-five thousand years. Burnet said, "These mountains we are speaking of, to confess the truth, are nothing but great ruins; but such as show a certain magnificence in Nature; as from old temples and broken amphitheatres of the *Romans* we collect the greatness of that people." By 1700, antiquarians had been delving for two centuries among the ruins of that departed grandeur.

Early Italian paintings of the Madonna and child and the Magi are set amid the ruins of the heathen past, ruins that had completely taken over the scene and were transformed in meaning by the eighteenth century. The blasted tree and the broken wall had connoted death and decay since the beginning of the Renaissance, but these symbols now suggested the good life that had vanished, a wistful and melancholy thought. The broken rocks represented time slowly working the cycle of empire. The sweep and grandeur of the past uncovered by archaeology was reaching the imagination of that growing audience with a "classical" education. The pilgrimage to Rome took on a new aspect, a veneration for that pagan past and its relics in every ancient city. Of the seventeenth-century paintings of ruins owned by Englishmen, H. V. S. Ogden writes, "Probably no other kind of landscape except the prospect was more admired during the second half of the century."[3] Englishmen thereupon examined their own parishes with pensive pride for sublime scenes and objects. There followed a rebirth of interest in medieval history and Gothic architecture.

Excavations at Pompeii and Herculaneum began in the second quarter of the eighteenth century and by mid-century were widely known and followed in the press. John Dyer's poem "Ruins of Rome" described "Laturnae's wide champaign, forlorn and waste . . . solemn, wilderness . . . deep empty tombs, gloomy caverns, the mouldering wall . . . whose dust the solemn antiquarian turns." To Dyer the sewers were fantastic caverns and Sibylline grottoes. He and Samuel Bowden wrote a poem on Stonehenge, and other poets soon began to celebrate ruined abbeys and castles in Britain. The landscape architect William Kent stuck dead trees in his landscape parks. Pope admired old walls. Ruins and Gothic edifices were constructed in the new informal landscape gardens, or "gentlemen's parks."

The scientific study of the rhythmic pulsing of nature reinforced concepts of a cyclical history. Southern artists such as Claude Gellée of Lorrain and Nicolas Poussin painted landscapes with classical temples and mythological associations. In the north Rubens and Ruisdael emphasized the purely visual details of crumbling facades. In Germany the revival of interest in medieval life and architecture was in step with the Christian symbolism of decay and revival. The dead tree continued to appear as a form of ruin, complicated by its other functions as home for wild animals such as bees, as phallic symbol, and as the log home of wild man.

Catastrophe as well as time was the creator of ruins. Rosa painted stormy scenes. Naturalists reinterpreted storm and quake as natural processes instead of punishment meted out by an angry God. Literary and artistic mood pieces used them to communicate horror or terror. The Lisbon earthquake of 1775 provided a new theme for John Dyer, becoming an esthetic event through the medium of the sublime. So had the esthetic of the sublime evolved since Thomas Burnet considered ruins merely chaotic and ridiculed the idea that they had visual appeal. But the ruins of a "broken world" continued to be revealed in miniature. Burnet said, "They make a great noise, but they might all be apply'd to the ruins of an old Bridge fallen into the water," which was exactly what happened.

The suspenseful Gothic novel was full of hidden passages and secret places. Ancient hermitages were turning up in cliffs or under city streets. The imitation of such settings in architecture, gardening, poetry, and painting coincided with a renewed interest in hidden openings, especially underground channels and caves. Nicholson calls the grotto "a minor manifestation of the widespread interest in the secret places of the earth, the first appeal of which was more to novelty and irregularity."

From prehistoric times, caves have fascinated men. The sublime esthetic lent itself this complex heritage, impelled by a new interest in ruins with dark passages from room to room. The cave is a *transporting* experience. It is a mnemonic of certain experiences that we know from dreams, art, or the kinesthetic sense of our own bodily internal space, "the very bowels of the earth." Mythical and religious travels to the other world characteristically enter underground empires, labyrinths, hollow mountains, and voids so great that they display a peculiar similarity to the desert or the heavens at night. In spite of whatever the geologists may have found since the beginning of the seventeenth century about the natural origin of caves, the setting of Dante's *Inferno* remains valid because it affirms a profoundly interior experience.

The roasting of souls has a geographical basis as well as a biological one: the fiery torture of disease when disease was considered punishment. Volcanoes spouting fire were an affirmation of the nature of hell; it is no wonder that dragons belch fire too. Christianity would be different had mankind evolved at one of those periods of the earth's history when volcanism and mountain-building were at a minimum. Possibly there is also a relationship between sacred caves and the distribution of limestone rocks and the geography of mystery religions.

The fiery part of the subterranean body of the earth is related to fire on its surface. Fire provides a manifold stimulus; its infrared radiation penetrates deeply, euphorically. Burning wood radiates odor, sound, and heat. Visually the fire, like the bird and the tree, is one of the supremely mutable, symbolic, iconic forms.

Wirtschaft is the ancient practice of controlled burning in agriculture. It persists today in parts of Africa, Europe, and America. It is an hysterical anachronism, wasteful and profligate in a crowded world. It frees for new cycling the mineral nutrients in dead organic materials, but those elements become subject to erosion, and the burning of organic debris destroys humus, which is necessary to the soil. The vegetation on lands that are periodically burned is gradually reduced to heat- and drought-resistant plants. Woodlands in the temperate climates become parklike, as the forest slowly declines. The ecologist Sir Frank Frazier Darling suggests that the emotional furor associated with subtle seasonal changes in human behavior may be the most important factor in perpetuation of such fires.[4]

Hesiod postulated a golden age of innocence in Arcadia, followed by fall due to original sin. The alternative speculation, notably by Lucretius, was the elevation of man from barbarism by the discovery of fire. Greek and Egyptian mythology confirm the antiquity of this idea. Citing Lucretius and Vitruvius, Boccaccio led the revival of an evolutionary or progressive theory as opposed to divine creation and supervision. The visual expression of this idea from Boccaccio's *Genealogia Deorum* is to be found in the paintings by Piero di Cosimo, a fifteenth-century Florentine.

The art historian Erwin Panofsky interprets Piero di Cosimo's forest fires, wild melees between men, beasts, and half-men, and incidents from the lives of the gods with theories of the origin of man.[5] Drawing upon the *Physiologus,* beastiaries, and encyclopedias, Piero di Cosimo created an ethnology before modern archaeology, anthropology, or paleontology, looming behind which is the forest fire, background to the violence of prehistory.

Piero di Cosimo inverted the meanings of rocky or forested wilderness and pastoral valleys. To the Christian ascetic, desolation and sterility had been associated with virtuous rejection of the pursuit of riches and hedonism. "To Piero," says Panofsky, "the same contrast means antithesis between the merciless hardships of unmitigated wildness and the innocent happiness of a pastoral civilization. . . . While reconstructing the outward appearances of a prehistoric world, Piero seems to have re-experienced the emotions of primeval man, both the creative excitement of the awakening human and the passions and fears of the caveman and the savage." The two pastorals, the innocent and the corrupt, are, he says, Vergilian and Ovidian. It was not the latter's approach in Piero di Cosimo, nor was it a wistful nostalgia of the former, but a conviction that the pastoral environment propels the advance of civilization.

Piero di Cosimo himself was a recluse. He disliked the city, noise, the church, hot food, and was terrified by lightning. He refused to have the garden plants trimmed, the fruit picked, or his workshop cleaned. He enjoyed the rain and apparently lived on hard-boiled eggs, which were prepared in large numbers in order to save, or to avoid, lighting a fire.

Flames occurred in the fantastic landscapes by Hieronymus Bosch about 1490 and broke out subsequently in the work of Patinir, Lotto, Giorgione, and Brueghel. There are other fantastic aspects in the work of these men. Together with Dürer and Leonardo these are the authors of "the first pure landscapes" of modern times. They contain incredible jagged rocks or knotted trees, aerial perspective, and other visionary forms. The painting of sublime landscapes came forth all at once, as though some fullness of life, manifestly urgent, overflowed. The sublime was an emerging perception of nature, not a vogue, style, or art cycle.

The primeval forest was to the North what rocks were to the Mediterranean: the wilderness barrier—mysterious, antithetical to man, and awful. The forest's harshness is reflected in early Celto-Germanic epics, distinguishing them from the Egyptian *Book of the Dead* and the Greco-Roman hero tales. In Greek tragedy men were fortuitously caught between two groups of contending deities, while the Gothic man conceived of his soul as a battleground between the powers of light and darkness in which God's victory was a human victory. Broadly speaking, the vast cosmic schemes of the Mediterraneans contrasted to the northerners' examination of minute details in the natural world that make broader inferences and induction possible. Galileo against Leeuwenhoek, the Rubens landscape against that of Rosa. Yet, no such generalization can be wholly true. Even so, the Old Testament tradition is Gothic in some respects. The Hebrews, says Charles Raven, took delight in the detail of a beautiful country. The Aristotelian heritage (Gothic in the sense above) tended to prevent the raising of questions that interested Kepler and Galileo. Gesner in the sixteenth century took up the science of life where Aristotle left off with the intimate and corpuscular approach. The teeming panoramas of Brueghel and Bosch represent a reunion of classical universality through Augustine and Plato with the proto-Christian enjoyment of the smallest configurations of the natural world and indigenous northern interest in the surroundings, which would lead to such works as Gilbert White's *Natural History of Selbourne* and to Izaak Walton.

The twelfth to fourteenth centuries saw a ferment of the rediscovery of ancient mythology, the ravages of contemporary plagues and malnutrition and new observations mixed in the sculpted figures of the cathedrals. Nicolas Pevsner in *The Leaves of Southwell* descries the profuse evidence of new observations of the environment in the leafy forms in the decoration of the cathedral.[6] Such realistic forms expressed stability and confidence, while abstract sculpturing indicated a withdrawal toward fundamentals, away from the specific conditions of everyday life. A widespread latent natural history as well as mythology provided a wellspring for the artist and philosopher to draw from. The craftsmen in stone who created the plant and animal forms in the Gothic cathedral reflect a prodigious revolution in sentiment and perception.

The primeval forest, which disappeared as the cathedrals were built, the "Great Mother Forest," as historian Attilio Gatti has called it, provided the motif for the architectural conception of the Mother Church. The extraordinary similarities between the interior of a virgin deciduous forest and the nave of a Gothic cathedral are conspicuous. A metaphor of forms and spaces within suggests nostalgia and profound emotion linking cathedral and the post-Pleistocene woodland, especially, the fears and religious insights that Celtic and Germanic peoples bore from that extinct natural community. Even the mild folk tales that reach American children from Germany and England display the fineness with which the temperate humid forest was woven into culture. This image of the cathedral has perhaps been put most eloquently by Oswald Spengler:

> The character of the Faustian cathedral is that of the *forest*. The mighty elevation of the nave above the flanking isles, in contrast to the flat roof of the basilica; the transformation of the columns, which with base and capital had been as self-contained individuals in space, into pillars and clustered-pillars that grow up out of the earth and spread on high into an infinite subdivision and interlacing of lines and branches; the giant windows by which the wall is dissolved and the interior filled with mysterious light—these are the architectural actualizing of a world-feeling that had found the first of all its symbols in the high forest with its mysterious tracery, its whispering of ever-mobile foliage over men's heads, its branches straining through the trunk to be free of earth. Think of Romanesque ornamentation and its deep affinity to the sense of the woods. . . . The history of organ-building, one of the most profound and moving chapters in our musical history, is a history of longing for the forest, a longing to speak in that true temple of Western God-fearing.[7]

The wild forest was the desert of the north, the hibernal antithesis of domesticated landscapes. There were hermits in it, but the most spectacular human occupants were the wild men, those who had fallen from grace. The wild man in the Middle Ages, like all the rest of nature, was perceived as a symbolic and allegorical form of disorder. "Just as the wilderness is the background against which medieval society is delineated, so wilderness in the widest sense is the background of God's lucid order of creation," says Richard Bernheimer.[8] Connotations of wilderness widened in the Middle Ages to embrace "everything that eluded Christian norms." The wild man and the witch enjoyed storms and lived in the roughest parts of the forest. Then, as the Middle Ages waned and the ancient forest disappeared, where once it had been right to slay or capture him, it became fashionable to "slip into the wild man's garb" as a repudiation of the hierarchic order of society. Affirmation of the nobility of the wild man as an escape from civilized evils represented a changing attitude toward the wilderness itself.

However vulgar, affected, foppish, and sentimental, such ideas marked a change in the relationship of man to nature, a renewed human wonder at the natural world, a revolution that has not yet run its course. Theoretical attempts to account for this new sensitivity were themselves part of that growing self-consciousness. After Dennis and Addison came Frances Hutcheson's *Enquiry into the Origin of Our Ideas of Beauty and Order*, which dealt with "sensations," and William Hogarth's *The Analysis of Beauty*, which also talked about persons of "sensibility." Finally, in 1757, Edmund Burke codified the effects of visible objects on the "passions" in *A Philosophical Enquiry into the Origin of Our Ideas of the Sublime and Beautiful*. He divided experience into the Sublime and the Beautiful on the basis of "subconscious" associations. The Sublime was stimulated by fear or the instinct for self-preservation; the Beautiful, by desire or the instinct for procreation. The subconscious to Burke meant temporarily latent associations by which a certain idea produced emotional responses, open to rational analysis. The Sublime was terrible (the ocean or snakes), obscure (lurking druids in the dark woods), powerful (as the bull, horse, gloomy forest, or howling wilderness), deprived (darkness, solitude, and silence), vast (cliffs), magnificent (the sky), and infinite.

Burke formalized the landscape esthetic. Walpole's Gothic novel *The Castle of Otranto* was calculated to inspire it; Dante was to be

reread for this newly defined pleasure. Ann Radcliffe brought the
novel of terror and the macabre to its acme near the end of the century. Like Walpole, who toured the Alps with Thomas Gray watching for appropriate scenes suggesting the paintings of Salvator Rosa,
Radcliffe's characters move through a series of Rosa-like scenes in
Italy. The windy solitudes in *Ossian,* a poem of 1763, provided her
with ideas. In contrast to the Italian scenery (which she had never
seen), the landscapes of heavy forest in her novels are thoroughly
Gothic. The German transcendentalists also found pictures essential.
Caspar David Friedrich, the painter, went indoors with sketches, put
them away, and, after a suitable wait, without again consulting his
sketches, painted the landscape. The wild forest was at the core of
works by Goethe, Tieck, Wagner, and Beethoven. The association of
the legendary German gods, the use of the holy grove as a symbol of
ritual worship, and the fantastic and fecund organic nightmare of the
northern forest metamorphized into fairy tales. George Boas writes:

> The forest primeval had disappeared from the Mediterranean
> basin generations before Homer. But in North Europe it still
> survived. Its darkness and its beasts, its wildness and mystery,
> were accessible to all who cared to investigate them. They were
> the home of the forebearers of Germans and Englishmen; they
> provided the *décor* for their rites. Consequently, if the men were
> to be admired so was their home. If they lived close to a state
> of nature, then Nature must not be the nature of Virgil and
> Theocritus, the smiling Sicilian fields; it must be the nature of
> north Germany, of Wales, of Scotland, the nature of rocky
> craig and tumultuous cumulus clouds, of great waterfalls; un-
> tamed by human art, raw, terrible, sublime.[9]

In America the sublime was peculiarly suitable to the perception
of Niagara Falls, the Hudson Valley, New England, parts of Virginia, and later the West. Louis Hennepin, a Flemish Jesuit, visited
Niagara Falls in 1678 to see the spectacle. Like Dennis in the Alps,

Hennepin was elated and yet fearful. "It was a great and prodigious cadence of water, to which the universe does not offer a parallel. . . . The waters which fall from this great precipice do foam and boil in a most astonishing manner, making a noise more terrible than that of thunder." There are scattered records from the following century that together faintly echo trends in England. Many historians have asserted that the wilderness was still too close for Americans to appreciate it in the way it was admired in Europe. But the typical gentleman was at least partly educated in Europe, and the regimen at Harvard and Yale was patterned closely after foreign schools. It was not the overwhelming abundance of wilderness in America that limited the degree to which the wilderness was admired during the nation's first two centuries, but the number of people with the suitable orientation. Mary Wolley has discovered about twenty writers who found parts of New England "romantic" before 1800, not including the many Europeans who had similar reactions.

Thomas Jefferson admired ruins while traveling in Germany, noting that Italian scenery was composed of "monuments of a war between rivers and mountains which must have shaken the earth itself to its center." He was among the first to enjoy sublime scenery in this country. In *Notes on Virginia* he wrote, "The Natural Bridge is the most sublime of nature's works. . . . If the view from the top be painful and intolerable, that from below is delightful in an equal extreme. . . . The rapture of the spectator is really indescribable."

The relationship of man to nature in nineteenth-century America cannot be intelligently understood apart from such sentiments and the perception of wild landscapes, or indeed, from the popularity and success of Ann Radcliffe's novels and those of her American imitator, Charles Brockden Brown. Washington Allston, the solitary, ambitious American painter whose *Storm at Sea* and *Elijah Being Fed by the Ravens* were both sublime and a new kind of achievement, greatly admired Salvator Rosa, German and English terror stories, the work of his friend Samuel Taylor Coleridge, and the books of Ann Radcliffe. He illustrated the American edition of her *The Mysteries of Udolpho* in 1795, and painted Spalatro's vision of the bloody hand from *The Italian*. He wrote of a French castle, "It had a most picturesque appearance as the first glimpse of morning fell on its mouldering towers. It stood on the brow of a high bank of the river which glittered at its base. The description of Mrs. Radcliffe was brought immediately to my recollection." A Unitarian minister admonished his congregation to distinguish between the moral and the natural sublime, warning them to shun the latter as it appeared in Mrs. Radcliffe's scene of the bloody hand. James Thrall Soby has discovered a similarity between George Catlin's description of the upper Missouri and the prose of Mrs. Radcliffe. William Cullen Bryant read *Romance of the Forest* while still a boy. Allston's landscape paintings, like Radcliffe's prose scenes, were constructed without field sketches and shared their strong visionary quality. The audience for whom they wrote or painted was, on the other hand, frequently engaged in travel to wild places, such as Niagara Falls.

Niagara Falls was a supreme spectacle. From the time of Hennepin visitors came in increasing numbers. An atmosphere of carnival stimulated daredeviltry and the sacrifice of animals in ships and rafts. Others found the experience deeply personal. The most passionate of the letters and records describing the falls were written by women. "It is now midnight," wrote one, "the roar of the waters agitates me. . . . I cannot sooth down my heart—it is kindled by deep working of the invisible. . . . My dreams are very wild here. I am not calm. A great voice seems to be calling on me. . . . I have felt a spell on my soul as if Deity stood visible there . . . I felt the moral influence of the scene acting on my spiritual nature, and while lingering at the summit alone, offered a simple prayer." Another ascribed to it a "terrible loveliness," and said, "I feel half crazy whenever I think of it." Harriet Beecher Stowe was reminded of images from Revelation and of the Great White Throne. To her, the mist seemed to be a rising soul. "I felt as if I could have *gone over* with the waters; it would be so beautiful a death; there would be no fear in it. I felt the rock tremble under me with a sort of joy; I was so maddened that I could have gone too, if it had gone." A tower was built on a small island at the lip of the falls.

The building of towers, chapels, and hotels near sites that attract travelers has been common from the earliest times. New England had no historic chapels or monasteries, but observation platforms and mountain houses appeared rapidly after 1820 amid impressive scenery. Most magnificent was the Catskill Mountain House on a high cliff overlooking the Hudson Valley above Palenville, New York. Its classic facade, razed in 1956, overlooked the scene where Americans were first awakened to esthetic enjoyment of the native landscape.

The Hudson Valley was settled by the Dutch early in the seventeenth century. For eighty years its real wild men, the Indians, were dangerous. One suspects that elements of the wild-man mythology from northern Europe were transferred to this new settlement. The English succeeded the Dutch, adopting and adding to local tradition. By Washington Irving's time, the valley had acquired a folklore, and this mythical and historical background opened the way for artistic and esthetic discovery of the Hudson. It is no accident that the Catskill Mountain House stood on the spot from which James Fenimore Cooper's Leatherstocking describes the sublimity of creation. A few hundred yards away is the clove or glen in which Washington Irving settled Rip Van Winkle for his twenty-year sleep. The immediate area surrounding the Mountain House is the region referred to as "the Catskills" until after the Civil War.

Even after mid-century, Irving wrote of the Catskills as though the ghost of Ann Radcliffe were guiding his pen:

The interior of these mountains is in the high degree wild and romantic; here are rocky precipices mantled with primeval forests; deep gorges walled in by beetling cliffs, with torrents rumbling as it were from the sky; and savage glens rarely trodden excepting by the hunter. With all this internal rudeness, the aspect of these mountains toward the Hudson at times is eminently bland and beautiful, sloping down into a country softened by cultivation, and bearing much of the rich character of Italian scenery about the skirts of the Apennines.

Here are locked up mighty forests that have never been invaded by the axe; deep umbrageous valleys where the virgin soil has never been outraged by the plough; bright streams flowing in untasked idleness, unburthened by commerce, unchecked by the mill-dam.

Rising more than three thousand feet above the Hudson Valley, the escarpment is surrounded by heavy forest, a contrast to the pastoral lowland. Henry T. Tuckerman, a writer, after strolling near the Mountain House, wrote: "We may imagine the effect of a lengthened sojourn in the primeval forest, upon a nature alive to its beauty, wildness and solitude; and when we add to these, the zest of adventure, the pride of discovery and that feeling of sublimity which arises from a consciousness of danger always pending, it is easy to realize in the experience of a pioneer at once the most romantic and practical elements of life."

Like many, he sensed the romantic danger of exploration, but more important, the experience of being the first man ever to see the place. As the English vicar William Gilpin wrote in 1782, in the forest one should "suppose the country to have been unexplored." Byron put this and related ideas so well in the nineteenth century that two generations of American travelers probably quoted him more frequently in their journals than any other English poet.

To sit on rocks, to muse o'er flood and fell,
To slowly trace the forest's shady scene,

Where things that own not man's dominion dwell,
And mortal foot hath ne'er or rarely been
To climb the trackless mountain all unseen,
With the wild flock that never needs a fold.

One of the fancied dangers of being the first into a wilderness was getting lost.

It was not necessary actually to enter the wild forest to enjoy the possibility of getting lost. Nathaniel Hawthorne, after driving near Northampton in a coach at night, wrote, "How very desolate looks a forest when seen in this way—as if, should you venture one step within its wild, tangled, many-stemmed and dark shadowed verge, you would inevitably be lost forever."

To be actually lost was the ultimate experience. In the Catskills this was possible in a circumscribed area, especially at night, but with near certainty of eventually reaching safety. This happened to Thomas Cole during a thunderstorm, when he found himself in one of the deep gorges:

> The truth at last crept over me. *I was lost*—lost past finding out or being found. . . . Again I tried to extricate myself from the windfall, with a desperate energy. I climbed and stooped, scrambled, crawled, and dodged. Now a limb struck me in the face, and I fell backwards among the brambles; then I made a misstep, or a rotten bough broke beneath my foot, and I plunged forward with a crash. . . . The dash of my footsteps, as I waded forward, rang strangely through the hollow cave, and I felt a wild and vivid pleasure as I advanced. I shouted, sang, whistled, for the very horror of the thing.

Charles Lanman, who admired Thomas Cole and had probably seen Cole's painting of the view from Round Top near the Mountain House, hiked up the mountain for a night out. In the middle of the night he arose and sat upon the big rock on the summit and looked toward the Hudson in the moonlight. "Oh, how can I describe the scene that burst upon my enraptured vision? It was unlike anything I had ever seen before, creating a 'lone, lost feeling' which I suppose could only be realized by a wanderer in the heart of an uninhabited wilderness."

Thus the idea of camping out and of the "adventure hike" was emerging. Cole, English-born, was an itinerant Ohio limner before coming east. While studying in England he had copied paintings by Richard Wilson. Bryant induced him to move up the Hudson from New York City, and he settled at Hudson, eight miles from Palenville and the Mountain House. From Hudson he occasionally commuted down the river to New York to speak at the American Academy of Design, commingle with colleagues, or meet a patron. Like the painters Thomas Doughty and Asher Durand he traveled widely over New York and New England, sketching.

Cole was among those who were ruefully aware of the scarcity of ruins in America. He wrote, "We feel the want of associations such as cling to scenes in the old world. Simple nature is not quite sufficient. We want human interest, incident and action, to render the effect of landscape complete." He sought out areas such as the lower Hudson and Lake George, which were associated with historical events. "If we were endowed with ruins we should not preserve them," complained another. "They would be pulled down to make way for some novelty. A striking instance of this tendency will be found in the fact that the last Dutch house in New York has disappeared. . . . We might have supposed that occupying so little space as they did, standing in streets with Dutch names, owned perhaps by men of Dutch descent, one, at least, of these relics of our olden time might have been preserved."

Even Indian legends could be worked into an appreciation of the time and history as a ruin, but few had been interested enough to preserve them. One writer lamented, "A scene of primeval nature and solitude . . . would that its stupendous scenery were linked with mighty incident and that its rare loveliness were clothed with the sacred vestment of traditionary lore! But alas! Its magnificent grandeur and picturesque beauty so fitted to figure in Indian romance or the settler's legend is sadly deficient in the hallowing charm of historic or poetic association!"

Less than a generation after the Presidential Range had been named in 1820, a disgruntled observer commented, "What a pity that the hills could not have kept the names which the Indian tribes gave to them . . . Webster, Clinton, Franklin, Monroe, Washington, Clay, Jefferson, Adams, Madison. What a wretched jumble!"

A family named Wiley living at Crawford Notch had been killed by a rock slide during a stormy night in 1826. Their undamaged house stood unoccupied for many years, gradually falling into ruined heaps. Cole wrote,

> We now entered the Notch, and felt awe-struck as we passed between the bare and rifted mountains, rising on either hand some two thousand feet above us. With the exception of a few curling round the airy pinnacles the clouds had now dispersed, and the sun shown down brilliantly upon this scene of wild grandeur. The sight of the Wiley House, with its little patch of green in the gloomy desolation, very naturally recalled to mind the horrors of the night when the whole family perished beneath an avalanche of rocks and earth.

A visitor said of the place, "The fleetingness of human life is the reflection which focuses itself upon the mind of the traveler, as he treads the deserted chambers of that lonely house." Another added that "the furrows and ruins of a number of avalanches, too, are visible at the sides of the mountains. These possess a melancholy interest from the fact that one of them . . . swept away an entire family." Links were being forged between the architectural and the natural ruin, and the observer was led to an examination of the natural processes that made ruins of the mountains as well as men's works and lives.

Theodore Dwight, who traveled widely in New England as had his Uncle Timothy, looked in vain for actual remains of the Indians. In northern New England he found "mighty rocks balanced on the hills . . . apparently artificial heaps of loose stones . . . and . . . the unaccountable lines and figures traced on many rude blocks of granite." Agassiz's first visit was still twenty years away and his discovery of the ice age far in the future. Dwight was probably looking at glacial deposits and scratches—erratics, moraines, and striae. Patriotism could make men yearn for ruins.

Looking at flood debris along the Saco River, Dwight added another type of natural "ruin" to the glaciated land. At the river's head he passed through Crawford Notch and down the Ammonoosuc, where there were signs of "general desolation" and the stream looked like an avenue with "impenetrable shades" on either side, arching over it like a "Gothic edifice." The debris on the floodplain looked like parts of a structure. "Ruins lie scattered and mouldering for miles down the course of the stream," he said of the trunks deposited by high water. A burned forest resembled the masts of all of Europe's ships moored together; the rocks from the walls of the notch suggested cannon shot; and the cliffs themselves brought to mind "a palace, and yonder a whole city in ruins."

Dwight had seen Hutton's book on uniformitarianism, which said that land surface is not static and that its evolution may be understood by its present processes. With Hutton's and Lyell's geology, fragments of rock were recognized as products of a process and at the same time as ruins. Of the tumbled piles of stone at the foot of the cliff faces between New Haven and Hartford, a guidebook said, "These fragments are the detritus or debris of these mountains, and everyone in the least acquainted with such countries, knows how much they always abound with similar ruins. . . . piled on one another in vast confusion. . . ."

Like Irving, Bryant, and Cole, Andrew Jackson Downing, a landscape architect, was embarrassed by a national architectural insufficiency. Some architectural ruins were built in imitation Gothic. Irving and Cooper had their homes redone. Others followed, such as John Cruger, who built crumbling arches on an island in the Hudson and scattered Mayan sculpture among them. Travelers reading European novels and poetry as they sailed up the river could see another ruined arch built on a high point near Hyde Park. Cole painted Gothic and classical fantasies and, with Downing and others, discovered substitutes. In Europe, John Ruskin spoke for all those, including the American artists, who went as "pilgrims" on the Grand Tour to Italy: "I could not even for a couple of months live in a country so miserable as to possess no castles."

Organic things could also be ruins. George P. Morris's poem "Woodman, Spare That Tree" was published not long before Downing wrote, "If we have neither old castles nor old associations, we have at least, here and there, old trees that can teach us lessons of antiquity, not less instructive and poetical than the ruins of a past age."

The primeval forest is a place of large trees, both living and dead. The dead trunks appealed to Cole as a form of organic ruin. Of a lake near the Catskill House, he said, "The dead trees are a striking feature in the scenery of the lake, and exceedingly picturesque—their forms rise from the margin of the deep, stretching out their contorted branches, and looking like so many genii set to protect the sacred waters. . . . What a place for music by moonlight." The water levels of that lake had been raised slightly by the construction of a dam, thereby inundating the roots of marginal trees and killing them. Tree ruins were multiplied by man in other ways, too. Farmers girdled them, or they died from fire injury.

Although there is probably no record of fires having been set to produce sublime ruins, fires were certainly lit for excitement. In this, the Americans continued the ancient pursuit of hysteria by conflagration. Charles Mason, for instance, enjoyed "the grandeur and terror of the scene" of a fire on Mt. Monadnock about 1820. "It was a beautiful spectacle and grand in itself, but rendered sublime and awful by the thought of the dread power." Some fires, like that on Monadnock, were started by hunters, others from land clearing. Panther and wolf hunts were staged in New England by large groups of armed men with packs of dogs. These chases sometimes lasted all night, or even several successive days and nights, suggesting Piero di Cosimo's fifteenth-century *Hunting Scene,* a wild melee of predatory men and animals against a background of burning forest. J. T. Headley, hiking in the Adirondacks, said that he "wanted to set fire to the trees on the summit . . . so as to present an unobstructed view," but he found the foliage too green to burn. Land clearing went on at a very rapid pace in the East during the first forty years of the nineteenth century. Travelers reported that they rode for days at a time in the smoke of burning logs. It was the traveler who could most fully lose himself in enjoyment of the world as a fiery spectacle. "We had a fearfully sublime example during the dry summer of 1864," wrote a traveler, "when the flames reached within a few feet of the outbuildings at the Mountain House . . . a view by night, of the mountains, with the flames rolling along their sides and summits, and shining forth from the trunks and tops of lofty forest trees, is a scene of exciting and appalling splendor, well nigh as great and imposing as an eruption of Vesuvius or Etna."

The wooden house was a poor ruin. It decayed too rapidly, failing to dramatize the slow ravagement of time. However, some travelers were very determined. Charles Lanman left his coach at Montpelier in 1845 and spent a morning idling in a ruined frame house, "musing upon its solemn admonition." The graveyard also offered a substitute, and with the coming of the new rural graveyards, it was possible to combine the pleasures of the pastoral imagery of the park with the sublime sense of time and the frailty of human life. Gray's *Elegy* was a specimen of the possibilities of such contemplation.

Best of all were the associations derived from historical incidents. "These scenes are classic," said Cole of Lake George, thinking of the Revolution, and he liked views of the Hudson "as seen from the rich orchards of the surrounding hills, hills that have a legend."

West Rock at New Haven recalled "a story of trial and fortitude, courage and magnanimity, the noblest friendship, and a fearless adherence to political principles from religious motives." This referred to the history of Judge's Cave on the top of West Rock, a hideout for pre-Revolutionary rebels.

Americans were eager to enshrine their forefathers' footprints. They doted on the Hudson with its two centuries of history, especially its Revolutionary War episodes and its great estates. According to a guidebook, "No place in the Union, probably, exceeds West Point in beauty of location and the stirring incidents connected with its early history," being "hallowed by the footsteps of Washington and Kosciusko."

Even Niagara Falls was improved by awareness of nearby battlegrounds. "The sensibilities of my heart had been powerfully awakened by what I had just heard of the dreadful scenes of Chippewa and Bridgewater," wrote a traveler, "and the roaring of the falls, which now becoming distinct, appeared like the sound of distant thunder, served to heighten my emotions." When the past failed as a source of recorded history and when Indian legend was inadequate, there were still men creating the future history of their own legends. In a sense, American landscape painting between 1800 and 1865 captured the sublimity of the wheel of time and the birth of empire in visible forms. The view from West Point up the Hudson, the tombstone, the relic, the historical marker, and the landscape painting yielded emotional accompaniment to the contemplation of time and God.

In the twenty-five years from about 1820 to 1845 Americans discovered their wilderness in a new sense. From Virginia north to the upper watersheds of the Hudson and Connecticut rivers there arose a new kind of artist-tourist. Much of their inspiration came from the eighteenth-century romanticism of Europe, but its focus on something approaching true wilderness stimulated an indigenous excitement that still characterized the wilderness "movement" at the end of the twentieth century. Immediately prior to the painting of Albert Bierstadt in the far West and the work of John Muir in California— both in mid-century—a form of wilderness experience took shape in the Northeast that made it possible to perceive the landscape in a way that remains sharply divided even today from the utilitarian mentality and "taming" ideal of most of the early settlers and their modern successors.

The terrible awe of God was made into an esthetic—or, if you prefer, the forests and mountains of the earth came to be revered with religious intensity. The enjoyment of primeval wilderness had not been possible before. Like other esthetic abstractions, the concept of the sublime was a portable emotion. In America it made the discovery of magnificent scenery possible, where none was before, by discovering in natural forms and processes manifestations of the omniscient and inexorable, which in Europe had been connected to mythological or historical events. The explicit focus of the sublime on virgin wilderness has created in the American character one of its few true idiosyncrasies: the emotional connection of nationalism with stupendous scenery, leading to the phenomenon of the preservation of wilderness areas.

ELEVEN

The American West as a Romantic Landscape

THE PLAINS

PERHAPS THERE IS no better example of the evocative power of natural landforms than the response of westering pioneers to the great plains. To many of the thousands who followed the Oregon Trail before 1850, the escarpments and sedimentary bluffs along the Platte River in western Nebraska were the structures of a ghostly architecture. The Reverend Samuel Parker wrote in his diary in 1835:

> Encamped today near what I shall call the old castle, which is a great natural curiosity . . . [it has] the appearance of an old enormous building, somewhat dilapidated; but still you see the standing walls, the roof, the turrets, embrasures, the dome, and almost the very windows; and the guard houses, large, and standing some rods in front of the main building. You unconsciously look around for the enclosures but they are all swept away by the lapse of time—for the inhabitants, but they have disappeared; all is silent and solitary.

These speculations were more than the whimsy of a saddlesore preacher. The journals of mountain men, farmers, speculators, and soldiers make similar comparisons. Their wonder is directed toward "rocks" called Steamboat, Table, Castle, Smokestack, Roundhouse, Courthouse, Jail, and Chimney. But why should these rocks have looked more like buildings than those back East? And why should they have made such an indelible impression on the traveler? These are problems in human ecology, in the formation of attitudes toward the landscape, in the fusion of an experience in nature with historical ideas of process and natural change; and they reveal the impact of strangely new places on the mindset of people from a distant world.

Proceeding northwest along the terraced banks of the Platte at a longitude just beyond 103 degrees, a few minutes south of the 42nd parallel, the "pioneers" were about six weeks past Independence, Missouri. The travelers hailed from several states, particularly eastern and midwestern. They were heterogeneous groups, numbering sometimes in the thousands. They were alike insofar as they shared the geological provincialism of men reared in the subhumid forest landscapes of America and Europe. They shared also the historical background and values of Protestant Yankees and Hoosiers of the 1830s and 1840s. After crossing the upland between the Platte forks, they had followed for almost two weeks the "shores" of what Washington Irving described as the "most beautiful and least useful" river in America. Because the Platte was a kind of linear oasis the itinerants were scarcely aware of the progressive alteration in vegetation and land forms.

At Scott's Bluff they had climbed more than three thousand feet above Independence, and had traversed the northern high plains from the oak-hickory forest to the margin of semiarid highlands, from regions of more than thirty inches of rainfall annually to under fifteen. Leaving the savannahs of the western boundaries of the forests, they had crossed the tall-grass prairies and the shorter mixed grasses, to the place where the upland vegetational cover ceased to be continuous—a significant point in the reduction of vegetational control on the geomorphic weathering and mass wasting. The travelers had also entered a region of greater daily temperature range, more numerous cyclonic storms, and less relative humidity, with varied and subtle effects on human senses and responses.

Plodding up the valley of the Platte, with its arm of forest, meadow, and savannah, the traveler penetrated unaware new surroundings. Then, in what is now Scott's Bluff County, Jailhouse Rock and Courthouse Rock appeared on the left horizon some fifteen miles away. As the column of wagons passed slowly to the right of these structures, more came into view, and finally an escarpment parallel to the trail about five miles from the river. This is Wildcat Ridge on present maps, more than thirty miles long, and sends three spurs north almost to the river's edge, the westernmost being Scott's Bluff.

The first fifteen miles or so produced a galvanizing impact on the observer. There had been intimations of things to come, such as buffalo trails that looked to one pioneer "like the once oft-trodden streets of some deserted city." The valley with its pleasant greenery had itself been suggestive; Rufus B. Sage observed that "everything had more the appearance of civilization than anything that I have seen for many days, the trees, the shrubs and bushes, grapevines, the grass—resembling blue grass—the singing of the birds in the trees, the sound of the ax cutting wood for breakfast." Then, as the typical westbound party drew abreast of the bluffs, a wave of astonishment swept through it. John Bidwell wrote in 1841, "The scenery of the surrounding country became beautifully grand and picturesque—they were worn in such a manner by the storm of unnumbered seasons, that they really counterfeited the lofty spires, towering edifices, spacious domes, and in fine all the beautiful mansions of cities."

Numerous observers discovered lighthouses, brick kilns, the capitol of Washington, Beacon Hill, shot towers, churches, spires, cupolas, streets, workshops, stores, warehouses, parks, squares, pyramids, castles, forts, pillars, domes, minarets, temples, Gothic castles, "modern" fortifications, French cathedrals, Rhineland castles, towers, tunnels, hallways, mausoleums, a Temple of Belus, and hanging gardens that were "in a tolerable state of preservation, and showing in many places hardy shrubs that, having sent down their long roots into partial openings of the supporting arches, still smiled in beautiful green, amid general desolation," according to J. Quinn

Thornton. Taken at a glance, the rocks "had the appearance of Cities, Temples, Castles, Towers, Palaces, and every variety of great and magnificent structures . . . splendid edifices, like beautiful white marble, fashioned in the style of every age and country," reported Overton Johnston and William Winter. Where more palpably than in America could such a jumble of architecture actually look like a city? A. Delano wrote,

> Here were the minarets of a castle; there the loopholes of bastions of a fort; again the frescoes of a huge temple; there the doors, windows, chimneys, and the columns of immense buildings appeared in view, with all the solemn grandeur of an ancient, yet deserted city, while at other points Chinese temples, dilapidated by time, broken chimneys, rocks in miniature made it appear as if by some supernatural cause we had been dropped in the suburbs of a mighty city—for miles around the basin this view extended, and we looked across the barren plain at the display of Almighty power, with wonder and astonishment.

But the cities were not often American. What cities came to mind?

> The mind was filled with strange images and impressions. The silence of death reigned over a once populous city, which had been a nursery of the arts and sciences, and the seat of a grand inland commerce. It was a Tadmore of the desert in ruins. [J. Q. Thornton]

What people had lived there?

> No effort of the imagination is required to suppose ourselves encamped in the vicinity of the ruins of some vast city erected by a race of giants, contemporaries of the Megatherii and Ichthyosaurii. [Edwin Bryant]

> Noble castles with turrets, embrasures, and loopholes, with draw-bridge in front and the moat surrounding it; behind, the

humble cottages of the subservient peasantry and all the varied concomitants of such a scene, are so strikingly evident to the view, that it required but little stretch of fancy to imagine that a race of antediluvian giants may have here swayed their iron sceptre, and left behind the crumbling palace and the tower, to all of their departed glory. [John K. Townsend]

What had happened to that vanished civilization? There was a room, suggested J. Q. Thornton, where "that monarch might have sat upon his throne, surrounded by obsequious courtiers and servile slaves, while the lifeblood of men better than himself was being shed to make him a holiday." Perhaps because of this degeneracy the city had been overwhelmed, "a people who had perhaps gone down into the vortex of revolutions . . . leaving no trace of their existence, save those remains of architectural grandeur and magnificence." From the position of the ruins some travelers reconstructed the probable course of the catastrophe, a series of pitched battles, slaughter, pillage, fire, and the "bodies in promiscuous piles about the gates."

The illusion was difficult to resist. The mirage "would deceive the most practiced eye were it not known that it is situated in a wilderness hundreds of miles from any habitation." There was bemusement and flashes of embarrassed self-consciousness. The Reverend Sam Parker declared that "one can hardly believe that they are not the work of art. Although you correct your imagination, and call to remembrance, that you are beholding the work of nature, yet before you are aware, the illusion takes you again, and again your curiosity is excited to know who built this fabric, and what has become of the bygone generations." Israel Hale rode twelve miles to inspect the incredible Chimney Rock:

> I could not help imagining that it might be the work of some generation long extinct and that it was erected in commemoration of some glorious battle or in memory of some noble

chieftain. But on arriving at the spot I could discover no marks
of hammer, ax, or chisel, no cemented joints by which it should
be cemented in one solid mass.

The first half of the nineteenth century was a time of geological
discovery. Its impact was felt by many who had little education but
had a workman's interest in minerals and rocks. By 1835 anyone who
thought about the new geological information at all was aware, however vaguely, of the process of change. It was a time of tension between the idea of a created static world and the discovery of a new
one in which time and nature seemed to carve the landscape.

Time, working the surface, made ruins. The ruin has a respectable
and venerable iconography: Christian symbolism, Renaissance veneration for classical antiquity, and the emergence of nationalism with
its celebration of the indigenous past. But the ruin's most provocative effect was as testimony to the ravages of time.

The Chimney, noted William Watson, "is composed of soft sandstone; and like the surrounding bluffs, is in a state of decay; and
nothing that I saw on the route put me so strongly in mind of my
approaching dissolution." One rock had "the appearance of a vast
edifice, with its roof fallen in, the great doorways partially ob-
structed, and many of the arches broken and fallen." The structures
were all magnificent, "but now lift up their heads amid surrounding
desolation; befitting monuments of man's passing glory, and of the
vanity of his hopes," sighed J. Q. Thornton. The description of the
cycle of empire postulated by several itinerants was exactly the view
of cyclic history that Thomas Cole had impressively depicted in his
five large paintings of *The Course of Empire*.

Because of its cut-and-fill nature, much of the Platte Valley is
without bluffs; in Scott's Bluff County not only has the river cut
bluffs, but they are sufficiently distant from the trail to be seen as a
whole. Semiarid climatic conditions begin to prevail at this longi-

tude, creating fundamental changes in erosion factors: Debris is rapidly removed; plants and their acid secretions do not gently round off the hilltops. The result is that the forms of the hills are no longer curved, and their slopes lose the S-shaped profile characteristic of a humid climate, with the result that, as they wear away, the mountains retreat as cliffs rather than lose height and steepness.

In Scott's Bluff County a tributary called Pumpkin Creek parallels the Platte and like it has cut deeply into the conglomerates, sandstone, and compacted alluvium. Wildcat Ridge is a neck of upland between the two valleys. The erosion of this ridge has penetrated it in several places, leaving isolated outlying remnants and sculpturing it with the aid of other climatic agencies into a maze of forms that show the differential erosion of the various materials. Architecturally, a single cliff is only a facade, a bas-relief, compared to the fully sculptured three-dimensional forms cut from the rock between these two streams.

The clear air and absence of trees made perspective exceedingly difficult for men whose visual habits had developed within a humid landscape. Three long dissected spurs running north from the ridge toward the Platte lent additional depth to the scene, creating the impression upon an observer of standing in the city rather than looking at a flat picture. The box canyons into which he looked, Horseshoe Flat and Cedar Valley, contained nothing to dispel the architectural image, their floors neatly terraced by the stream.

In this way the ceaseless process of geomorphic change had staged a scene that caught the imagination, evoking an esthetic developed around ruins, and perceptual experience may have been heightened by novel physical circumstances. Rocks of certain angular shapes may always mean "man-made structure" to European-Americans because of an indelible association of form with human works. J. Z. Young has suggested that large structures, notably cathedrals, are, because of their permanence, ultimate symbols of the most human of qualities—the striving for perfection and permanence of communication.[1] Thousands of people moving up the Platte in the 1840s left their names, destination, and the date carved and written on every available surface along the Oregon Trail.

The illusion of architecture associates these structures with nobility and with a dramatic and violent history. Revolution against autocracy and despotism was fresh in mind and yet distant enough to be part of history. Although professing opposition to it, Americans seemed strangely receptive to the external forms and appurtenances of aristocracy. In addition, the Mediterranean and Near Eastern heritage of classical history was associated with architecture. A prebiblical myth involved the rebuilding of ruined cities in the desert by heroic measures. W. H. Auden probed the idea briefly in *The Enchafèd Flood* and indicated the effects of its imagery on the literate mind of the nineteenth century. The mystery of the Lost Tribes was a living issue. The expressions of human experience in the American West fell back on imagery that had come from the deserts of Transjordan, Asia Minor, and the Nile fringes. From it came the inception and pursuit of a national concept of reclamation and the compelling idea that only good can come of unlimited irrigating, reclaiming, and populating the deserts. No complete explanation of the formation of the American's ideas of the West could afford to omit the significance of desert or semiarid land forms as a challenge.

THE PARKS

On Sunday evening, August 21, 1870, Lieutenant Gustavus C. Doane, U.S. Second Cavalry, stationed at Fort Ellis, Montana, received orders to choose a sergeant and four privates for a mission of "important military necessity" and to prepare to depart the following morning. A perceptive and vigorous man of thirty, Doane was soon to discover that his mission had no more military significance than protection from Indians of a half-dozen sightseeing tourists.

The party that left Bozeman at 11:00 A.M. on the twenty-second was an exceptional group. General Henry D. Washburn, its leader, had prevailed upon General Phil Sheridan to order the escort, over the objection of the Fort Ellis commander that his troops were already too widely scattered fighting Indians for the safety of the fort. A veteran of the Civil War, Washburn was then Montana's surveyor-general. With him was Nathaniel Pitt Langford, President Andrew Johnson's territorial governor-appointee and U.S. collector of internal revenue. Langford, who later became famous as a vigilante, a describer of nature in Victorian euphemisms, chronicled the enterprise that was to become known as the Washburn-Langford-Doane Expedition. Its objective was to explore the upper Yellowstone River and to verify or discredit a half-century's accumulation of rumors about a forest of geysers, huge waterfalls, and fantastic rainbow-colored hot springs where it was possible to hook a trout in one shimmering pool and flip it into a boiling pink and yellow caldron to cook it.

With Washburn also came Probate Court Judge Cornelius Hedges, the party's most truly literate member. A New Englander (Yale '53), Hedges had taught school and practiced law and was destined to forty years of prominence in the public affairs of Montana. His daily experiences went into a diary with a poetic flourish and reference to the Lake Poets, Poe, or classical literature. There was also Truman C. Everts, state assessor of internal revenue; Lyman Trumbull, assistant assessor and son of an Illinois senator; Samuel T. Hauser, president of the Helena First National Bank and later state governor (who kept a diary of the expedition, too, written rapidly with a soft lead pencil in a miniature pocket journal); and Warren C. Gillette and Benjamin Stickney, two prominent merchants of Helena, where most of the party lived. At the last minute a ne'er-do-well named Jake Smith enrolled. It turned out that Jake cheated at cards, slept on guard, and generally proved the habitual foil to his upright companions.

All were keen outdoorsmen except Everts, the assessor, who allowed his horse to stray, became befuddled and separated from the party while it was enroute through a pine forest near Yellowstone Lake, and was lost for thirty-seven days. Everts' horse stampeded when he dismounted to look for tracks, and with it went his gun. He accidentally broke his glasses. Nearsighted, he stumbled through snowstorms and lived on roots in an area where Jim Bridger had reported that even the crows carried provisions. Everts discovered after two desperate weeks that he could make fire with his field glasses. Weakening, he was stalked by a mountain lion and was incoherent when two trappers finally found him. Meantime, the expedition had become history and returned to Helena with its entourage of cooks and packers after delaying to search for the assessor. Everts soon became something of a national hero and wrote a book about his adventure.

The loss and rescue of Everts caught public interest, which was further fired by articles by Langford and Hedges. A tale of wonders from such reputable citizens could not be ignored. The Honorable David E. Folsom, a wealthy rancher who had come west with Langford, declined to accompany the Washburn Expedition in 1870 because he had seen Yellowstone the previous year. His descriptions were so incredible that he had ceased talking publicly for fear of being permanently labeled a liar. An article he and a companion had written about the geysers was rejected as fiction by a national magazine, although it found a publisher elsewhere.

Near the end of the expedition Hedges had proposed that the area should be preserved as a public park. All but Smith enthusiastically concurred, and the party returned from the wilderness determined to get congressional action. General Washburn went to Washington and Langford toured the eastern lyceum circuit in the winter of 1870–71. Their efforts resulted in the government's Hayden Expedition the following summer. This was an official party, ponderous with scientific talent, and included the photographer J. B. Jackson and the painter Thomas Moran. Moran's huge panoramas of the Yellowstone Valley overwhelmed spectators, including congressmen, and the government eventually paid him ten thousand dollars for two of them (one now hangs in the secretary of the interior's conference room and the other in the Smithsonian Institution). By act of Congress, Yellowstone became the world's first national park in 1872.

This extraordinary event occurred when Indians were still a danger in Yellowstone. The general atmosphere was one of gold-hunting, root-hog-or-die, cut-out-and-get-out, where wilderness seemed to be civilization's worst enemy; of a national orgy of westering, land speculation, and claim-staking. In Yellowstone a huge piece of wilderness was preserved by Congress, two thousand miles from Washington, D.C., with no means of enforcing such preservation except by appointing Langford park superintendent without funds or help. It is reasonable to ask what the rationalizations were for reserving a slice of the unlimited green cheese which to some seemed as remote as the moon.

There was awareness in 1872 that natural resources were wasting—the last great herd of buffalo was already tottering and industrial logging with its trail of waste had moved into the South—but not even the most altruistic or simple congressmen assumed that sealing off the Yellowstone Plateau from claims would help diminishing resources. The act was compounded of admiration for scenery and the idea that awe and beauty were morally uplifting. (The vote was along party lines, the Republicans winning.) In short, the National Park Act had the insubstantial and obscure reference of an act of faith.

The gentlemen on the Washburn Expedition and their counterparts with Hayden are the key to the existence of the national parks. Their diaries of the trip reveal the themes on which they became arbiters of American nature esthetics. The account by Lieutenant

Doane is sensitive, even brilliant. He rejoiced in the distant views and natural curiosities. He was the party's most indefatigable hunter and explorer. His sparkling report, long since buried in the army's morgue of official papers, comes through even today with good sense and the freshness of discovery. Part of it was written in spite of the agony of an infected thumb which had so drained his resources that he slept solidly for thirty-six hours after Langford lanced it with a pocket knife.

The image of the Yellowstone compounded by the educated men with Hayden and with Washburn, by Folsom, by one William Lacy, a Virginia planter who was there in 1863, and perhaps a few others, was a different Yellowstone than that seen by scores of men who had been there before them. Mountain men like Jim Bridger, John Coulter (who was there in 1806), and Joseph Meek lived on the edge of danger with a casual humor almost unknown today; to them Yellowstone was a great natural joke, a campfire tale come true. The fumaroles looked like the chimneys of Pittsburgh. To unnumbered and unnamed bands of trappers and gold seekers it was merely a passing curiosity. The relatively unique vision of the men with Washburn had to do with contemporary esthetics and an acquired virtuosity. As a contemporary writer said of the western mountains, "One must carry something of culture to them, to receive all the benefits they can bestow in return." This requisite cultural baggage, laboriously transported into virgin territory, produced the first national park.

Langford published his journal as *The Discovery of Yellowstone National Park*. That is, the area contained features that seemed like a park and worth preserving to him and his companions, if not, for instance, to the fifty or so trappers who were there with Bridger in 1846. It did not need to be constructed, as did Central Park. The secret was that to Langford the landscape looked anything but wild. This was due mostly to coincidence. The natural land forms and vegetation of Yellowstone resembled certain humanized landscapes plus objects that were considered an improvement on wilderness, such as ruins.

On the surface, any reference to ruins reflected the social status of the class that indulged in art collecting. Ruins were evidence of the great wheel of time, invoking images of classical antiquity, and cyclic flow in which empires grew, flourished, and decayed. From the time of the Italian Renaissance this idea had captured the modern mind, and it was further stimulated by new approaches to the study of history in the eighteenth century. For all their protestations against aristocratic postures, clichés on independence, and disavowals of the physical artifacts of a class society, Americans never seriously questioned the social value of national tangible evidence of power, wealth and history.

Writers, then painters and poets, had injected the symbolic ruin into general Western cultural heritage. The eighteenth-century English had discovered their own ruined abbeys, walls, and relics, and built fabrications in their estate pleasuring grounds. Well-to-do Americans toured Europe's great ruins and returned home to lament that "we have neither old castles nor old associations." Why should I visit America, asked John Ruskin, where there are no castles. Patriotism wanted suitable icons. George Washington had not slept in enough places to go around, or in the kind of places that became durable ruins. Meantime, exploration in South America, Africa, and the South Pacific, as well as the United States, showed that ruins were where you found them. The Washburn party in the upper Yellowstone canyon observed rock formations that were geologically and architecturally suggestive. Their resemblance to buildings was so insistent that the educated imagination needed little prompting. They welcomed the "ruins" along the Yellowstone with passion, with all the momentum of American tourists unleashed in Rome or the Rhineland. While Hudson Valley aristocrats were copying old

Gothic facades or wishing they could import Scottish castles intact, Langford, Hedges, and Doane were discovering an unchartered heritage of castles, fortresses, and ramparts already in the American landscape. Minarets, watchtowers, and turrets lined the canyon of the Yellowstone where Folsom, silenced by embarrassment for the extravagance of his fantasies, confided to his diary "a huge rock that bore resemblance to an old castle; rampart and bulwark were slowly yielding to the ravages of time, but the old turret stood out in bold relief against the sky. . . . We could almost imagine that it was the stronghold of some baron of feudal time and that we were his retainers returning laden with the spoils of a successful foray." The geysers were fountains, and the terraced hot springs were exactly the kind of adjunct that one might expect in a villa garden.

The geology of these natural ruins was new to men from a humid environment. The climate that sculptured these rocks architecturally is characteristic of the continental interior of the American West. While pictures of the geysers of New Zealand and Iceland had appeared in popular literature, and everyone "knew" what a desert or mountain range looked like, the Western European esthetic of natural beauty nonetheless contained little imagery of angular desert geology. Perhaps this element of novelty rendered it easy to perceive a rectangular block or wall-like cliff as an edifice. It may be asked what cultural conditioning would be necessary to combine the human inclination to associate natural rectilinear forms with an intelligent builder. The journals of the Washburn Expedition leave no doubt that the haunting architecture of the Yellowstone's filagreed cliffs delighted Americans who were wistfully conscious of a national cultural shortcoming. Entertaining the pleasant illusion that the rocks were the ruins of buildings led to an equally gratifying dream that the area had formerly been inhabited by a highly civilized and artistic people who, like the ancient Greeks and Romans, had vanished, leaving their works to the amazement of future generations. At the same time, these gentlemen were interested in the rock itself. American geology had outstanding professionals, like John Wesley Powell, who was busy in the Colorado gorge, and good amateurs as well. The men of the Washburn party knew that these rocks were ruins in their own right. Looking out from what was to be named Mt. Washburn, Doane grasped at once that the whole plateau was a complex volcano. And chemical and mineralogical observation occupied much of their time.

The architectural qualities of Yellowstone's rocks added dimension to their geology. The same processes that sheared fragments from the Pantheon fractured the canyon walls. Natural ruins and man's ruins met in the same arena of time, victims together of weather and climate, so that the American West could evoke as much of a stunning grasp of time's wheel as could Europe. Together, the architectural and geological curiosities formed a basis for literary and pictorial description of great empires, which centered on the imagery of the ruin.

There was also a moral and allegorical aspect of the ruin in the wilderness. In the mythology of the ruined city, where man's evil had brought the retribution of catastrophe, a hero appears to build a new and better society. The Washburn party arrived at Yellowstone in a spirit of evangelical fervor, but the "city" could not be rebuilt because the values of the myth had been rearranged. In the nineteenth century the city had become a symbol of man's depravity, whereas in the classical view it had been the normal arena of life. One no longer went into the wilderness penitently, for meditation and self-denial, but to immerse oneself in untarnished creation and to confront its virginal sanctity. Since the ruin had come to be seen as both a natural curiosity and a picturesque monument, this conflicting heritage of ideas could be resolved: in preserving Yellowstone park it was implicit that reclamation must follow, but the public was not to come as settlers and builders. The wilderness must remain wilderness, and the ruins forever ruins. It was the character of the pilgrims themselves that was to be reconstructed.

Of course natural ruins do not wholly account for the popularity of Yellowstone, since the West is full of rectangular erosion. The vertical dimensions of the landscape were very great and the local relief on an enormous scale. From high points the landscape was most impressive; any mountain looks bigger from the top of another mountain. The horizontal scale was vast, partly because of the transparency of the dry air. In combination, the novelty of these situations is likely to be emotionally dazzling with mystic overtones; it becomes an encounter with cosmic forces. Such a view permitted sweeping observations and composition of verbal panoramas, counterparts to the pictures being painted by Frederick Church and Albert Bierstadt. While comparable scenery was found in certain parts of the eastern United States and in Europe, Yellowstone's fame suggests that release from the limits of the customary horizons prepared the tourist for transcendental amazement in the West.

Reaction to the "wonder" did not require the educated eye and was more common than the baggage of the educated gentlemen. Geysers, falls, lakes, and canyons were Yellowstone's wonders. Falls have been primary attractions for a thousand years. Their peculiar fascination is not associated with fashions in esthetics or refined tastes. The awe with which they are regarded is not and perhaps cannot be intellectualized. Falls are as fundamental to the wonder of nature as the spontaneous belief that there is a spirit in things with motion. Falls belong to a category that includes fire, clouds, and even trees tossing in the wind. Natural wonders that do not move, but in which vitality is immanent, suggest the human body. Mountains, forests, large rivers, lakes, caves, and geysers are anatomical. These partly account for the curiosity that lures people into the landscape and especially to the national parks.

The spiritual impact of these wonders elicited biblical quotations from the men with Washburn, including a psalm by the taciturn leader himself. As the group sat around the campfire, Washburn intoned, "When I behold the work of Thy hands, what is man that Thou art mindful of him!" Having looked at the lower falls all day, Langford wrote, "I realize my own littleness, my helplessness, my dread exposure to destruction, my inability to cope with or even comprehend the mighty architecture of nature. . . . We are all overwhelmed with astonishment and wonder at what we have seen, and we feel that we have been near the very presence of the Almighty. . . . exhibitions which suggest no other fancy than that which our good grandmothers have painted on our boyish imaginations as a destined future abode." "The beauty . . . is overpowering," wrote Doane, "transcending the visions of the Moslem's Paradise." Paradise involves the Garden of Eden, and the garden to nineteenth-century English and Americans meant the landscape park, a descendant of the paradise garden by way of the classical pastoral and the village green. The "natural" garden or "park" was the estate grounds, landscaped to blend into the countryside. The park was a particular association—planned randomness—of scattered trees, lawn, and winding streams connecting lakes. It looked somewhat like paintings of Arcadia or of paradise. It was both an abstraction from nature and a figment of human experience, roughly equivalent to the pastoral landscape of mixed forest and meadow from which modern European man emerged. The English landscape park was not properly a wonder, although it inherited artificial mounts and grottos; not a ruin, although ruins were constructed to add to the effect; nor yet merely panoramic, although the views were sweeping and extensive.

As a symbol of refinement and well-being, the park became important to Americans who were eager to keep up with their English cousins. With the professional aid of Andrew Jackson Downing, the Hudson River estates developed "pleasuring grounds" on the English model. Nor was the gentleman's park limited to the wealthy; Frederick Law Olmsted's Central Park proved in 1858 that in America every man could have his park. Thousands picnicked in similarly planned pastoral grounds in the new rural cemeteries near Boston and Philadelphia. Although considered "natural," these parks were carefully planned, planted, and manicured. They were far from the original wilderness which the pioneers had to invade, cut down, and humanize in order to establish agriculture.

This was the visual surprise of the Western wilderness: truly wild places that resembled civilization's most ornamental achievement— the estate park—which was, in turn, linked with an image of paradise. William Gilpin's *The Parks of Colorado,* published in 1866, was a description of genuine wilderness, although a park had never been wilderness in Europe.

The association of park landscape and paradise is apparent in American landscape paintings of the time like Thomas Cole's *The Expulsion from Eden.* Members of the Washburn Expedition wrote about paradise with its fountains. They found in Yellowstone "innumerable groves and sparkling waters, a variegated landscape of surpassing beauty." Standing on the lake shore with its grassy meadows, it seemed to the observer "almost incredible that so tame and so quiet a scene could be found in the midst of a region usually so wild and terrible." Nearby there was a "beautiful park of firs with a broad meadow just in front. No artificial arrangement of trees could have been more perfect." It was the sort of landscape that Constable had painted at Vivenhoe Park, a grassy retreat insulated from the outer world by distant groves, a solitude where cattle or deer munched the turf and gracefully composed themselves into groups.

The existence of the natural park in America, like that of the architectural land forms, resides ultimately in unique climatic areas, usually at altitudes of at least four thousand feet. Where a region of natural grasslands, prairie, tundra, or marsh adjoins a forested area, there is usually a transition zone in which there are scattered trees with grassy areas between them. In the Rocky Mountains, open areas with scattered aspens succeed the destruction of the forest by fire, and there were many natural fires before white men appeared. At higher elevations where forests approach the limits of their range, regrowth after a fire may be slow and spotty, with lichens, grasses, and flowering herbs filling in the open places. Sometimes the high meadows have the environmental conditions of tundra, and elsewhere the vicissitudes of soil moisture prevent forest growth by providing too little or too much soil water during the growing season. In the valleys, which are often surrounded by dense forest, there may be open meadows with scattered deciduous and evergreen trees, which most nearly approximate the lawn park, usually on flat, poorly drained ground. Many of these flats are beaver meadows (former beaver ponds that have been filled with organic material and alluvium). These natural parks usually have low soil temperatures and pockets of water-saturated soil. The grazing animals that substitute for cows or sheep of the English park are the elk, mule deer, antelope, and moose, assisted by many minor lawn mowers in numerous rodents and rabbits. Only in midsummer are the high country parks comfortably warm for people; at that time green, flowery, and virginal. They are seen mainly by tourists who come from lower elevations, and the altitude probably contributes subtly to the observer's sense of exhilaration.

Similar parks exist in the Cascade and Sierra mountains. Yosemite Valley offers precisely the same combination of major features: the unusual visual experience, the natural wonders, the waterfalls, the architectural geology, and the natural paradise or garden park. Yosemite was withdrawn from homesteading and reserved as a park eight years before Yellowstone, but instead of becoming a national park at that time, it was ceded to California on the condition that it be preserved, becoming a national park in 1890. The history of its esthetic discovery is a remarkable parallel to that of Yellowstone. The gentlemen who "discovered" its natural beauty were a minority of all who saw it first in 1851 and 1852, but they brought "something of culture" to the valley, and their almost unbelievable reports stirred men of similar enthusiasm who in turn exerted their influence on Congress. It is significant that Frederick Law Olmsted, who was professionally weaned on the parks of Europe and who helped design Central Park, had a hand in preserving Yosemite.

In the case of both parks, their establishment came about at the end of an era in which nature had been philosophically regarded as benign and beneficent. It was the time of the omniscient naturalist, unlimited natural bounty, and an agrarian national orientation. After Yellowstone it was nearly twenty years before a second national park was established, then with a new social and scientific justification. The wonder, the ruin, and the natural park were a creative combination in the era of nature love; discovered during the exploration of the West where unique geomorphic forms and vegetational communities combined cultural images and natural pride. Civilization and wealth traditionally coincided with the architecture and parks. It took educated tourists to recognize these similarities, men who wished that America were more embellished.

ESTHETIC FAILURES OF THE LATER PARKS

The sublime wonder, ruin, and English-type lawns in remote places were the component images that made Yellowstone and Yosemite seem worth preserving. What can be said of the system of national parks today? Together with national monuments, there are now more than two hundred. (A national monument is proclaimed by the President; a national park is established by Congress.) An integrated system with a philosophy of administration came when Stephen Mather organized the Park Service in 1916. Four-fifths of its areas have been added to the system since then. The high proportion that fail to meet the criterion of looking domesticated or improved is striking. The newest are desert, swamp, or dense forest with few of the traditional esthetic qualifications except that they are wonders. They are not even that in the usual sense of a visible object; they are abstract wonders. The whole swamp (as in the Everglades) or forest (as in the Olympic Rain Forest) is conceptualized as a wonder. The totality has become the wonder rather than large panoramas.

This evolution of wilderness esthetics began with a few individuals far back in the nineteenth century, such as William Cullen Bryant, George Catlin, Henry Thoreau, and Thomas Cole, who urged public preservation of natural relics. At that time it was perhaps too improbable and unexciting—even against progress—to get much public support. Yet, it has never died. Naturalists have continued to espouse it. Their argument is an intellectual complement to the emotional appeal of wonder preservation. Yellowstone provided the political machinery and the precedent for reserving other areas. Surprisingly few scenically undesirable areas got into the system by public or political pressures. Many members of the National Park Service are naturalists, and a philosophy of supreme sample relic preservation has marked the thinking of that agency and its supporters. But there is a great difference between the concept of pictorial beauty based on paradise and scientific arguments for preserving relic samples of wilderness. It takes a great deal of argument to persuade an American to *resist* the exploitation of natural resources in the name of progress. A combination of deeply set cultural images could persuade him in the Yellowstone, but where no such images exist the proposal loses its immediate self-evident justification.

In spite of the strategic role of the desert in our religious history, the relatively new desert parks have not been esthetically assimilated. Although there has always been some pressure to open the parks to commercial exploitation, those pressures are directed to the unpark-like parks. Dinosaur National Monument, a desert park, was considered a weak link if not an Achilles' heel in the park system by the purest school of commercial developers. Presumably, the legal establishment of water, timber, or mineral use in one park would open up the others by precedent. In a five-year struggle between developers and preservers in the 1950s, the fundamental question was whether or not the monument actually contained a sufficiently spectacular synthesis of the traditional park landscape—although it was never put in these words. The preservers published photographs of vast panoramas, architectural rocks, and a rippling river. The developers concentrated on pictures of arid "waste" and the lake they wished to create—the latter having its own esthetic value. More recently, the attack was turned on the Grand Canyon. For closely similar reasons it is not surprising that the tropical marshes of the Everglades National Park and the rain forest of the Olympic National Park are two of the most embattled areas in the system. Both contain desirable material resources, and neither are conventional parks. Central Park was originally conceived as a kind of large estate ground for the opulent villas that would surround it, but at the same time it was to be a congenial space for public outings and thus fulfill a social necessity. But there seems to be no natural place for a picnic in the heart of the Everglades, among the dripping ferns of the rain forest, or on the Grand Canyon's rocky perimeter. Moreover, the outing has taken on a new and nationally economically sanctioned and commercialized recreational dimension; the parks have emerged in its vernacular as playgrounds for the millions. Present-day recreation, which is often defined as a negative value, as escape from an unpleasant environment or boring routine, is replacing the pilgrimage that had moral uplift or natural wonders as its objective. This version of the national park is only another form of commercial exploitation, not because of its motives, but because people so motivated require so many props, machines, and controls on nature. The original park, which in Europe was a humanized landscape in harmony with intense human pressures, could, like Central Park, sustain heavy traffic without deterioration. The American national parks of the original type, like Yellowstone and Yosemite, are by comparison fragile, because however much they resemble the gentleman's park superficially, they have reached their lawn-tree state in the relative absence of human tread. Even so, they are more resilient in the face of an onslaught by tourists than unparklike parks. Lawn and trees are hardy associates of human activity, but not so the environments where living things endure on a more tenuous and less recuperable basis, as in the desert or cold forest, or even in the rich subtropical places of superabundance, where the pattern is small numbers of many kinds of organisms in a competitive balance that man joggles easily. In such places popular use depends on renovating and artificializing. No "national playground" is consistent with the outdoor museum, wilderness relic, or natural shrine in those environments that cannot stand much tampering.

The natural museum is an intellectual counterpart to the sensory catharsis of natural parks. The outdoor museum has a patriotic-historical value insofar as it involves the preservation of native life and original landscapes, although this, strangely, does not seem to be a particularly cherished idea. There is more enthusiasm for the preservation of natural areas for scientific research on the nature of natural processes, the study of systems too elaborate to be mocked-up in the laboratory.

Its value is potentially very great to a mechanized society that periodically gets itself into dust bowls, floods, and other catastrophes. Natural relic preservation may prove to have value also as a storehouse of plant and animal species that are otherwise becoming extinct and which at any time may become useful in medicine, industry, or agriculture. In addition, there are numerous educational uses of such natural areas. To an open-minded and reasonably intelligent observer the various scientific needs of outdoor museums and natural areas arc reasonably convincing: proponents, even if romantic, scarcely give the impression of being harebrained. Yet, a very small number of people are directly involved. Just as it was a small number of people who established the first parks, on the basis of a refined nature esthetic. But there was an equalitarian yearning for such upper-class tastes. The public and its Congress knew what a "temple of nature," a "natural Wonder," or a "gentlemen's park" might be, but a forest that is a "natural community representing the bio-ecological climax" is apt to get the axe as soon as it can be converted into cardboard at a profit.

While the natural area idea finds its way into wider awareness and public acceptance, there is also some new appreciation of the lawnless parks. As the artist races forward with new visual abstraction, the casual tourist follows his cold trail. If the desert is not a garden in the usual sense, it does have color, and Americans have discovered color fairly recently. A rather wide public enjoyment of Bryce and Zion national parks is not based entirely on architectural fantasy. The Painted Desert was added to the Petrified Forest National Monument in 1932—twenty-six years after the monument was established. The impressionist spectrum in painting quickened by the invention of color film has finally enabled large numbers of people to achieve or retain the pleasure inherent in color vision. Perhaps the abstract form is next, and Anglos may hope to attain the sophisticated level enjoyed by the Navajos in this respect. On the other hand, there may be limits to the rate at which the public will accept abstractions by art in its dominion over the beauty of nature. Friends of the parks may hope that there will never be an epitaph for an exploited Everglades reading "When Nature Failed to Copy Art."

Whether the parks can survive the interval before the emergence of a suitable public esthetic is uncertain. There are two ways in which a continuation of conflict could be averted. The first would be to give up the controversial areas in the face of growing commercial demands and economic pressures, and retreat to the conventional parks for a concerted defense. This would consolidate the park system and enable a society with rather specific esthetics to preserve the whole system. An example of one of the first parks to be sacrificed would be the rain forest of the Olympic Peninsula, most of the Olympic National Park. Nearby chambers of commerce would enjoy a brief burst of progress, parts of a local economy would boom temporarily, a few thousand more homes would be built faster (but not at a lowered cost), a lumber company or two would be appeased politically, and the only forest of its kind would vanish without a chance of returning. Desert parks, in much the same fashion, might eventually produce sugar beets under irrigation or become practice ranges for new weapons.

An alternative would be the playground policy, taking all comers whatever their motives and desires. This is the "recreational" route along which the Park Service is apparently being impelled. There is a certain amount of education available to the park visitor, but the major effect is instead to whittle the wilderness to fit the pastoral playground picture—an undertaking that, incidentally, would be much less expensive in some mountain and forest areas outside the parks proper. Many tourists do not get beyond the engineering of "visitor hours" or "visitor dollars." The veneer of comfort and excitement has been well built. The tourist may never suspect that he is not getting all nature has to offer.

Amiable diversions for all comers are popular with the public: swimming pools, beauty parlors, bars, dance floors, gift shops, movies, and other entertainments to shake off the horrors of the highway. Perhaps scattered lawns and trees will be built into the Everglades, Death Valley, and the Olympic Forest. By clearing a few extra feet of mangrove, cactus, or hemlock, it would be possible to surround the playground with the "necessities" of life, not perhaps on the scale that Central Park is circumscribed, but ultimately approximating a refined, though busy, midway.

Historian James P. Gilligan says, "The real democratic significance of our parks may not be in providing access and accommodations to everyone, but in holding a few undeveloped areas where high quality recreation benefits can still be obtained by those willing to make the effort. . . . Most endeavors to retain such areas for a relatively small number gradually yield before the demands of an eager traveling public, which has not yet grasped the full significance of our national park system."

The usual traveler can engage in contemplation of a geyser only so long. If the Park Service were not to divert the traveler with entertainment he might move on to complementary activity elsewhere and his space would be available for someone else. He might discover that he actually prefers the race track or Hoover Dam and go there next year instead. It seems possible that much of the present tourist pressure on the parks is not so much an expression of a desire to see certain wonders as it is a function of a footloose population, high-speed automobiles, convenient highways, and the sheer pleasures of motion and movement.

The case seems dark for holding undeveloped areas for unique wilderness values. The parks may dissolve into playgrounds for mass use. This would save the newer parks from the clutches of the developers, if dismemberment by the construction of semi-amusement facilities could be called saving. In 1966 the Park Service undertook a ten-year building program. Conservationists worked for greater appropriations from Congress on the erroneous assumption that they were helping to preserve the parks. Many national park areas have remained pristine because the Park Service has been too poor to build roads into them. The back country represents administrative poverty.

The dilemma would seem to be almost beyond solution, although an answer presumably lies somewhere between opening the parks to material exploitation or, in order to perpetuate politically a "preservation" policy, holding unlimited open house for an endless thundering herd. The Park Service may be too retiring or too hot on the scent of power and empire in the bureaucratic jungle to try rationing the use of wilderness parks. No one has expressed surprise that Dinosaur National Monument was saved from progress (i.e., high dams) in the 1950's by thousands of people who never saw that monument. Yet, those citizens aimed tons of mail at their congressmen, not to save Dinosaur for science, not to spite Utahans, not even to preserve a place for their next summer's vacation. The wilderness evidently has value beyond such motivations. The developers' schemes for the unparklike parks carried the assumption that these are less defensible—lacking the association of cherished images—and therefore their despoilation in the name of improvement would be unopposed. This hunch was wrong. The public reaction was a slowly augmenting, enormous cry of protest, climaxed by a national uproar that drew the critical examination of relatively uninterested politicians and economists. The economies of the whole Upper Colorado River Project, of which the Echo Park Dam in Dinosaur was only a small part, was impugned. The anguished cry for values that were intangible nearly swept away the whole scheme. To salvage the huge project, President Eisenhower, Secretary of the Interior Douglas McKay, the state governors, and the officials of the Upper Colorado River Development Commission withdrew their support of the dam in Dinosaur. Theirs was a political reaction. But the tide of protests against dams in the park had not to do with politics or economics.

What the conservationists apparently wished to save was a fragment of the earth's primeval wilderness big enough and genuine enough to satisfy the imagination, particularly the urban mind. It is neither wholly an intellectual nor wholly a cultural matter, but partly the expression of an impulse to hold on to an aspect of the environment that has always been real to humanity: the uninhabited place and the reality of wildness and danger.

There is more to it than place. It is wildness from which we, as living things, have come, and it represents the natural landscape with its creatures which has surrounded the habitations of humans for millennia. It extends to individual species in that wild community. For example, a part of the same emotion was directed toward saving the "vanishing" whooping crane. People worked to save the last thirty-odd birds, irrespective of the fact that they had no more idea of seeing a wild whooping crane than they did of camping at Dinosaur. Both are symbols foolish to ignore, and yet we pass over this strange behavior as though we had every intention of saving the cranes in order to make them into hats. There are numerous other animals whose survival is cherished for similarly symbolic reasons.

As for the landscape itself, however much it resembles Arcadia, paradise, or the ruins of Greece, and whatever vast, nervous body of recreationists go to the parks for want of somewhere better to go, it seems apparent that the response is to the lure of far-off unknown places, to the eternal challenge and enigma of forest and desert, the spirit of risk, and the promise of the not-yet domesticated lands. It would be surprising indeed if the wilderness that surrounded us so long did not occupy a place in the process of thought itself. Fears have in a sense become needs. Until recently there have always been unexplored regions relatively near at hand. The western public lands are as near today to New York as the Catskill escarpment wilderness was a century ago.

The desert, swamp, and rain-forest parks are conspicuously unlike traditional pleasure grounds. The unparklike parks fail as public commons because they have a unique function of their own, which playground use will destroy. Perhaps we could survive without that function, though we may not survive without the kind of concern of which wilderness preservation is an example.

It is fair to ask at this point why in a general consideration of man and nature we have examined the beginnings of Yellowstone and Yosemite and the recent parks in detail. The answer is that they are, or were, the world's most extraordinary examples of the preservation of whole landscapes, of the defense of unmodified segments of nature. It is important to ask what those responsible thought they were doing. In large part we have seen that they thought they were perpetuating something resembling traditional values, or ideal scenery. But they were involved in an experience that had been recognized for more than two centuries as "sublime" and which had been reduced by vulgar imitation to sentimentality and damned by literary critics as affectation.

THE PRESERVATION OF NATURE

I do not wish here to attempt to defend the sublime, but rather to say something further about preservation. Among those professionals in the modern world who stand between ourselves and nature, who are our agents, as it were—the agricultural engineers, hydrologists, farmers, foresters, mining engineers, public land bureaucrats, contractors, and planners of various sorts—there is a generally held distinction between *conservation* and *preservation,* and a common misunderstanding about them. Conservation means efficient use and naturally, with the vast needs of humanity, includes an ideal dispensation of most of the world. Preservation means a special type of land reservation for esthetics, recreation, or science. In this view the first is a general philosophy, the other a very specialized form of land use. All of these "resource" people, especially the foresters, are at pains to remind the public of this distinction, lest a groundswell among gardeners, bird watchers, and other "nature nuts" against the devastation of the world environment take the form of more preservation. The "land managers" have been making this point now for so long that they are always ready with outrage against any such attempts. They learn in college an indignation and righteous humanitarian horror of "locking up" the raw materials used by our civilization. They have not been above showing that preservation is immoral and un-American, since it "wastes" those resources we could otherwise use. The posture is completed, of course, by their magnanimous agreement that we may properly have a little bit of preservation, as they know that man has emotions and does not live by bread alone. Certainly it will chagrin many of them to hear such generosity and common sense called an exploiter's game. But the error in their view can be demonstrated in a five-minute lesson in biology. We must first dispose of the alternatives—conservation ("wise use") and preservation ("nonuse") which they offer, and look at all human activity in nature as falling along a graded scale of environmental modification. There is a polarity indeed in land use, but the actual events always fall in the tension zone between them and never at the extremes. Something is preserved and something used in every situation. The thing kept or lost is always a species of organism. I shall take, somewhat arbitrarily, five examples of use intensity and try to show how and why preservation is the dominant element in each, in all land use.

I. The conventional idea of preservation is setting apart an area with a minimum of human intervention, at least by agricultural and technological man. Such a landscape is protected from change by man in its growth and reproduction, and from interference in its catastrophes as well. Forests may be blown about by storms or knocked down by slides, or live out their lives in a process of gradual replacement. Invasion by and extinction of organisms tend to be very slow.

The area remains an essential expression of geological, climatic, and evolutionary processes acting on a biota. This is preservation *sui generis*. Its protection from modern man extends even to the *individual* organism. It is most commonly practiced in scientific natural areas where men come as students and witnesses.

II. The second example is the protection of species or their niches. The individual organisms are not sacrosanct, but populations of indigenous organisms and the place which they occupy in nature are. The soil and the particular structure of the natural community with its populations of native organisms are preserved. The size of the populations may be manipulated and harvest made by man. Modest alterations in food chains are made without otherwise changing the qualitative aspects of the system. As hunter, forester, or gatherer, men impinge mainly quantitatively on the system. Though draining off substance and energy, they preserve the stability and productivity of the community. The great majority of biotic interrelationships and dependencies remain intact, for only in their preservation is an enduring harvest of the native species insured. By focusing on the harvest component of the infinitely complex metabolic system, one may be misled into speaking of "use" as opposed to preservation. But the overriding essential is that the community is preserved as a group of populations or a taxonomic mosaic.

III. More intensive use occurs at a third level of preservation. Here the basic energy flow structure is preserved, but substitutions are made in the food webs. These substitutions are both intentional and incidental. Individual organisms are not protected; indeed, whole populations may be manipulated, even extinguished or added. The additions are mostly domestic or "camp follower" or pest species. In admitting domestic plants and livestock, their parasites and symbionts are admitted as well. In some pastoral economies these introductions have been made so gradually that the underlying energy pattern or *ecosystems* have been sustained; these attenuated natural communities continue without breakdown. A preponderance of native forms—plants, birds, reptiles, especially invertebrates and soil microbes—are merely adjusted quantitatively.

The visible scene seems utterly transformed. This is due to the scope of human vision and our preoccupation with domestic species. We see the landscape, the mesocosm. We do not see an environment or a community, but a field with its orchards or cattle. These few species, because of their size, give a distorted impression of the amount of modification. It is important to remember that at this *trophic* level of preservation thousands of native species continue to share space and support each other, to interact among themselves and with introduced species in transferring nutrients and energy. Except for competitors with man at the peak of the ecological pyramid, even the vertebrate components of these systems—the rabbits, squirrels, and moles—are preserved.

IV. At a further degree of modification, new plants are introduced that dominate the energy-fixing process. Competitors and parasites are combatted at all levels. There is a gross rearrangement of the community, with large amounts of life removed, as in truck farming and other agricultural crop production. Yet, even though the principal consumer is man or domestic animals, all breakdown, decay, and other transformation processes are carried on by wild organisms. The actions of other invertebrates are also utilized in the preservation of the soil. In effect, this preserves the complex of biogeochemical cycles characteristic of the area. These are the fundamental ties of unity. The removed materials must be replaced with other organic and chemical equivalents, but the nature of these patterns is still determined by the climate and geology of the area and sustained by bacteria and fungi.

The increasingly demanding routine of modern agriculture—

rotation, cultivation, fertilization, weed, pest, and disease control, hormone applications, harvest techniques, seed and plant treatment—is the price paid for the preservation of the element cycles. Even the most intensive irrigation vegetable farming depends essentially on the preservation of a natural exchange soil system about which relatively little is actually known except that its details are formidably complex and obscure, dependent upon hundreds of kinds of microbes that must be preserved.

V. The preceding type grades off through hydroponics to a final type, included primarily for reasons of symmetry. This assumes an ultimate ability to control or dispense with the ecosystem, to undertake at a physiological level only the preservation of energy capture, transfer, and amino-acid synthesis. Individuals, species, populations, food webs, trophic pyramids, and even the nutrient cycles would be abandoned. There are some people who neither want a world occupied exclusively by a single multicellular species (man) nor believe it possible. With it comes artificial photosynthesis, *in vitro* tissue culture, genetic control, and the pursuit of the synthetic protein. The question could be raised for this category as well as any of the others, whether man can be psychologically healthy in it.

Even in such a world, however, the fixation of energy would be contingent upon chemical and thermodynamic factors operating now in nature. These determine all transfer and are governed by the laws of thermodynamics and the operation of biochemistry and biophysics. These processes are coextensive with the life of cells, which in turn form organisms and populations. Even if man were to extend his protoplasm so that it occupied a large fraction of the solar system, he would be dependent upon stable systems described by cellular and solar physics, a relationship constituting a sort of cosmic ecology whose integrity would have to be preserved.

The following table summarizes the various levels of nature preservation:

TYPE	PRESERVED	TYPICAL HUMAN ACTIVITY	USED
I. *Sui generis*	Forests, lakes, deserts	Observing	Space, air
II. Niche	Population	Hunting, gathering, forestry	Some individual organisms
III. Trophic	Food chains	Pastoralism	Domestic animals
IV. Ecosystemic	Biogeochemical cycle	Agriculture	Domestic plants
V. Thermodynamic	Cellular organization	Bioengineering	Elements, energy

From this series it may be seen that the preserved component is far more basic and more massive than the harvestable or modified component and that the stability of the system is more important than its manipulation. The absence of man in the food chains does not necessarily render a type worthless; it may be particularly important in the study of natural processes critical to the other types. For man's economics the efficiencies of types II, III, and IV are probably low compared to that conceivable in V. Insofar as resource use is successful and enduring (i.e., there is conservation) at each level, there must be a clear understanding of what must be preserved. This has not always been the case because of the exaggerated importance of the directly usable forms and materials.

Historically it appears that the world is moving in both directions from type III. In one direction, lands formerly used extensively for grazing and forestry are converted into farming. Agriculture itself increases in intensity, approaching the laboratory conditions of V. In the opposite direction, lands used for hunting and forestry are more explicitly designated. Activities not compatible with them are given over to parks and nature reserves. The amount of land committed to type I continues to increase. This need not be alarming because the effectiveness of IV and V will not be measured by the acre, and as they become more efficient there will be more land available—at least until the bulk of humanity spills over into them.

At all levels how much is harvested is less important than the preservation of a stable continuum. The different levels have different proper rates of human use. Type III imposes, for instance, a pace harmonious with the characteristic rate of population adjustment, soil formation, and food-chain stabilization. The tempo in IV may be faster, limited by rates of carbon and nitrogen fixation, other oxidations, the addition of chemical substrate, and the flow of gases and fluids at various temperatures. The tempo innate to each type is enormously important and often overlooked. Indeed, the rate at which significant change occurs in type I coincides with climatic change, continental uplift and erosion, and organic evolution and is fast becoming the only place where these tempos can be seen manifested in the landscape by the sensitive observer.

The appreciation of preservation as the essential transaction puts conservation, resource use, and the man-nature relationship itself in a new and somewhat unfamiliar light. Henry Thoreau's famous statement that "in wildness is the preservation of the world" ceases to be ambiguous and inoperable in the modern world when wilderness, as the collective of wild things, is seen to be an epitomization, indeed an abstraction, like mankind or truth. But it also has biological reality. In wilderness are preserved *all* kinds of plants and animals, *all* those interconnecting events that are the physiology of life. We ourselves do not need all of them to live (for example, the lion catching the deer), but their loss is a diminution of the whole for which there is no remaining equivalent, like a small amputation. When we cease to preserve a predatory relationship, such as the lion and deer, by allowing the destruction of its participants, we have paid a price for some "necessary" advance in our civilization. The price is a diminishment. Such increments are cumulative, like the effects on the body of ionizing radiation. The irony is that well-being does not demand the sacrifice of the beauty of the world, which is the esthetic experience of its physiology. The real distinction between type I and the others is that there is nothing unique to types II to V, nothing which is not found in I. As we have seen, II–V are conversions, deletions, and substitutions, largely rearrangements of the patterns of I. There is nothing wrong with any of these preservation-use intensities; no human experiment in the use of nature is immoral. But nature is events, not stuff. The wilderness is like a great river of events, diverted by men into this or that irrigation ditch. Any number of patterns of ditches are possible—as long as the river flows.

NOTES

PREFACE

1. Ivan Illich, *Gender* (New York: Pantheon, 1982).

CHAPTER ONE: THE EYE

1. *Scenery and the Sense of Sight* (Cambridge: Cambridge University Press, 1935).
2. *The Gothic Cathedral* (New York: Pantheon, 1956).

CHAPTER TWO: ON ANIMALS THINKING

1. "Homage to Santa Rosalia, or Why Are There So Many Kinds of Animals," in Hutchinson, *The Enchanted Voyage and Other Studies* (New Haven: Yale University Press, 1962).
2. Table from Harry Jerison, *The Evolution of the Brain and Intelligence* (New York: Academic Press, 1973).
3. A parallel process of the evolution of tactical social hunting and cunning escape in the open may also account for the intelligence of the marine mammals. It probably also accounts for the intelligence of many of the rodents.
4. "Brain Size and Hunting Ability in Earliest Man," *Current Anthropology* 9 (1968).
5. *Beastly Folklore* (Metuchen, N.J.: Scarecrow Press, 1968).
6. There are some cases of autistic children whose recovery is initiated by giving them a pet; that is, they first speak by speaking to or about the animal.
7. *The Orphic Voice* (New Haven: Yale University Press, 1958).
8. "Suggestive Hallucinogenic-Derived Motifs from New World Monumental Earthworks," unpublished ms.
9. Personal communication, 1977.

CHAPTER THREE: THE MENTAL MENAGERIE

1. With the qualification that our hunter-gatherer forebears ventured into open country and, like all social predators, developed group defenses against other carnivores.

2. "The Seeing Eye," *Landscape* 9, no. 1 (1959).

3. In the social sciences, the "wolf-children" literature is one of those jokes, like patent-medicine cure-alls, for which there are always buyers. The lost infant raised by animals is represented as still crawling at the age of eight or ten, having never had humans to "teach" it to walk. Since the only way you could keep a normal human child from beginning to walk would be to tie it down, the evidence for the wolf-child's animal past convinces only those who have assumed uncritically that a child must have human adult supervision in the initiation of walking.

4. *Vision and Design* (London: Chatto & Windus, 1920).

5. A remark, possibly apocryphal, attributed to Ronald Reagan, then governor of California.

6. *The Savage Mind* (Chicago: University of Chicago Press, 1966).

7. *Animal Land: The Creatures of Children's Fiction* (London: Hutchinson, 1974).

8. Roderick Nash calls "The Rights of Rocks" the final field of ethical concern, which, at an interpersonal, strictly human level, reaches its ultimate dispensation in the mineral world. I suspect that he is wrong, and that mountains, streams, caves, and some rocks were first venerated early rather than late in the evolution of human consciousness.

9. That Disney films often show the predator as necessary to biological systems does not change their essential conceit, that at best predators are necessary evils. Sympathy is always with the prey, which, in the films as in nature, usually escapes.

10. On the face of it, such a cycle would seem difficult to break,

but the infantile characteristics of adolescent behavior are the signs of an inward regression that makes early experience possible. For a few months, there is a kind of insect metamorphosis allowing deep tissues of thought to be renewed.

11. *The Uses of Enchantment* (New York: Alfred A. Knopf, 1976).

12. "Anthropomorphism" is an overworked and misused word anyway. Literally, it means "the doctrine of ape- and monkey-like forms," since it refers to anthropoids, which are the primates except for its most primitive group, the prosimians. In our neo-Cartesian culture, to anthropomorphize is to endow an animal with bogus humanity. In this sense, the term has a destructive effect on understanding, for it closes the door on the processes common to humans and other animals by simply declaring them illusory.

13. Lévi-Strauss, *The Savage Mind*.

CHAPTER FOUR: THE METAPHYSICAL BEAR

1. Quoted in Joseph Fontenrose, *Orion: The Myth of the Hunter and the Huntress* (Berkeley and Los Angeles: University of California Press, 1978).

2. *The Goddess* (New York: Crossroads, 1980).

3. "Bear Mother," *Journal of American Folklore* 59 (1946).

4. *The Archetypal Image of Mother and Daughter* (London: Routledge & Kegan Paul, 1967).

5. "Adaptability and Human Genetics," *Proceedings of the National Academy of Science* 60, no. 1 (1968).

6. *Many Winters* (Garden City, N.Y.: Doubleday, 1981).

CHAPTER SIX: THE DANCE OF NEOTENY AND ONTOGENY

1. Kenneth Keniston says, "The *extent* of human development is dependent upon the bio-social-historical matrix within which the child grows up; some developmental matrices may demonstrably retard, slow, or stop development; others may speed, accelerate,

or stimulate it. . . ." ("Psychological Development and Historical Change," in Robert Jay Lifton and Eric Olson, eds., *Explorations in Psychohistory* [New York: Simon & Schuster, 1974]).

2. The infantilizing effect of domestication on animals has other effects far beyond the animals. Incorporated into the human social system as its lowest-ranking members, their subservience becomes part of a hierarchic scale of authority and right. Toward the animals themselves, the human feeling for their otherness evaporates in material values and sentimental affiliation. See Calvin Martin, "Subarctic Indians and Wildlife," in Carol M. Judd and Arthur J. Rays, eds., *Old Trails and New Directions: Papers of the Third North American Fur Trade Conference* (Toronto: University of Toronto Press, 1980).

3. Daphne Prior, "State of Surrender," *The Sciences* 11, no. 1 (1971).

4. *The Time Falling Bodies Take to Light* (New York: St. Martin's Press, 1981). See his concept of enantiodromia, p. 131.

5. *Countertransference* (New York: International Universities Press, 1979).

6. The fear of strangers in the child peaks at about three months, then subsides. But defective nurturing heightens this reaction and perpetuates it as an obsession for the familiar (Gordon W. Bronson, "The Development of Fear in Man and Other Animals," *Child Development* 39, no. 2 [June 1968]). Erik Erikson sees this fear of strangers (and strange animals and flora) as "the first fear of alienation," the "dread of being left alone in a universe without a supreme counterplayer," a mixing of anxiety and rage that "persists into all later phases of life and can pervade a widening range of relationships" (*Toys and Reasons* [New York: W. W. Norton, 1977]).

7. Erik H. Erikson, "Play and Actuality," in Lifton and Olson, eds., *Explorations in Psychohistory.*

8. In describing childhood thought as "iconic representation" (as opposed to infantile "sensory motor" perception or "acting out"), Jerome Bruner notes that children vary in their capacity for imagery, commenting that those with "low imagery" tend to replace it with language. These latter, "intellectually more supple," are held to have superior powers of conceptualization, but a "conventionalized memory," and lose the ability to preserve the distinctive quality of perceptual experience (*Studies in Cognitive Growth* [New York: John Wiley, 1975]). It seems likely that such individuals (or such behavior) and their literary emphasis would be favored in societies rejecting icons and leaping forward to the symbolism of the printed word.

9. Much of the loneliness, sense of isolation, fragmentation, and crises of alienation of modern people—and, to some degree, the loss of "meaning" in their lives—is due to the collapse or subversion of Eliade's "maturational psychodynamics of adolescence." Erik Erikson describes it as "a loss of things to be true to," malfunctions of identity psychology, avoidance of commitment, the denial of ancestors and repudiation of the significance of the past, hypermobility, and excessive abstract idealism ("Youth, Fidelity and Diversity," in Alvin E. Winder and David L. Angus, eds., *Adolescence: Contemporary Studies* [New York: American Book Company, 1968], and Joseph L. Henderson, *Thresholds of Initiation* [Middletown, Conn.: Wesleyan University Press, 1967]).

10. The term "inclusionist" is used here following Frederick Elder, who has described environmental attitudes as styles of inclusionist (seeing the world as a single reality) and exclusionist (believing that spiritual and human interests are independent of the natural realm) thought. See *Crisis in Eden* (New York: Abingdon Press, 1970).

11. Edith Jacobson, *Psychotic Conflict and Reality* (New York: International Universities Press, 1967).

12. The fanatic anality of Protestantism and capitalism has been fully discussed in Norman O. Brown's *Life Against Death* (Middletown, Conn.: Wesleyan University Press, 1959). The Reformation, he says, was not due to toilet training but was "an eruption of fresh material from deeper strata of the unconscious, made possible by a large-scale transformation in the structure of the projective system (the culture). The dynamic of history is the slow return of the repressed."

13. *The Universal Experience of Adolescence* (New York: International Universities Press, 1964).

14. Erikson, "Youth, Fidelity and Diversity"; Claire Russell and William S. Russell, "The Sardine Syndrome," *The Ecologist* 1, no. 2 (1970).

15. Joseph Chilton Pearce, *Magical Child* (New York: Dutton, 1977).

CHAPTER SEVEN: THE DOMESTICATORS

1. The best evidence for the ponderous emergence of agriculture is the carbon-14 dating of the oldest-known samples of the various domesticated plants and animals. Most of the community of cultivated forms does not appear in the first seven thousand years (Colin Renfrew, *Before Civilization: The Radiocarbon Revolution and Prehistoric Europe* [London: Cambridge University Press, 1979]).

Adina Kabaker, "A Radiocarbon Chronology Relevant to the Origins of Agriculture," in Charles A. Reed, ed., *Origins of Agriculture* (The Hague: Mouton Publishers, 1977).

2. "World as View and World as Event," *American Anthropologist* 7 (1971).

3. José Ortega y Gasset, *Meditations on Hunting* (New York: Scribner's, 1972). The idea of "attention" can be seen as a cultural style, as in Ortega y Gasset, or as an organizing concept in neuropsychological processes. If the hunter's attention were in some

sense "superior" then perhaps the question is whether it touches on child rearing for us today. For the scientific end of this spectrum, see Monte Jay Meldman, *Diseases of Attention and Perception* (New York: Pergamon Press, 1970).

4. Phenology is what the mature naturalist finally comes to. Much of Henry Thoreau's journal in the nineteenth century, like the work of Aldo Leopold in the twentieth, is given to the dates of first appearance—of flowers blooming, the passage of migratory birds, and so on. Their liveliness depends on a deeper understanding and a more refined sense of mystery.

5. Place to Australian aborigines is continuous with the identity structure of the adult. It is embedded there as a result of a combination of daily life and formal ceremony during the first fifteen to twenty years of life. It is not unreasonable to suppose that something like it gave shape to the religious life and the personality of the prehistoric hunter-gatherers of Eurasia and Africa. For the Australians, see Amos Rapoport, "Australian Aborigines and the Definition of Place," in William Mitchell, ed., *Environmental Design: Research and Practice* (Los Angeles: University of California Press, 1972).

6. Defensive personal space is analogous to territoriality in animal breeding space. The most scholarly work on the latter remains Robert Ardrey's *The Territorial Imperative: A Personal Inquiry into the Animal Origins of Property and Nations* (New York: Atheneum, 1966). But Ardrey's leap from typical animal territoriality to human war was unjustified: organized human invasion by force is probably due to the breakdown of human social behavior rather than its healthy expression, likely regressive and infantile.

7. The making of boundaries in a deforested terrain is done in terms of familiar landforms or, lacking those, man-made rock piles. Jane Ellen Harrison long ago pointed out that the "worship of stones" originated as "boundary" markers between the living

and the dead. "Hermes is at first just a Herm, a stone or pillar set up to commemorate the dead. . . . In his lifetime a man went to his father or his grandfathers, to his elders for advice. . . . So when the Herm gets a head and gradually becomes wholly humanized, among a pastoral people he carries on his shoulders a ram, and from the Ram Carrier, the Criophorus, Christianity has taken her Good Shepherd" (Jane Ellen Harrison, *Mythology* [New York: Cooper Square, 1963]; see also Nelson Gulic, *Rivers in the Desert: A History of the Negev* [New York: Farrar, 1959]).

8. The Great Mother Earth has been described at length in many works, notably those by Eric von Neumann, Joseph Campbell, Homer Smith, Henri Frankfort, Mircea Eliade, and Simone de Beauvoir. No single figure is more indicative of the tendency of farming peoples to extrapolate their place in the cosmos from the symbiosis between infant and mother. The force of such an image draws directly from individual infancy. Whether or not the emotional states and metaphors inspired by early experience suffuse a society in immaturity and incompetence may depend on what the "benign elders" do with that inspiration in the initiation of adolescents and the education of young adults. If the goddess is seen as erratically undependable and possessive, she may hold her "children" in infantile bondage. If her children carry her image as a model of a matrix, as an understanding of the world, then she may have served to liberate them to further growth.

One may wonder whether the increasing anthropomorphism of the goddess over the centuries of early agriculture did not make it more difficult for the child to project the maternal spirit onto nature in general.

9. Representation of the gods as humanlike among many cultures often shows them riding on certain animals. No mounted figures appear before domestication, and they occur in hierarchic, anthropomorphizing religions. Riding-on, which connects the per-

sonhood of the god with his appropriate ancestral animalhood, is a retreat from the world-at-large as signifying or symbolizing. To ride on is, after all, to be once again carried, a childish perceptual style.

10. R. E. Money-Kryle and others believe paradise to be the sub-adult's re-vision of the "disappearing breast." The whole literature of paradise is fraught with mammary allusions (R. E. Money-Kryle, *Man's Picture of His World* [London: Duckworth, 1968]). Harold F. Searles discusses Hudson's *Green Mansions* as an adolescent fantasy. The ideal of purity, he says, is akin to childish love of one's mother. From it, in late childhood, arises idealized nature as part of a similar projection. "In *Green Mansions* Abel, I believe, fails to carry through to this final differentiation of himself as a full-fledged human being. Those persons who, like Abel, fail to make this final achievement of normal adolescence apparently continue throughout their lives to identify themselves more with Nature than with mankind" (*The Nonhuman Environment in Normal Development and in Schizophrenia* [New York: International Universities Press, 1960]). One is tempted to point the finger at naturalists, nature lovers, preservationists, and so on—but perhaps prematurely. Elsewhere Searles and others point out that inadequate mothering may result in the individual's lifelong overdependence on objects in the search for his own mature identity. If this means materialism, accumulating and hoarding of things, and identity by acquisition, then the technocratic wasters of nature today have no reason to snort down their noses at the romantic childishness of those who sometimes seem to confuse wilderness with paradise.

11. "Nostalgia for Paradise in Primitive Traditions," in Eliade, *Myths, Dreams and Mysteries* (New York: Harper & Row, 1960).

12. The idea of a declining world is reviewed in Clarence Glacken's *Traces on the Rhodian Shore* (Berkeley: University of California

Press, 1967) and is explained in Christian theology by the Fall. The Christians had abundant evidence to go on, as the Mediterranean world was physically deteriorating. According to R. O. Whyte, the destruction of the great juniper forests of Persia began after 5000 B.C. Grazing, dry farming, and charcoal burning turned Syria into a vast overgrazed steppe. Erosion produced the "colossal silt load of the Tigris and Euphrates," and vegetational collapse *resulted* in locust infestations. Kilns, smelters, and urban construction put further demands on the forests. Whyte adds, "For these reasons combined with the clearance of land for cultivation, the forest resources of our region were dissipated unwisely, and on a vast scale. The bald mountains and foothills of the Mediterranean littoral, the Anatolian Plateau and Iran stand as stark witnesses of millennia of uncontrolled utilization." What made it worse was increased rainfall from 5000 to 2000 B.C., which cushioned the effects of land abuse somewhat, followed by two thousand years of profound aridity, which aggravated them ("Evolution of Land Use in South-Western Asia," in L. Dudley Stamp, *A History of Land Use in Arid Regions* [Paris: UNESCO Arid Zone Research, vd. 17, 1961]). With the spread of Western ideologies and Christianity north into Europe on the heels of agriculture, the image of a "declining" world was convincing in spite of the rich virginal fruitfulness of the fertile lands.

13. The garden image of paradise is apparently a debased figure. But "Adam" means "red" and has to do with men of the red upland soils rather than the black cultivated ones. Geographically, Eden was a steppe plateau, the home of hunters and gatherers. The yearning that the myth first expressed must have been that of disillusioned tillers of the soil for a long-lost life of freedom and relative ease (Nigel Calder, *Eden Was No Garden: An Enquiry into the Environment of Man* [New York: Holt, Rinehart & Winston, 1967]).

14. Arnold Modell, *Object Love and Reality* (New York: International Universities Press, 1968).

15. The distinction between grain- and root-farming cultures has been cited as the basis of fundamental differences of outlook between Occident and Orient. Briefly, the thesis is that the root crops of southeast Asia required fewer and simpler techniques of cultivation, were perennials instead of annuals, stored less well than grain, concentrated less energy, were grown in small, mixed assemblages instead of large monocultures, required less irrigation, and fermented differently. The result is that the husbandry of Asia was more in harmony with the inward and passive mysteries of the feminine principle. The Great Mother in the West was more readily subordinated to the calculating and regimenting masculine ideal (Edwin M. Loeb, "Wine, Women and Song: Root Planting and Head Hunting," in Stanley Diamond, ed., *Culture in History* [New York: Columbia University Press, 1960]).

16. In the north the same generative forces making luxuriant crops and cattle can spill over as swarms of pests and malignant forms of decay. Without constant vigilance, root and vine eat away at human works, forest invades the field, and marsh and fen overwhelm man-made drains. But in the subarid subtropics, where agriculture began, fertility is more clearly benign, a counterforce to the dry and sterile nonlife.

The deep human need for name learning and classifying that emerges in the individual with speech itself continues throughout life in satisfactions rooted in our sense of order. Conversely, when categories are not so clear it is perceptually and psychologically troubling to us. I have sometimes felt that this esthetic pleasure of things-in-their-place was a strong element of the beauty of the desert fringes, where agriculture began. There each plant and each mountain is a separate being, totally visible and clearly what it is. All differences seem emphasized—day and night (with their short twilight), wet places and dry places, life and nonlife, sky and earth. The human impact on dry lands tends to further exaggerate some of these differences. While one cannot conclude from this that desert people have any less subtlety of thought, there is available to them a world of visible contrasts that may be seen as evidence of a fundamental and pervasive rule of dichotomy in the universe.

17. "An Ecological Perspective on the Eastern Pueblos," in Alfonso Ortiz, ed., *New Perspectives on the Pueblos* (Albuquerque: University of New Mexico Press, 1972); see Mircea Eliade, "Nostalgia for Paradise in Primitive Traditions," and *The Quest* (Chicago: University of Chicago Press, 1969). Celebrations are widely reported in which group release also found expression in sadistic spectacles: bulls and bears or death fights of men and animals. Because of the disorder in their lives, says Paul Ford, the agricultural pueblo people of southwestern America have periodic festivals in which all rules are broken and norms of behavior violated. In these orgies the tribe dissipates its burden of dissonance and incongruity, gaining control over it by enacting it, and starts fresh from that chaos which is felt to be a necessary prelude to the rejuvenation of society, just as it is in the generation of the individual.

18. Harold F. Searles, "Non-differentiation of Ego Functioning in the Borderline Individual and Its Effect upon His Sense of Personal Identity." Paper presented at the Sixth International Symposium on the Psychotherapy of Schizophrenia, Lausanne, Switzerland, 28 September 1978.

Farmers, assuming nature to be conscious but not very bright, acted out what they wanted her to do, ritually copulating in the fields so that they, like the crops in which they saw themselves mirrored, also might be fruitful. As larger human numbers became advantageous, the spacing of children shrank from three or four years to one, aided by a reservoir of village wet nurses and the availability of more caretakers. Sixteen children in a lifetime would not be unusual, perhaps four times the number born to the woman in a hunting-gathering society (Richard B. Lee, "Population Growth and the Beginnings of Sedentary Life among the !Kung Bushmen," in Brian Spooner, ed., *Population Growth: Anthropological Implications* [Cambridge, Mass.: Massachusetts Institute of Technology Press, 1972]).

What seems at first a convenient arrangement—mother substitutes and surrogates—can disturb the infant, sometimes with lifelong effects. The infant is normally imprinted by its own mother during the first weeks of postnatal life. Loss of the mother, even for periods of hours or days, can result, says Anthony Storr, in a permanent attachment to her, tainted by fear, distrust, reclusiveness, and the tendency to extend this tormenting connection to an ambiguous entity, such as society or the earth, a distrust of the world, and a failure of courage in anxiety lest the support system disappear again and again. The child fails to develop the confidence necessary for achieving the independence necessary to move toward a freedom from maternal symbiosis (*The Dynamics of Creation* [New York: Atheneum, 1972]), remaining at a vague, juvenile identity level. Thus villagers do have a strong sense of belonging to the land and become fierce patriots and willing subordinates in societies that control the food supply by controlling maternal processes, invidiously and ritually.

19. Marshall Sahlins, *Stone Age Economics* (Chicago: Aldine, 1972).
20. Searles, "Non-differentiation of Ego Functioning."
21. John Yudkin, "Archaeology and the Nutritionist," in Peter J. Ucko and G. W. Dimbleby, eds., *The Domestication and Exploitation of Plants and Animals* (Chicago: Aldine, 1969). Richard B. Lee, "What Hunters Do for a Living, or, How to Make Out on Scarce Resources," in Richard B. Lee and Irven DeVore, eds., *Man the Hunter* (Chicago: Aldine, 1968).

Trade and markets do not increase the culinary opportunities beyond the possibilities in a wilderness except for the wealthy. Even now, the modern supermarket, with all its opulence, has an illusory diversity. Family buying habits are highly predictable and repetitive, a continuation of normal immature tastes and unconscious dependence on the literal use of food as part of a self-identity structure.

22. "The Spirit of the Gift," in Sahlins, *Stone Age Economics*.

23. A good example might be music. In conventional history/progress thinking, the complexity and quality of music have steadily grown from something repetitive and simple like the Kalahari bushman's plucking his bowstring to the symphonies of the nineteenth century. But Susanne Langer observes that "the great office of music is to . . . give us an insight into . . . the subjective unity of experience" by using the principle of physical biology: rhythm. Its physiological effect is to reduce inner tensions by first making them symbolically manifest, then resolving and unifying them (*Feeling and Form* [London: Routledge, 1953]). The more complex the music, the more fundamental the problem; or, the more elaborate the music, the more fragmented the vision of the world.

24. For the effects of domestication on the physique and behavior of animals, see H. Spurway, "The Causes of Domestication: An Attempt to Integrate Some Ideas of Konrad Lorenz with Evolution Theory," *Journal of Genetics* 53 (1955); Erich Isaac, "On the Domestication of Cattle," *Science* 137 (1962); and E. B. Hale, "Domestication and the Evolution of Behaviour," and other papers in E. S. E. Hafex, ed., *Behaviour of Domestic Animals* (New York: Williams & Williams, 1962).

25. Wilhelm Stekel, "The Animal in Fantasy," *Patterns of Psychosexual Infantilism* (New York: Evergreen, 1959).

26. "The Strategy of Ecosystem Development," *Science* 164

(1969). I am aware that the concept of the climax has fallen into disfavor among some ecologists in recent years, but it remains useful in speaking of the appearance of the world to an observer in the course of an ordinary lifetime.

27. Ortega y Gasset, *Meditations on Hunting*.

28. The attendant executive diseases center around the dysfunctional effects of protracted stress. What Searles says of the child who is given "responsibility" for events he cannot actually control is surely indicative of physiological and psychological pathology in a culture determined to "control the environment." Searles, "Non-differentiation of Ego Functioning in the Borderline Individual."

29. "State of Surrender," *The Sciences* 11, no. 1 (1971). With agriculture, there arose scheduled work routines. Edith Jacobson says that repetitive work conceals psychosis, which erupts when the individual leaves the job or even takes a vacation (*Psychotic Conflict and Reality* [New York: International Universities Press, 1967]).

30. This is because others in the family may use the child to complement their own defective egos (Harold F. Searles, *Countertransference* [New York: International Universities Press, 1979]).

CHAPTER 8: TEN THOUSAND YEARS OF CRISIS

1. "Conquest of the Land through Seven Thousand Years," USDA Agricultural Information Bulletin No. 99 (Washington, D.C.: Soil Conservation Service, 1953).

CHAPTER 9: THE DESERT FATHERS

1. Of course, individual historians have struggled against the rules. For example, Ellsworth Huntington's theory early in the twentieth century that national traits could be in part explained by local climate appealed to a widely shared intuitive feeling for connectedness between the human and natural. He was roughly

handled by his critics, in part because his timing was bad. He wrote as the foundations for existentialism were being laid, as reductionism dominated biology, and as the psychology of James Watson emphasized the conditioning of the individual, turning psychology toward experimental atomism and clinical manipulations, the Adlerian therapies of "making yourself," the declarations of independence from biology by the social sciences, and the repudiation of evolution. The theology of Karl Barth, the "new criticism" in art, and all rejection of "determinism" by intellectuals and academics built contempt for the natural history of man.

2. The scorn for the work of Konrad Lorenz, Robert Ardrey, Desmond Morris, and Edward Wilson for their naturalization of man is not surprising. The revulsion they evoke seems to derive from the assertions of the desert fathers of the West: the absolute distinctions between man, nature, and the supernatural (Aldous Huxley, "The Desert," *Tomorrow and Tomorrow and Tomorrow* [New York: Signet, 1964]).

3. Part of the difference between the Egyptian stasis and what would become history in the minds of the Semitic sons of old Sumer is due to the differences in their rivers: the Nile flooding peacefully and cyclically, the Euphrates violently and erratically (Henri Frankfort, "Egypt: The Nature of the Universe," *The Intellectual Adventure of Ancient Man* [Chicago: University of Chicago Press, 1946]).

4. The Four Horsemen are formulated as the chief forces of history (Jacques Ellul, *Apocalypse: The Book of Revelation* [New York: Seabury, 1977]).

5. This cycle combining ecological and social bases in the rise and fall of the desert empires can be seen in the joint reading of four essays: R. O. Whyte, "Evolution of Land Use in South-Western Asia"; W. C. Lowdermilk, "Conquest of the Land through Seven Thousand Years"; Robert L. Carneiro, "A Theory of the Origin of

the State," *Science* 169 (1970); and Franklin Russell, "The Road to Ur," *Horizon* 14 (1972).

6. When they settled, the Hebrews were on dry marginal land instead of rich bottomlands. Even here uncertainty persisted, so that the eruptive quality of events was not reduced as it might have been by the relative certainty of crop success known to those on lower lands. This could have only perpetuated the association of morality and climate and the synonymy of failure and punishment.

7. The "desert ways" of the Kenites, Kenizzites, Calebites, Yerahmilites, and Rachabites in the Negev, says Nelson Gulic, were "idealized in the religious philosophy of Israel." These were simplicity, austerity, selflessness, "prophetic ideals"; the "leanness, clarity and uncompromising qualities of Sinai and the Southland were favorably contrasted with the abominable fertility practices and idolatry of the Canaanite civilization." Of the Negev, "the very ground became and remained the touchstone enabling the peoples of the Exodus and their descendents to find and ever renew their spiritual values." Gulic speaks of "the kind of clarity and puritanism that are characteristic of the desert atmosphere . . . the rockbound realities of inner attitudes and concrete actions of love and mercy and justice" (*Rivers in the Desert: A History of the Negev*).

8. "The Desert."

9. In an unpublished and untitled, perspicacious essay written while he was a student at Williams College in 1968, David Klemm, now a professor of theology, perceived that the "environmental crisis" was, in fact, related to the concept of history. He analyzed Paul Tillich's highly praised *The Courage to Be* (Yale University Press, 1952), in which Tillich's idea of being versus nonbeing was coupled to the act of self-affirmation and creation by man, including his technology. Klemm writes, "This attitude—

production is progress, progress exists for itself, man has ontic destiny—represents an obsession with history and seems like a justification of self-glorification on a historical plane by nations (as in the American attempt at genocide of the native Indians for reasons of progress and destiny) or by individuals (the reality-transforming assassination of Robert Kennedy)."

Klemm notes that "the correlation of Being and History, as per Tillich, cuts man off from nature and the mystery of life. Modern culture has made that correlation and history becomes its 'ultimate concern.'"

"The terror of history," Klemm concludes, "lies in the great destruction it has wrought on our planet and our people, and in the perversion of our natural religious sensitivities to place and the source of Life." In this connection, see also Kai Nielson, "On Taking Human Nature as the Basis of Morality," in John J. Mitchell, ed., *Human Nature: Theories, Conjectures, Descriptions* (New York: Metuchen, 1972).

10. Any number of Holy Land places are celebrated and are the goal of a passionate tourism. But this is largely literal, childish behavior in a religious view that celebrates nonplace. Even the betrothal between Jehova and Israel did not include a participatory role for nature—the promised land being more a dowry than a member.

It has been argued that the Old Testament is a nature-sensitive document (see, for example, Eric G. Freudenstein, "Ecology and the Jewish Tradition," *Judaism Magazine* 14, no. 4 [Fall 1970]). But the argument stands up only in contrast to other parts of the book—the "thou shalts" and the "thou shalt nots" directed toward duties in property, not beings. The celebration of natural beauty and the cautionary words against abuse of soil or livestock do not refer to an independent reality so much as respect for providential

mastery and rights in property. It is, however, true, says Henri
Frankfort (*Kingship and the Gods* [Chicago: University of Chicago
Press, 1948]), that much of the reference to nature in the Old
Testament is poetic—in the modern sense of man "expressing his
moods in its imagery . . . but never sharing its mysterious life,
never an actor in the perennial cosmic pageant."

11. The ambiguity of Christian spokesmen on the responsibility
of Christianity for the destruction of nature is an extraordinary
example of the problem of just what "Christian" or "Jewish"
means: its orthodox position or the culture of which it is part? Are
what were once heretical views that were later incorporated part
of the official church or not? Is the Manichaean thought of Augustine, for example, to be regarded as contrary to Christian teach-
ing or as part of it? I think that the dominant religion of a society
is always in some degree responsible even for the ideas and behaviors of its heretics and opponents because its collective perceptions
and values are far broader and more general than its formal apparatus and heretics are usually believers who simply want to re-
vise details.

12. *In Bluebeard's Castle* (New Haven, Conn.: Yale University
Press, 1971).

13. *The New Polytheism* (New York: Harper & Row, 1974).

14. *The Ideological Imagination* (Chicago: Quadrangle, 1972). Gordon W. Bronson says that such aversive reactions peak at about
three months in the infant, then subside. Psychiatric "problems,"
however, heighten this fear reaction and result in a continuing obsession with the familiar. I conclude from this that a society in
whose interest fear and hostility toward strangers were desirable—
as among the military, for example—would find means of tweak-
ing mother-infant relations so that such "psychiatric problems"
occurred ("The Development of Fear in Man and Other Ani-

mals"). Erik H. Erikson sees this fear of strangers (and strange animals and flora) as "the first fear of alienation," the "dread of being left alone in a universe without a supreme counterplayer," a mixing of anxiety and rage that "persists into all later phases of life and can pervade a widening range of relationships" (*Toys and Reasons*).

15. *Bird in the Bush* (New York: New Directions, 1959).

16. Noting that Palestine was only about one hundred by sixty miles, Watsuji Tetsuro observes: "That small tribe of Israel has forced Europeans to believe for over 2,000 years that the history of Israel, in fact, reads almost like that of the whole human species" (*Climate and Culture* [Hokuseido Press, 1961]). George Williams's *Wilderness and Paradise in Christian Thought* (New York: Harper & Row, 1962) is pertinent here, in terms of the European elaboration of metaphors of "desert," "wilderness," "paradise," and so on. But a more literal transfer also took place. As temperate climate climaxes were broken by the march of civilization, they inevitably became slightly more xeric. Grasslands tended to become deserts and, indeed, to be called deserts from the first by Europeans (Martyn Bowden, "The Great American Desert," in Martyn Bowden and David Lowenthal, eds., *Geographies of the Mind* [New York: Oxford University Press, 1976]).

17. An excellent example of this is given by Richard Rabkin: "A curious natural phenomenon is the extended predator-victim relationships of distinct animal groups, such as that between hyenas and wildebeests. When a hyena pack picks off newborn wildebeests on the plains of Africa one option is to focus upon the individuals involved. . . . The hyena . . . is the proverbial despicable coward who terrorizes the innocent and the weak. The mere sight of him arouses our dislike; his elimination is the strategy of choice. . . .

"From another approach, this encounter can be said to have, at least, the virtues of being genuine and authentic. As such, we can appreciate that 'this is darkest Africa.' . . . Thus, Norman Mailer has defended . . . the 'authenticity' of the juvenile delinquent's act of smashing an old storekeeper over the head with a gun. More abstractly, Camus' hero Meursault in *The Stranger* has an icono-clast's view of the individualistic position, and does not construct events in sequence but simply considers the raw facts; . . . Camus indicates that the former orientation has the virtues of genuineness and authenticity. . . . The hyena's career is to be a scavenger; the natural history of his species inevitably leads to such behavior.

"Finally, adopting . . . [a] cyclical viewpoint, there is a sudden expansion of focus. The hyena and wildebeest disappear as struc-tures, as individuals. . . . There exist two systems, the wildebeest herd and the hyena pack. . . . It becomes evident that the hyena pack lives in harmony with other systems such as the bird flock or the jackal pack, which also live together with it and the wildebeest herd. On reflection it becomes apparent that the elimination of hyenas would eliminate the wildebeests; the herd would overgrow its food supply, its composition would tend toward old, feeble, sick animals, disease would spread, and so forth. . . .

"What starts out in the historical framework as a repellent sit-uation involving the individual hyena and the newborn wildebeest becomes in this model a repetition, a cycle that has long endured. To save individual wildebeests may ultimately endanger the entire herd. This 'ecological consciousness,' as the conservationists call it, challenges much of Western political and religious philoso-phy" (*Inner and Outer Space* [New York: Norton, 1970]).

18. "The Child and the Mother in Arab-Muslim Society," in L. Carl Brown and Norman Itzkowitz, eds., *Psychological Dimen-sions of Near Eastern Studies* (Princeton, N.J.: Darwin Press, 1977). In the same volume, psychiatric illness is rated at over 50 percent in a Lebanese village under study (compared with 80 percent in

midtown Manhattan) (Herant Katchadourian, "Culture and Psychopathology").

19. Rudolf Eckstein and Elaine Caruth, "From Eden to Utopia," *American Imago* 22, no. 1 (1965).

20. See, for example, Peter Blos, "The Child Analyst Looks at the Young Adolescent," *Daedalus* 100, no. 4 (1971).

21. Following Arnold Van Gennep's *The Rites of Passage* (Chicago: University of Chicago Press, 1960), Eliade has carefully set out the initiatory sequence in its most widespread and general form: preparation of the sacred ground and isolation of the candidates, instruction of the novices, physical ceremonies (circumcision, tooth extraction), ritual pantomimes ("death," "rebirth"), and dietary and other prohibitions (*Rites and Symbols of Initiation* [New York: Harper & Row, 1958]). The literature on the psychology of adolescence by Erickson, Anna Freud, Blos, and Kiell correlates the social events under Eliade's "benign intercession of elders" with the psychological "readiness" of the adolescent for the tests, special knowledge, new kinships, and the rites of expulsion, exile, and incorporation.

22. *The Masks of God,* vol. 1: *Primitive Mythology* (New York: Viking, 1959).

23. According to Jay Y. Gonen, patriarchal societies frustrate the adolescent's transferral of his love of mother to others or to nature. This results in a massive repressed rage toward the father, especially among competing sons. The harsh authoritarianism is intended to "control sexual love toward the mother." Tenderness is allowed but all expression of sensuality is redirected to prostitutes. The neurotic love of the adolescent therefore includes "an overwhelming desire to rescue the beloved." A society that manipulates and destroys the natural world as though it were a woman in chattel evokes a minority of antagonists bent on saving her, whose arguments seem romantic to the more "realistic" majority. The

"nature lovers," acting on a muted rage and the guilt over their hostility, seek punishment from the dominant authorities or perhaps by a natural calamity. The sons of the patriarchs who are redirected toward prostitutes perceive nature as fallen, undeserving of their tenderness, freeing them to exploit it with callous disregard for its own inner state. Both nature destruction and preservation can be interpreted in these terms as an unresolved oedipal problem—which is not an unexpected analysis if desert-mindedness is a destructuring of late childhood developmental processes (*A Psychohistory of Zionism* [New York: Mason/Charter, 1975]).

24. Edith Jacobson speaks of this "acting out" behavior as "unwillingness to accept and adjust to reality," a "global projection identification" in which external objects become unacceptable parts of the self, to be changed via political or legal means," an attitude leaning toward "megalomaniac ideas" (*Psychotic Conflict and Reality*).

25. Ideologists tend toward totalism, says Gonen: "Persons with a negative identity . . . resort to a rigid ideology to achieve totality at the expense of wholeness" (*A Psychohistory of Zionism*).

26. Tetsuro says of the desert peoples, "Man does not wait passively for nature's blessings; he makes active incursions into nature's domain and succeeds in snatching a meagre prey from her. This fight with nature leads directly to a fight with the other man; it is like two sides of a coin—on the reverse side the fight with nature, the fight with man on the obverse." "God was the realization of the oneness of man in his struggle against nature, so there are here no marks of the deification of the forces of nature" (*Climate and Culture*).

27. The terrorist is the supreme revolutionary, the extreme ideologist, acting out responses to "the demands of inner change" that may be impossible if he is trapped in an immature society.

In totemic thought, the outer world is transformed metaphorically; in Neolithic thought, this metaphor was emphatically maternal; in Western thought, the metaphor is denied, leaving the adolescent to act on the literal-mindedness of his childhood and direct the transforming impulse to political ends. Idealism appears to become inflamed and insatiable. The effect in the long run, says Steiner, is a loathing of an impossible goal, a desire for war "for the sake of identity," a "nostalgia for disaster." The need for rebirth is projected upon the world, so that it, rather than one's own childish self, is to be destroyed (*In Bluebeard's Castle*). See Hannah Arendt, "Ideology and Terror, a Novel Form of Government," *Review of Politics* 15 (1953). Arendt holds that totalitarian thought of the past century finds intellectual support in the Darwinian theory of evolution and that violent revolution and tyranny are therefore presented as extensions of a "natural" process. In this, Arendt is insufficiently critical. Herbert Schneidau is more accurate when he says: "We have been misled by a spurious analogy with evolution and maturation into believing that ours is the 'normal' way to think" (*Sacred Discontent*).

28. The similarity of modern Americans to drifting Bedouin nomads is a penetrating criticism. Islam, or "submission," has perpetuated with gusto the tides of skirmishing that go on endlessly in the Near Eastern desert. Its best description may still be Robert Doughty's *Deserta Arabia*—a hard-line, calculated balance of accommodation and hospitality motivated by suspicion and vengeance, loyalty and deception, the exaltation of will and honor, rituals of procedure, overdefined boundaries, overstructured sensory modes, fantasies of scheming enemies, fatalism, discipline, hierarchic relationships, goal-oriented behavior, anxiety, hostility, and despair. Islam, in its perpetual crises, dreams of extrication by a heroic outsider, a rescue, escape, or messiah—sharing this with older Arabic attitudes and the Hebrews, Jews, and Chris-

tians. Deliverance of this kind is premised on the model of centuries of equestrian strife and the unpredictable, calculating judgment of the worth of those in need of help from distant warlords or petty chiefs, who may or may not come to their aid.

29. Gonen discusses the psychological problems of people without a place or home as centering on their loss of identity. To this they respond with the "hyper-vigilance of the haunted, the alert scanning of the insecure, and the continuous suspiciousness of the vulnerable" (*A Psychohistory of Zionism*). See also Lewis H. Lapham, "The Melancholy Herd," *Harper's,* July 1978.

30. M. von Senden, *Space and Sight* (London: Methuen, 1960).

31. This statement is not an attack on Jewish mothers, but I suspect that the literature on Jewish mothers by Jewish sons bears out an obsessive syndrome between them that may indeed be related to the theme of this essay. On the whole, however, I see the failure of nurturance among Jews, as among Christians and Muslims, as reflecting not one or the other of the parents, but rather the whole of the nurturing activity of society common to the Western experience. As for the fearful child shutting down because of a fearful mother, see Joseph Chilton Pearce, *Magical Child*.

CHAPTER TEN: THE VIRGIN DREAM

1. *Natural Religion and Christian Theology* (Cambridge, England: Cambridge University Press, 1953).

2. *Mountain Gloom and Mountain Glory* (Ithaca, N.Y.: Cornell University Press, 1959).

3. *Taste in Landscape in the Seventeenth Century* (Ann Arbor: University of Michigan Press, 1956).

4. *West Highland Survey: An Essay in Human Ecology* (Oxford, England: Oxford University Press, 1955).

5. *Early Netherlandish Painting: Its Origin and Character* (Oxford, England: Oxford University Press, 1954).

6. *The Leaves of Southwell* (London: Penguin, 1945).

7. *The Decline of the West* (London: Allen and Unwin, 1918).

8. *Wild Men in the Middle Ages* (Cambridge, Mass.: Harvard University Press, 1952).

9. *Essays on Primitivism and Related Ideas in the Middle Ages* (Baltimore: Johns Hopkins University Press, 1935).

CHAPTER ELEVEN: THE AMERICAN WEST
AS A ROMANTIC LANDSCAPE

1. *Doubt and Certainty in Science* (Oxford, England: Oxford University Press, 1950).